D1481715

HARVARD EAST ASIAN MONOGRAPHS

90

Studies in the Modernization of
The Republic of Korea 1945-1975

Education and Development in Korea

126°　　　　127°　　　　128°　　　　129°

North Korea

Kŭmhwa
Sokch'o

KYŎNGGI　Ch'unch'ŏn
KANGWŎN
Ŭijŏngbu　　　　　Kangnŭng

38°

Mukho
Pukp'yŏng
Samch'ŏk

Inch'ŏn　Seoul　Wŏnju
Chŏngsŏn

Yŏju
Suwŏn
Ansŏng　Ch'ungju
37°

**NORTH
CH'UNGCH'ŎNG**

Ch'ŏnan

Ch'ŏngju　Ŭmsŏng

NORTH KYŎNGSANG

**SOUTH
CH'UNGCH'ŎNG**

Taejŏn

Yŏnmu

Changhang　　Kimch'ŏn
Kunsan　I-ri　　　　　P'ohang
Okku　Chŏnju
36°

Taegu　Kyŏngju

Yellow Sea

NORTH CHŎLLA

SOUTH KYŎNGSANG

Pŏpsŏngp'o

Chinju　Chinhae

Kwangju　　Samch'ŏnp'o
Pusan
35°

SOUTH CHŎLLA
Sunch'ŏn　　　Changsŭngp'o

Mokp'o　Yŏsu
Mijo-ri

Sin'gŭm-ni

34°

128°　　　129°

East Sea

THE REPUBLIC OF KOREA

CHEJU ISLAND　Cheju

Sŏgwip'o

126°　　127°

0　20　40　60　80　100　120　140　160
KILOMETERS

0　20　40　60　80　100
MILES

LC 67 .K6 E34

Education and development in
Korea /

Studies in the Modernization of
The Republic of Korea: 1945-1975

Education and Development in Korea

NOEL F. McGINN
DONALD R. SNODGRASS
YUNG BONG KIM
SHIN-BOK KIM
AND
QUEE-YOUNG KIM

PUBLISHED BY
COUNCIL ON EAST ASIAN STUDIES
HARVARD UNIVERSITY

Distributed by
Harvard University Press
Cambridge, Massachusetts and London, England
1980

WITHDRAWN
RITTER LIBRARY
BALDWIN-WALLACE COLLEGE

© Copyright 1980 by
The President and Fellows of
Harvard College

The Council on East Asian Studies at Harvard University publishes a monograph series
and, through the Fairbank Center for East Asian Research, administers research projects
designed to further scholarly understanding of
China, Japan, Korea, Vietnam, Inner Asia, and adjacent areas.

The Harvard Institute for International Development
is Harvard University's center for interdisciplinary research, teaching, and technical assistance
on the problems of modernization in less developed countries.

The Korea Development Institute
is an economic research center, supported in part by the Korean government
that undertakes studies of the critical development issues and prospects of Korea.

Library of Congress Cataloging in Publication Data

Main entry under title:

Education and development in Korea.

(Studies in the modernization of the Republic of
Korea, 1945-1975) (Harvard East Asian monographs ; 90)
Bibliography: p.
Includes index.
1. Education—Economic aspects—Korea.
2. School management and organization—Korea.
I. McGinn, Noel F., 1934- II. Series.
III. Series: Harvard East Asian mongraphs ; 90.
LC67.K6E34   370'.9519   79-26384
ISBN 0-674-23810-9

Foreword

This is one of the studies on the economic and social modernization of Korea undertaken jointly by the Harvard Institute
for International Development and the Korea Development
Institute. The undertaking has twin objectives; to examine the
elements underlying the remarkable growth of the Korean
economy and the distribution of the fruits of that growth,
together with the associated changes in society and government;
and to evaluate the importance of foreign economic assistance,
particularly American assistance, in promoting these changes.
The rapid rate of growth of the Korean economy, matched in
the less developed world (apart from the oil exporters) only by
similar rates of growth in the neighboring East Asian economies
of Taiwan, Hong Kong, and Singapore, has not escaped the
notice of economists and other observers. Indeed there has been
fairly extensive analysis of the Korean case. This analysis, has

been mainly limited to macroeconomic phenomena; to the behavior of monetary, fiscal, and foreign-exchange magnitudes and to the underlying policies affecting these magnitudes. But there are elements other than these that need to be taken into account to explain what has happened. The development of Korean entrepreneurship has been remarkable; Korea has an industrious and disciplined labor force; the contribution of agricultural development both to overall growth and to the distribution of income requires assessment; the level of literacy and the expansion of secondary and higher education have made their mark; and the combination and interdependence of government and private initiative and administration have been remarkably productive. These aspects together with the growth of urban areas, changes in the mortality and fertility of the population and in public health, are the primary objects of study. It is hoped that they will provide the building blocks from which an overall assessment of modernization in Korea can be constructed.

Economic assistance from the United States and, to a lesser extent, from other countries, has made a sizable but as yet unevaluated contribution to Korean development. A desire to have an assessment undertaken of this contribution, with whatever successes or failures have accompanied the U.S. involvement, was one of the motives for these studies, which have been financed in part by the U.S. Agency for International Development and, in part, by the Korea Development Institute. From 1945 to date, U.S. AID has contributed more than $6 billion to the Korean economy. There has also been a substantial fallout from the $7 billion of U.S. military assistance. Most of the economic assistance was contributed during the period before 1965, and most of it was in the form of grants. In later years the amount of economic assistance has declined rapidly and most of it, though concessional, has been in the form of loans. Currently, except for a minor trickle, U.S. economic assistance has ceased. The period of rapid economic growth in Korea has been since 1963, and in Korea, as well as in other countries receiving foreign assistance, it is a commonplace that it is the receiving country that is overwhelmingly responsible for what growth, or absence of growth, takes place. Nevertheless, economic assistance to Korea was exceptionally large, and whatever contribution was in fact made by outsiders needs to be assessed. One of the studies, *The Developmental Role of the Foreign Sector and Aid,* deals with foreign assistance in macroeconomic terms. The contribution of economic assistance to particular sectors is considered in the other studies.

All the studies in this series have involved American and Korean collaboration. For some studies the collaboration has been close; for others less so. All the American participants have spent some time in Korea in the course of their research, and a number of Korean participants have visited the United States. Only a few of the American participants have been able to read and speak Korean and, in consequence, the collaboration of their colleagues in making Korean materials available has been invaluable. This has truly been a joint enterprise.

The printed volumes in this series will include studies on the growth and structural transformation of the Korean economy, the foreign sector and aid, urbanization, rural development, the role of entrepreneurship, population policy and demographic transition, and education. Studies focusing on several other topics—the financial system, the fiscal system, labor economics and industrial relations, health and social development—will eventually be available either in printed or mimeographed form. The project will culminate in a final summary volume on the economic and social development of Korea.

Edward S. Mason
Harvard Institute
for International Development

Mahn Je Kim
President,
Korea Development Institute

A Note on Romanization

In romanizing Korean, we have used the McCune-Reischauer system and have generally followed the stylistic guidelines set forth by the Library of Congress. In romanizing the names of Koreans in the McCune-Reischauer system, we have put a hyphen between the two personal names, the second of which has not been capitalized. For the names of historical or political figures, well-known place names, and the trade names of companies, we have tried to follow the most widely used romanization. For works written in Korean, the author's name appears in McCune-Reischauer romanization, sometimes followed by the author's preferred romanization if he or she has published in English. For works by Korean authors in English, the author's name is written as it appears in the original publication, sometimes followed by the author's name in McCune-Reischauer romanization, especially if the author has published in Korean also. In ordering the elements of persons' names, we have adopted a Western sequence—family name first in all alphabetized lists, but last elsewhere. This is a sequence used by some, but by no means all, Koreans who write in English. To avoid confusion, however, we have imposed an arbitrary consistency upon varying practices. Two notable exceptions occur in references to President Park Chung Hee, and Chang Myon, for whom the use of the family name first seems to be established by custom and preference. Commonly recurring Korean words such as si (city) have not been italicized. Korean words in the plural are not followed by the letter "s." Finally, complete information on authors' names or companies' trade names was not always available; in these cases we have simply tried to be as accurate as possible.

Geographic Terms (from largest to smallest)

Urban
  si – city
  pu – old term for a city
  ku – borough
  tong – precinct; (see rural tong)
  t'ong – sub-precinct
  pan – neighborhood

Rural
  to – province
  kun – county
  ŭp – town (formerly the county seat)
  myŏn – township
  tong – group of villages
  i (~ri, ~ni) – village
  purak – hamlet

Contents

Contents

Contents

Tables

Figures

Abbreviations

CLEP	National Council for Long-Term Educational Planning
EPB	Economic Planning Board
FAO	Food and Agriculture Organization
GDP	gross domestic product
GNP	gross national product
KCCI	Korean Chamber of Commerce and Industry
KEDI	Korean Educational Development Institute
OECD	Organization for Economic Cooperation and Development
OLA	Office of Labor Affairs
OM	Overall Modernization (scale)
ORD	Office of Rural Development
SKIG	South Korean Interim Government
SNU	Seoul National University
UNESCO	United Nations Educational, Scientific, and Cultural Organization
UNKRA	United Nations Korea Reconstruction Agency
USAID	United States Agency of International Development
USOM/K	United States Overseas Mission/Korea

Preface

Long the "Hermit Kingdom" or the "Forgotten Nation," the Republic of Korea[1] today attracts the world's attention, and especially that of leaders and planners in other parts of the developing or Third World. For fourteen years Korea has enjoyed one of the highest rates of economic growth of any country in the world. Its annual rate of per capita increase in gross national product (GNP) (7.7 percent in 1962–1974) has been equaled or surpassed only by a handful of countries in the world, and by only one other less-developed Asian country (Singapore).

At the same time, the distribution of income in the Republic of Korea is more equal than in all but a very small number of non-socialist countries, including those (such as the United States and Sweden) that have achieved the highest levels of economic activity. Perhaps as a consequence, perhaps as a contributing factor, Korea also has enjoyed during those four-teen years a period of political stability uncommon among countries in which rapid economic and social transformation is taking place. Since 1945, Korea has moved from a state of poverty characterized by periodic hunger to a situation in which all members of society appear to have their basic needs met, in which unemployment is low, and in which there are few instances of conspicuous consumption or ostentatious displays of wealth. These accomplishments are all the more extraordinary given the conditions under which they were realized.

Korea is a country deprived of rich natural resources. What known mineral deposits and forests there are on the Korean peninsula went to North Korea in the partition of 1945. The Republic of Korea crowds more than 30 million people into a land mass scarcely bigger than New England, crossed by mountains, endowed with relatively little arable land. Thirty years of occupation under the Japanese left little in the way of industrial development in the south, and few trained people. Much of what little physical capital the Republic had was destroyed during 1950–1952, as invading armies from the north twice occupied more than half the territory of the Republic of Korea, living off the land, and scorching the earth as they retreated. The threat of another invasion, real in the minds of political leaders and many citizens alike, has required the Republic to carry the burden of an excessively large military force. In 1973 per capita military expenditures were U.S. $41, smaller than only four countries (Egypt, Albania, Jordan, Syria) with similar levels of GNP, and four times public expenditures on education.[2]

Leaders of other developing countries, also faced with bur-geoning populations, scarce resources, and political pressures for growth, might be expected to look closely at the experience of the Republic of Korea to determine whether the factors leading to success, to the "Korean miracle," could be duplicated in their own countries. What made Korea "modern" might be transferable to countries seeking through modernization to better the conditions of life of their populations.

The series of monographs of which this study is a part addresses the issue of what factors did in fact contribute to the Republic of Korea's "modernization," to the phenomenal economic growth and highly equitable distribution of income that have been achieved. Some observers have explained the phenomenon simply, in terms of the massive amounts of capital aid and technical assistance that Korea received, mainly from the United States. As another volume in this series indicates, capital aid was large, but is not sufficient to account for the phenomenon. Other observers have suggested that it was the choice of technology for exports that allowed Korea to grow so rapidly. Other explanations are sought in foreign trade, exchange rate, and monetary policies; in political organization; in the unique character of the Korean people.

This volume focuses on the contribution of *human* resources to the development of the Republic of Korea. Although poor in land and minerals, Korea is rich in culture and education, and some see in the high levels of educational attainment among the Korean population, and the almost insatiable demand for further learning, the explanation of the nation's rapid development of economic activity. Typical of the widespread enthusiasm for education as a major factor in the modernization of Korea is this statement by UNESCO: "The remarkable and rapid economic growth that has occurred in Korea over the last decade has been based to a large degree on human resources, and education has assisted in the production of a literate and industrious people."[3] The arguments to support these conclusions are:

1) Korea has (compared to other countries at a similar level of GNP) a highly developed educational system, which reaches all its population.
2) This educational system was developed after 1945.
3) There is a close secular relationship between the expansion of education and the growth of the economy.

4) The content of Korean education fits the economic requirements of the country and is a "modernizing" influence.

This study seeks to test these propositions. To do so it provides
a description of the growth and development of education in the
Republic between 1945 and 1975 and then an analysis of interactions between changes in education and changes in the
economy and society. The history includes information about
the structure and content of education, curriculum, and student
flows; it also describes governmental and foreign financing, the
role of foreign technical assistance, and current conceptions of
the role of education in the development of a new society. We
then proceed to the analysis of how education is affected by
and contributes to other sectors of society in Korea. This inquiry
may be of interest (and perhaps even of use) to planners and
policy-makers in education and human resources development
in other countries.

An additional objective is to evaluate current theories that
attempt to explain the relationship observed in history between
education and economic growth. A casual examination of
Korea's experience suggests that the relationship between education and economy has been especially neat and clear. An
analysis of the Korean case could, therefore, be helpful to
administrators, policy-makers, and social scientists who are concerned with education and development, but confused as to
which theory should be followed in proposing change in
educational systems.

ONE

The Development of Education Since 1945

How does one go about assessing an education system's contribution to economic growth? Typical of many analyses has been a simple (and, we believe, simplistic) comparison of some measure of the outputs of education (for example, years of schooling of the working population) with some measure of economic activity or product. But hidden within those measures may be unique entities: one year of schooling in a traditional Confucian school bears little resemblance to one year in an American school; growth in economic product shared by only a tiny fraction of the population has a different significance and content from growth distributed fairly equitably.

Besides, given an interest in transferring some part of the Korean lesson to other countries, what is most important is to understand how and why education made its contribution. Unless we can identify the mechanisms, the policy instruments as they are called, that resulted in education influencing growth, we gain little from demonstration of an association between the two.

That identification requires a close-up view of the history of education and economic development in the Republic of Korea. Most of our attention will be on the period from 1945 to 1975, but it will be impossible to ignore the legacy of Japanese colonialism. Some attention will have to be paid to the evolution of the structure of the educational system. That is dull material but, as there have been relatively few changes, we can breeze through it.

More interesting is consideration of how goals for education have changed with changes in political leadership. One has to distinguish between public pronouncements by national figures, objectives of those who make the operating decisions in the system, and expectations of parents and students. The significance of goals can be checked by analysis of attempts to rationalize investments in education, by examination of measures of effort such as financing, quality, and quantity of teaching, and by matching content of input with expected outcomes.

We begin our evaluation of the Korean miracle by looking at what education has been like. Following a description of structure, we look briefly at the direction of the system. Have goals emphasized economic growth? Are goals translated into curriculum? Has planning been effective? Finally, we ask, Has quality improved? Has output growth matched increases in inputs?

THE STRUCTURE OF EDUCATION

There is little that is unique about the present structure of the school system of Korea. Under the Japanese, formal schooling consisted of six years of primary school, five years of secondary school, and four years of higher education. Under the U.S. Military Government that took power in 1945 this 6-5-4 pattern was altered to a 6-6-4 pattern, common in the United States. The Education Law of 1949 specified primary education as compulsory, and divided secondary education into a four-year middle school and a high school of two or three years' duration. With the advent of the Korean War, these plans were abandoned, and the present 6-3-3-4 pattern was adopted (see Figure 1). The structure looks much like that found in most countries today.

Table 1 presents enrollments in the various levels of the formal system from 1945.[1] Primary school enrollments grew rapidly after the Liberation, at about a rate of 8 percent per year between 1945 and 1952 (see Table 2). Expansion was most rapid before 1950; during the war enrollments actually declined. As more and more of the school-age population was taken into primary school, the rate of growth declined, to about 5.5 percent per year between 1952 and 1960. Enrollments declined in absolute numbers after 1970 as the backlog of unsatisfied demand of children older than the age group was met and as population growth rates declined.

Middle school enrollments grew at about 8 percent per year between 1952 and 1960. With the elimination in 1969 of the screening examination that limited access to middle school for primary school graduates, enrollments increased even more rapidly. The rate of increase between 1965 and 1975 was 11 percent per year.

Under the Japanese system, graduates of vocational secondary schools were not eligible for admission to higher education. The system adopted after 1945 eliminated the formal barrier for vocational school graduates and Figure 1 does not distinguish between general or academic high schools and vocational high schools. As we shall see later, however, graduates of the two kinds of schools do not follow the same career lines.

Until 1973, each high school gave its own admission examination. Students could apply for admission to any high school of their choice anywhere in the country. Because some academic high schools had a reputation for preparing students well for

FIGURE 1 The School System

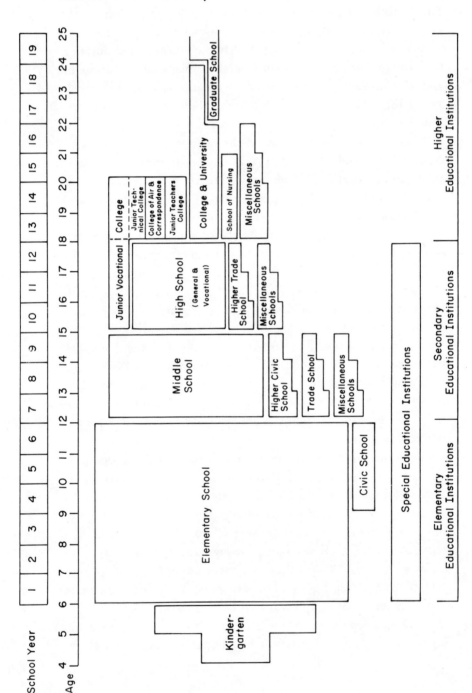

Source: Ministry of Education

TABLE 1 Increase in School Enrollments, 1945–1975

Type of School	1945	1952	1955	1960	1965	1970	1975
Elementary Schools	1,366,024 (100)	2,369,861 (173)	2,947,436 (216)	3,622,685 (265)	4,941,345 (362)	5,749,301 (421)	5,599,074 (410)
Middle Schools		291,648 (100)	475,342 (163)	528,614 (181)	751,341 (258)	1,318,808 (452)	2,066,823 (709)
Academic High Schools	50,343 (100)	59,421 (118)	141,702 (281)	164,492 (327)	254,095 (505)	315,367 (626)	648,149 (1,287)
Vocational High Schools	33,171 (100)	74,463 (224)	118,911 (358)	99,071 (299)	172,436 (520)	275,015 (829)	474,868 (1,432)
Higher Ed. Institutions	7,819 (100)	34,089 (436)	80,391 (1,028)	101,045 (1,292)	141,626 (1,811)	193,591 (2,476)	296,640 (3,794)

Source: Ministry of Education, *Statistical Yearbooks of Education*

Note: Indexes of increase are in parentheses, 1945 = 100.

TABLE 2 Rate of Growth in School Enrollments, 1945–1975

Type of School	1945–1952	1952–1960	1960–1970	1970–1975
Elementary	8.2	5.4	4.7	–0.5
Middle	—	7.7	9.6	9.0
High School	7.0	8.8	8.4	13.7
Academic	2.4	13.6	6.7	15.5
Vocational	12.2	3.6	10.7	11.5
College	23.4	14.5	6.7	8.9

Source: Based on Table 1.

the admission examination to the universities, they attracted the brightest (or highest-scoring) students. In 1973, the central government announced its intention to administer a national high school examination. Students now can apply to any school only within their area. The examination is given first to students applying to vocational high schools, and high scorers are placed before the academic high school examination is given. Only students who do not apply or who are not admitted to vocational high schools can apply to academic high schools. Seoul (the capital, with about 16 percent of the nation's population) has been divided into five residential districts and one common district. Each residential district is supposed to contain an equal balance of schools of high and low prestige, but the common district contains only prestige schools. Students whose scores are not high enough to get them into the common district are randomly assigned to a school in the residential district. A similar system is to be developed for Pusan and other areas of the country.[2] The importance of the examination system will be made clear later.

Under the U.S. Military Government (1945–1948) enrollments in academic high schools grew slowly (2.4 percent per year), while those in vocational high schools (which include the American-type comprehensive high school) grew rapidly. After 1952 this pattern of growth was reversed. During the first years of the Park Government (1962 on), vocational high school education again grew more rapidly than academic high schools, but this pattern was reversed in 1971–1975, despite government policy to enroll about two-thirds of the high school population in vocational high schools.

Higher education includes not only four-year colleges and universities but also two-year junior colleges, two-year teacher training colleges, technological institutes, and other post-secondary institutions. As Tables 1 and 2 show, enrollments in these schools grew most rapidly immediately after the Liberation from the Japanese, and have declined in rate of growth since that time. (It should be noted that high rates of growth in the late 1940s reflect the small base, rather than a large absolute growth.) Of approximately 300,000 students in formal higher education institutions in 1975, about 209,000 were in four-year colleges, 9,000 in junior teachers' colleges, 4,000 in junior colleges, and 59,000 in junior technical colleges.

Not all the expansion of enrollments has resulted from governmental action. As Table 3 shows, the private sector accounts for a large and increasing share of education in Korea. Only at the primary and middle levels, where there has been a public commitment to universal education, has the government acted to increase its share of enrollments in schools. The expansion of private education indicates a high unsatisfied demand for education, a theme to which we shall return several times.

Entrance to four-year colleges and universities has been determined by an entrance examination since 1968. Students are assigned to the institution of their choice according to their scores on the examination. Because of the belief that graduates from several of the universities (Seoul National, Yonsei, Korea) have a better chance of obtaining government employment upon graduation, places in those universities are in high demand, while provincial universities may have assigned to them students who are low scorers on the examination. Since 1971, the government has attempted to limit the expansion of higher education enrollments. The number of students at each college is fixed and

TABLE 3 Public School Share of Enrollments at Various Levels

	Percentage of Students in Public Schools		
	1965	*1970*	*1975*
Elementary	99.5	98.9	98.8
Middle School	55.6	51.4	59.4
Academic High	42.5	40.0	39.6
Vocational High	61.2	51.9	47.6
Junior College	3.2	0	0
Junior Technical	55.0	50.0	32.0
Junior Teaching	100.0	100.0	100.0
College and University	27.4	24.6	27.2
Graduate School	42.9	39.1	30.5

Source: Ministry of Education, *Statistical Yearbooks of Education 1965, 1970, 1975.*

adjusted by the government on the basis of manpower demand forecasts.

A university must have at least one graduate school. In 1975 there were 82 graduate faculties with 13,870 students enrolled. Graduate studies generally follow the American model.

Junior technical colleges began in 1963 as a post-middle school, five-year professional training program. In 1974 the government decided to upgrade these to junior technical colleges. Primary school teachers have been trained in junior teachers' training colleges since 1961, while secondary school teachers are trained in 24 four-year colleges of education.

All primary education in Korea is coeducational. As Table 4 shows, large numbers of single-sex schools exist at the secondary level. Most of the women's higher education institutions were begun in order to provide women with greater opportunities for further education.

Although less important in terms of number of students, there are several other educational institutions in Korea worthy of mention. The civic school system was begun in 1946 by the U.S. Military Government as a means to provide basic education for children and adults out of school. At one time, hundreds of

TABLE 4 Distribution of Schools by Sex, 1975

	Boys	Girls	Coeducational	% Enrollments Female
Primary	0	0	6,367	48.4
Middle	505	398	1,064	42.2
Academic High	267	227	179	41.7
Vocational High	190	116	173	33.3
Junior Technical College	3	35	50	25.4
Junior College	1	4	5	62.1
Teachers' College	0	0	16	58.0
Colleges or Universities	1	13	58	26.5

Source: Ministry of Education, *Statistical Yearbook of Education, 1975.*

thousands of students were enrolled in the basic civic schools, acquiring fundamental literacy and numeracy. But with the expansion of educational opportunity at the primary level to all regions of the country, the need for this institution has declined. While in 1947 there were 15,400 civic schools, by 1975 there were only 26. Civic high schools service youths and adults who are graduates of primary or civic schools. They provide middle-school level instruction. Numbers enrolled in these schools have increased slowly, growing from 34,000 in 1949 to 53,000 in 1975. All but a small fraction of the civic high schools are under private auspices. Korea also has a variety of non-accredited secondary and college-level schools or academies that provide non-degree courses in a variety of subjects. Total enrollments in these schools, almost all run by the private sector, were 62,000 in 1975.

Adult education is also provided through the Korean Junior College of Air and Correspondence, a program begun by Seoul National University in 1972. It provides programs in home economics, business management, public administration, agriculture, and primary education at the junior college level.

Admission to the program is restricted to high school graduates. In 1974 there were 19,000 students enrolled.

Literacy programs in Korea were important between 1945, when the adult literacy rate was estimated at 22 percent, and the early 1960s, by which time the rate had risen to 80 percent. The 1970 Population Census established a literacy rate of 88 percent. Adult education also is provided by voluntary organizations. Of these the most important are the YMCA, Korean Mothers Association, and Korean Association of Women College Graduates. The Korean mothers' club movement is claimed to have contributed to the decline in the birth rate during the past ten years.

Agricultural extension services in Korea are provided through the Office of Rural Development (ORD), which disseminates farming technology through guidance workers and farm training centers, rural youth programs, and public information documents and broadcasts. In 1972 the ORD ran 11 provincial farmer training centers, and provided 20,000 farmers with one to two weeks' training; the office also maintained 113 country centers and trained 180,000 leaders for two to six days. About 600,000 young people participated in 4-H activities. Formal training was limited to 500 who received three months' supervised work on a model farm, and 2,000 who received a three-week course in basic farm construction skills. The ORD links in with the activities of 115 secondary-level vocational agricultural schools enrolling 40,000 students, and with the 17 university faculties or colleges of agriculture and 7 junior colleges of agriculture.[3]

The Office of Labor Affairs (OLA) runs publicly supported training centers for industrial workers. In 1972 these centers trained 14,000 workers in classes, and another 4,400 by correspondence. Between 1967 and 1972, it is estimated that about 140,000 workers were trained by the OLA, and in factories. In 1974 legislation was passed to require all firms of 500 or more employees to provide in-plant training of craftsmen. Approximately 15,000 workers were being trained in 45 firms in 1974.[4]

Other educational resources in Korea include libraries, museums, expositions, concerts, plays, lectures, and similar activities. Libraries have expanded rapidly since 1955, as shown in Table 5. In addition to 106 national and public libraries, there are about 35,000 village libraries. These are impressive resources. Could they have helped spark an economic boom? Are they a result of central government planning?

TABLE 5 Books Held by Various Libraries
        (1,000s)

	1955	1968	1975
Public	476.8	864.4	1314.7
College and University	1297.0	1693.3	6335.3
School	403.5	5991.0	7013.7
Special	187.4	1113.9	1367.0

Sources: Chu-Chin Kang, "Library System in Korea," *Koreana Quarterly* 11.4:62–66 (winter 1969–1970); Ministry of Education, *Statistical Yearbook of Education 1975.*

ADMINISTRATION OF EDUCATION

The history of the administration of schools in Korea can be divided into three major periods, corresponding to the nature of the national government. These periods are: the U.S. Military Government from 1945 to 1948; the First Republic (the Rhee regime) from 1948 to 1960; and the Third Republic (the Park regime) from 1961 to the present. (The Second Republic—the Chang Myon regime resulting from the Student Revolution—endured less than one year.) Each of these periods has left its special stamp on the character of the educational system.

THE U.S. MILITARY GOVERNMENT PERIOD
The American liberators had a clear vision of how education would make Korea a modern democracy and mandated three major changes: the system would provide equal opportunity for

all; it would be controlled at the local level to reflect the heterogeneity of the population; and it would strive to develop in students self-reliance and responsibility. To achieve equal opportunity the U.S. Military Government made great efforts to provide educational facilities for all students, at no cost to the students or their parents. Primary education was ordered as coeducational, compulsory, and free to all students. The U.S. Military Government encouraged the creation of school boards at the kun (county) level, with an eye toward adoption of a local school tax. Educators free from Japanese influence were hired to write curricula and textbooks.

Many of the elements created originally under the U.S. Military Government were adopted into the Constitution of the First Republic and written into the Education Law. The Constitution specified: "All citizens shall have the right to receive an equal education correspondent to their abilities . . . compulsory education shall be free . . . independence and political neutrality of education shall be guaranteed." The Education Law created school districts at the county level with corresponding Boards of Education, as well as at the level of province and nation. Primary schools were to be financed in part by the national treasury, and in part through an education tax levied by provincial and municipal governments. The law also created, however, a national Ministry of Education with power to standardize all education in Korea (much as is done at the state level in the United States).

THE FIRST REPUBLIC (THE RHEE REGIME)

The troubled days of the Rhee regime made difficult the realization of the ambitions of the Education Law. In 1949, the central government could provide only 15 percent of the revenues needed to finance primary schools, and local governments only 10 percent. The other 75 percent of the funds for local schools were collected through Parent-Teacher Associations (PTAs). Originally begun under the U.S. Military Government as a means to supplement inadequate teacher salaries, and to increase parental involvement in school decision-making, the PTAs actually operated as tuition-collection agencies: children whose parents could not afford the "voluntary contributions" often were denied admission to school. The government assumed a larger burden of the support of public secondary education, paying half of teachers' salaries (upward of 70 percent of annual costs) from the national treasury and half from provincial government funds. Tuition fees levied on public college and university students were an even smaller portion of the total cost, about 5 percent of total expenditures in 1949 coming from tuition fees, and the rest from the national government.[5]

Increasing political instability and a resulting tightening of control by a threatened central government postponed the elections necessary to create local school boards. The Ministry of Education urged that board members be appointed; opposition political groups pressed for local elections. Increasing subversion and finally the outbreak of war in 1950 moved the government to impose total centralization of authority in education. The organization of education for war involved not only new curricula, but also tight control over educational practices. For example, the government organized "screening committees for the purification of teachers," to weed out persons who had collaborated with the Communists or who in other ways were of doubtful loyalty to the government. As a result of the screening committees, about one-fourth of the total elementary and secondary school teacher force lost their certificates and were removed from their posts.[6]

School districts were not created formally until 1952, when the National Assembly passed legislation providing for districts and boards at the central, provincial, and local (county) levels. The central board consisted of 30 members, 20 appointed by the President and 10 representing Seoul and the nine provinces. The provincial boards were composed of representatives from the counties, and chaired by the Provincial Governor (a political appointee). Local boards represented the various wards and townships, and were responsible for the selection of the local superintendent of education. The county board's authority was limited to primary schools; secondary schools were controlled at the provincial level.

Despite these efforts to create strong local boards, the national Ministry of Education assumed increasing power over the content and direction of educational activities. This seems a result of both increasing interest in economic planning (and consequently the need for central direction) as well as efforts to consolidate political power at the national level. Anti-communism and national security were used as means to mobilize teachers and students in massive demonstrations of support for the government,[7] and opposition efforts to put into practice legislation creating local educational autonomy met with failure.[8]

THE THIRD REPUBLIC (THE PARK REGIME)

With the establishment of the Park regime in 1961, control of the educational system was further centralized. Local school boards were abolished and education offices established in cities and counties. The Central Board of Education, reformulated by law in 1963, had not yet been appointed in full by 1973. There is a direct chain of command from the President to the Provincial Board of Education. The Board is chaired by the Provincial Governor (appointed by the President), and includes the Superintendent (appointed by the President but nominated by the Provincial Board), and five members appointed by the Provincial Assembly. Local education officers are nominated by the Superintendent and appointed by the President. Myung Han Kim comments:

> It is an inescapable fact that the appointments of these top-ranking administrative posts are usually made in the political arena. As a result the positions of higher educational status, such as those of superintendent and chief education officer in each city and county, have been mostly occupied by political appointees rather than carefully selected professional educators.[9]

FINANCING OF EDUCATION

The importance of education is seen clearly in the growth of expenditures on schooling. But what also emerges from the analysis is the government's ability to transfer the cost of education to the private sector.

Central government spending on education has increased many fold in real terms since 1948, as is shown in Table 6. Emphasis on education, at least as measured by central government expenditures, rose sharply around 1960, when education captured a larger share of the government budget. The real value of these expenditures on education has increased a little more than 3 times since 1960, although the ratio of education to total central government expenditures has remained about the same. Similarly, central government expenditures as a proportion of GNP have remained fairly constant, and less than 3.0 percent.

Data on educational expenditures (which here means *direct* expenditures) before 1966 are limited to those incurred by the central government. Table 7 summarizes all sources of educational finance since 1966. In-school expenditures are the expenses incurred in the construction and operation of schools. They may be financed by central and local governments, by students and their families, or by private foundations. Out-of-school expenditures include expenses incurred mainly by students, in the form of books, school supplies, transportation, extracurricular activities, and room and board. In 1974, for example, slightly less than one-fourth the primary school students received textbooks free of charge. About one-third the primary school students received a meal service provided by the government.

As Table 7 shows, total expenditures for education were about 7.7 percent of GNP in 1975, a decline from 1971 when expenditures on education were 9.8 percent of GNP. For the 1966–1975 period, total expenditures increased at a rate of 8.6 percent per year, slightly less than the annual growth rate of the GNP. Expenditures grew more rapidly than the

TABLE 6 Central Government Expenditures on Education, 1948–1975

	Central Government Expenditures on Education (million *wŏn*)		Ratio of Central Government Expenditures on Education (%)	
	Current price	*1970 price*[a]	*to Government Budget*	*to GNP*
1948	2	n.a.	8.0	n.a.
1951	15	n.a.	2.5	n.a.
1954	575	7,668	4.0	0.9
1957	3,217	16,495	9.2	1.6
1960	6,237	28,611	14.9	2.5
1963	10,523	28,596	13.8	2.2
1966	24,346	40,510	17.2	2.4
1969	57,301	66,091	15.5	2.8
1972	116,577	91,289	16.4	3.0
1975	199,776	90,642	15.5	2.2

Source: Yung Bong Kim, "Education and Economic Growth," Working Paper 7605, Korea Development Institute, October 1976, p. 29.

Note: [a]Deflated by GNP deflators.

GNP until 1971, but have lagged behind since then. The change appears to be mainly a result of the reduction of the rate of increase of government expenditures on education. This shows most clearly in an examination of in-school expenditures. They increased at a rate of 19.6 percent between 1967 and 1971, but in 1971–1975 grew at a rate of only 1.4 percent per year. The real value of government expenditures on education actually *decreased* in 1973. The proportion of total educational expenditures that the government finances has declined from 33.5 percent in 1971 to 30.9 percent in 1975.

Table 8 provides a more detailed breakdown of in-school expenditures by source of finance. As the table shows, the central government's share of these expenses has declined from 59.9 percent in 1968 to 48.9 percent in 1975. Because these are total expenditures for all levels of education, they make the contribution of local government seem very small. Since 1962 the central government has attempted to equalize public expenditures among primary school districts across the country by means of formulas that distribute national funds on the basis of local need and local ability to pay. Local sources have provided between 20 and 25 percent of the total amount of local education expenditures at this level.

Three-fourths of government expenditures on education have been spent for compulsory education. In 1974, for example, the government assumed only 12 percent of total in-school costs for non-compulsory education. As non-compulsory education expands, therefore, the share of expenditures borne by students and their families increases. It should be noted that, even at the compulsory level, costs to students and their families are relatively high. In 1974, Yuksŏnghoe (voluntary parent-teacher association) fees amounted to 28 percent of the public budget for compulsory education.[10]

Our estimates of out-of-school expenditures are based on a survey conducted by the Manpower Development Research Institute in 1970, and data on enrollments. Table 9 assumes that the 1970 figures for per-student expenditures remained constant

TABLE 7 Education Expenditures by Sources of Finance
(million wǒn)

	1966	1967	1968	1969	1970
			In current prices		
A) In-School Expenditures	45,647	58,953	73,997	107,708	156,139
	(50.3)	(52.3)	(53.8)	(58.5)	(62.1)
Government	25,188	35,787	39,543	61,910	81,815
	(27.7)	(31.8)	(28.8)	(33.6)	(32.5)
School Juridical Persons	1,251	3,495	5,122	6,556	9,705
	(1.4)	(3.1)	(3.7)	(3.6)	(3.9)
Students	19,208	19,671	29,332	39,242	64,619
	(21.2)	(17.5)	(21.3)	(21.3)	(25.7)
B) Out-of-School Expenditures	45,142	53,708	63,493	76,580	95,149
	(49.7)	(47.7)	(46.2)	(41.5)	(37.9)
C) Educational Expenditures (A+B)	90,789	112,661	137,490	184,288	251,288
	(100.0)	(100.0)	(100.0)	(100.0)	(100.0)
			In 1970 constant prices		
A) In-School Expenditures	75,952	86,063	96,602	124,231	156,139
Government	41,910	52,244	51,623	71,407	81,815
School Juridical Persons	2,082	5,102	6,687	7,562	9,705
Students	31,960	28,717	38,292	45,262	64,619

TABLE 7 (continued)

	1971	1972	1973	1974	1975	1966–1975 Average
	In current prices					
A) In-School Expenditures	196,309 (63.3)	234,629 (63.0)	257,984 (61.6)	321,164 (59.8)	409,520 (59.1)	
Government	103,928 (33.5)	122,684 (32.9)	127,187 (30.4)	161,770 (30.1)	213,859 (30.9)	
School Juridical Persons	9,505 (3.1)	9,334 (2.5)	12,399 (2.9)	17,186 (3.2)	20,828 (3.0)	
Students	82,876 (26.7)	102,611 (27.6)	118,398 (28.3)	142,208 (26.5)	174,833 (25.2)	
B) Out-of-School Expenditures	113,653 (36.7)	138,063 (37.0)	160,832 (38.4)	216,368 (40.2)	283,472 (40.9)	
C) Educational Expenditures (A+B)	309,962 (100.0)	372,692 (100.0)	418,816 (100.0)	537,532 (100.0)	692,992 (100.0)	
	In 1970 constant prices					
A) In-School Expenditures	176,062	183,735	184,406	181,244	185,808	
Government	93,209	96,072	90,913	91,292	97,032	
School Juridical Persons	8,525	7,309	8,863	9,699	9,450	
Students	74,328	80,353	84,630	80,253	79,325	

TABLE 7 (continued)

	1966	1967	1968	1969	1970
			In 1970 constant prices		
B) Out-of-School Expenditures	75,111	78,406	82,889	88,328	95,149
C) Educational Expenditures	151,063	164,469	179,491	212,559	251,288
D) GNP	1,719,180	1,853,010	2,087,120	2,400,490	2,589,260
E) C/D (%)	8.8	8.9	8.6	8.9	9.7
F) A/D (%)	4.4	4.6	4.6	5.2	6.0
			Growth rates (%)		
A) In-School Expenditures		13.3	12.2	28.6	25.7
Government		24.7	-1.2	38.3	14.6
School Juridical Persons		145.1	31.1	13.1	28.3
Students		-10.1	33.3	18.2	42.8
B) Out-of-School Expenditures		4.4	5.7	6.6	7.7
C) Educational Expenditures		8.9	9.1	18.4	18.2
D) GNP		7.8	12.6	15.0	7.9

TABLE 7 (continued)

	1971	1972	1973	1974	1975	1966–1975 Average
			In 1970 constant prices			
B) Out-of-School Expenditures	101,931	108,115	114,962	122,104	128,617	
C) Education Expenditures	277,993	291,850	299,368	303,348	314,425	
D) GNP	2,826,820	3,023,630	3,522,720	3,825,500	4,107,710	
E) C/D (%)	9.8	9.7	8.5	7.9	7.7	8.8
F) A/D (%)	6.3	6.1	5.2	4.7	4.5	5.2
			Growth rates (%)			
A) In-School Expenditures	12.8	4.4	0.4	-1.7	2.5	10.5
Government	13.9	3.1	-5.4	0.4	6.3	9.8
School Juridical Persons	-12.2	-14.3	21.3	9.4	-2.6	18.3
Students	15.0	8.1	5.3	-5.2	-1.2	10.6
B) Out-of-School Expenditures	7.1	6.1	6.3	6.2	5.3	6.2
C) Education Expenditures	10.6	5.0	2.6	1.3	3.7	8.5
D) GNP	9.2	7.0	16.5	8.6	7.4	10.2

Source: Yung Bong Kim, "Education and Economic Growth," p. 30.

Note: Figures in parentheses are the composition of educational expenditures.

TABLE 8 In-School Expenditures by Sources, 1966–1975
(million wŏn)

	1966	1967	1968	1969	1970
I. Central Government	24,778	31,330	44,332	58,923	77,713
	(54.3)	(56.0)	(55.4)	(54.7)	(49.8)
General Account	19,292	24,557	35,332	45,269	58,205
(−) Rents & Fees	284	299	338	398	440
(−) Expenses for Government Administration	59	55	136	115	138
(−) Academy of Science and Arts Organizations	86	114	172	174	232
Economic Development Special Account	5,927	7,272	9,660	13,144	19,074
(−) Cultural Organizations	12	31	14	9	–
SNU Special Account	–	–	–	533	1,244
Claim Fund Management Special Account	–	–	–	673	–
II. Local Government	410	1,447	1,211	2,987	4,102
	(0.9)	(2.6)	(1.5)	(2.8)	(2.6)
Total Expenditure	25,641	32,869	44,623	60,192	79,892
(−) Rents & Fees	2,739	3,266	4,249	5,675	8,262
(−) Local Education Grants	903	989	2,174	3,001	4,120
(−) Local Grants for Compulsory Education	19,784	25,034	33,960	44,850	58,446

TABLE 8 (continued)

	1971	1972	1973	1974	1975
I. Central Government	98,477	118,764	119,478	151,981	200,270
	(50.2)	(50.6)	(46.3)	(47.2)	(48.9)
General Account	74,460	94,475	99,485	134,338	180,381
(–) Rents & Fees	463	630	720	815	873
(–) Expenses for Government Administration	404	361	921	846	1,136
(–) Academy of Science and Arts Organizations	342	350	376	737	637
Economic Development Special Account	23,777	n.a.	17,751	14,647	21,252
(–) Cultural Organizations	–	–	–	613	2,334
SNU Special Account	1,384	1,943	4,259	5,649	3,617
Claim Fund Management Special Account	65	39	–	358	–
II. Local Government	5,451	3,920	7,709	9,789	13,589
	(2.8)	(1.7)	(3.0)	(3.1)	(3.3)
Total Expenditure	103,113	123,793	130,895	168,090	220,073
(–) Rents & Fees	12,666	19,143	23,543	34,500	42,293
(–) Local Education Grants	5,297	16,416	–	–	163,360
(–) Local Grants for Compulsary Education	72,685	76,493	97,727	121,996	–

TABLE 8 (continued)

	1966	1967	1968	1969	1970
Total Expenditure (continued)					
(–) Subsidies	1,583	2,105	3,015	3,596	4,788
(–) Endowments	222	28	14	83	174
III. School Juridical Persons	1,251	3,495	5,122	6,556	9,705
	(2.7)	(6.2)	(6.4)	(6.1)	(6.2)
Educational Expenses	8,815	11,573	16,171	19,414	23,914
Property Furtherance	–	1,953	2,744	3,471	6,726
(–) Rents & Fees	7,564	10,031	13,793	16,329	20,935
IV. Students	19,208	19,671	29,332	39,242	64,619
	(42.1)	(35.2)	(36.7)	(36.4)	(41.4)
Rents & Fees	10,587	13,597	18,380	22,402	29,638
Others	8,621	9,084	10,952	16,840	34,981
V. Total In-School Expenditures (I+II+III+IV)	45,647	55,943	79,997	107,708	156,139
	(100.0)	(100.0)	(100.0)	(100.0)	(100.0)

TABLE 8 (continued)

	1971	1972	1973	1974	1975
Total Expenditures (continued)					
(−) Subsidies	6,645	7,491	1,364	1,042	428
(−) Endowments	369	330	552	763	403
III. School Juridical Persons	9,505	9,334	12,399	17,186	20,828
	(4.8)	(4.0)	(4.8)	(5.4)	(5.1)
Educational Expenses	33,311	42,576	50,371	49,247	65,599
Property Furtherance	5,413	4,482	7,091	11,708	12,254
(−) Rents & Fees	29,219	37,724	45,063	43,769	57,025
IV. Students	82,816	102,611	118,398	142,208	174,833
	(42.2)	(43.7)	(45.9)	(44.3)	(42.7)
Rents & Fees	42,349	57,497	69,326	79,084	100,191
Others	40,527	45,114	49,072	63,124	74,642
V. Total In-School Expenditures (I+II+III+IV)	196,249	234,629	257,984	321,164	409,520
	(100.0)	(100.0)	(100.0)	(100.0)	(100.0)

Source: Yung Bong Kim, "Education and Economic Growth," p. 33.

Note: Figures in parentheses are the composition of in-school expenditures.

TABLE 9 Out-of-School Expenditures
(million wŏn)

	1966	1967	1968	1969	1970	1971	1972	1973	1974	1975
					In 1970 constant prices					
Primary School	35,158	36,629	37,751	38,246	39,103	39,499	39,277	38,694	38,194	38,037
Middle School	17,595	19,536	21,705	24,474	27,773	31,727	34,702	37,558	39,532	41,465
High School	12,328	12,594	13,780	15,222	17,070	18,773	21,326	24,582	28,739	32,664
College & University	10,031	9,647	9,653	10,385	11,203	11,932	12,810	14,128	15,639	16,431
Total	75,112	78,406	82,889	88,327	95,149	101,931	108,115	114,962	122,104	128,597
					In current prices					
Primary School	21,130	25,091	28,917	33,159	39,103	44,041	50,157	54,133	67,680	83,878
Middle School	10,575	13,382	16,626	21,219	27,773	35,376	44,315	52,544	70,051	91,389
High School	7,409	8,627	10,556	13,198	17,070	20,932	27,233	34,390	50,925	71,991
College & University	6,028	6,608	7,394	9,004	11,203	13,304	16,358	19,765	27,712	36,214
Total	45,142	53,708	63,493	76,580	95,149	113,653	138,063	160,832	216,368	283,472

Source: Yung Bong Kim, "Education and Economic Growth," p. 34.

during the period. This is unlikely, and it is probable that the real level of out-of-school expenditures is much greater and the rate of increase larger than shown in Table 9. As the table shows, the overall expansion of out-of-school expenditures is attributable mainly to the expansion of middle and high school enrollments.

The results of the prior tables are summarized in Table 10, which shows educational expenditures assumed by students and their families from 1966 to 1975. In Korea, students' families are the source of approximately two-thirds of the expenditures on education. The proportion declined until 1969, reflecting increased government investment in education, but has increased from 1970 on. The per-student cost of primary education increased by 1 per cent between 1966 and 1975, while costs for middle school increased by 12 percent, high school 6 percent, and college and university 41 percent. (These cost figures reflect only the increase in in-school expenditures, since we do not have data on out-of-school increases.) Given the improvement of the economy, however, the cost of education as a proportion of real disposable income has actually declined in recent years, as shown in Table 11.

Overall, the history suggests that, while the central government may have directed the expansion of education, and contributed to it, much of that growth was not a result of formal policy. What were official goals for education?

EDUCATIONAL GOALS AND OBJECTIVES

Changes in government have not been accompanied by major changes in goals for education. In March 1946, under the U.S. Military Government, the National Committee on Educational Planning adopted these goals for the new educational system:
   1) Formulation of character which is realized in international friendship and harmony as well as in national independence and self-respect

TABLE 10 Educational Expenditures Paid by Students
(million wŏn)

	1966	1967	1968	1969	1970
A) In-School Expenditures	19,208	22,681	29,332	39,242	74,619
Rents and Fees	10,587	13,597	18,380	22,402	29,638
Others[a]	8,621	9,084	10,952	16,840	34,981
B) Out-of-School Expenditures	45,142	53,708	63,493	76,580	95,149
C) Expenditures Paid by Students (A+B)	64,350	76,389	92,825	115,822	169,768
D) Total Educational Expenditures	90,789	112,661	137,490	184,288	251,288
E) C/D (%)	70.9	67.8	67.5	62.8	67.8

	1971	1972	1973	1974	1975
A) In-School Expenditures	82,876	102,611	112,398	142,208	174,833
Rents and Fees	42,349	57,497	63,326	79,084	100,191
Others[a]	40,527	45,114	49,072	63,124	74,642
B) Out-of-School Expenditures	113,653	138,063	160,832	216,368	283,472
C) Expenditures Paid by Students (A+B)	196,529	240,674	273,230	358,576	458,305
D) Total Education Expenditures	309,962	372,692	418,816	537,532	692,992
E) C/D (%)	63.4	64.6	65.2	66.7	66.1

Source: Yung Bong Kim, "Education and Economic Growth," p. 36.

Note: [a]Includes school-support fund, experimentation and practical training expenses, and student self-governing expenses.

TABLE 11 Enrollment Ratios, Real Disposable Income per Household, Cost of Education, and Number of Persons per Household, 1966–1975

	1966	1967	1968	1969	1970	1971	1972	1973	1974	1975
Enrollment Ratio (%)										
Middle school										
Male	51.31	51.99	53.28	55.91	61.33	66.18	68.42	72.96	76.03	79.49
Female	31.25	32.45	33.71	36.25	40.59	45.71	48.70	53.03	57.14	62.44
Both	46.69	42.55	43.84	46.42	51.33	56.32	58.92	63.33	66.89	71.27
High school										
Male	34.05	31.90	33.42	33.24	33.70	33.83	35.62	38.61	43.31	47.09
Female	18.57	18.11	19.42	20.29	21.25	22.02	23.30	26.15	28.79	31.22
Both	26.55	25.22	26.64	26.98	27.68	28.13	29.67	32.57	36.53	39.44
College and university										
Male	9.80	8.80	8.36	9.20	9.69	9.86	9.67	9.31	9.52	9.51
Female	3.13	2.95	2.79	2.86	2.96	3.17	3.35	3.36	3.59	3.67
Both	6.60	5.97	5.67	6.13	6.43	6.62	6.61	6.43	6.65	6.69
Ratio of Cost of Education to Real Disposable Income (%)										
Middle School	11.5	10.8	10.3	10.4	10.8	11.3	11.1	8.9	8.1	n.a.
High School	18.2	17.6	17.4	13.5	15.8	13.4	14.4	12.5	10.6	n.a.
College and University	40.4	41.6	41.5	38.4	44.5	40.7	42.3	34.6	32.4	n.a.
Number of Persons per Household	5.62	5.79	5.76	5.68	5.37	5.32	5.27	5.22	5.17	5.13

Source: Yung Bong Kim, "Education and Economic Growth," p. 40.

2) Emphasis on individual responsibility and a spirit of mutual assistance: enforcement of a spirit of faithful and practical service
3) Contribution to human civilization by originating science and technology and by refining and emphasizing national culture
4) Cultivation of a spirit of persistent enterprise by elevating the physical standards of the people
5) Cultivation of sincere and complete character by emphasis on the appreciative and creative power of fine arts.[11]

These goals later were adopted by the Rhee Government without major change and were embodied in the Education Law. The ultimate goal of Korean education is prescribed in Article 1, as follows:

> Education shall aim at, under the great ideal of *hongik in'gan* (benefits for all mankind), assisting all people in perfecting individual capability, developing the ability for independent life, and acquiring citizenship qualifications needed to serve for the democratic development of the nation and for the realization of human co-prosperity.

The ideal of *hongik in'gan* was "an ancient notion of the general weal" and had been the guiding philosophy in Korea for many centuries.

To realize these goals, more specific objectives were adopted, as follows:

1) Cultivation of knowledge and habits needed for the sound development and sustenance of body and of indomitable spirit
2) Development of patriotic spirit for the preservation and enhancement of national independence and values for the cause of world peace
3) Succession and development of national culture and contribution to the creation and growth of world culture
4) Cultivation of truth-seeking spirit and of the abilities to think scientifically, act creatively, and live rationally
5) Development of the love for freedom and of high respect

for responsibilities necessary to lead well-harmonized community life with the spirit of faithfulness, cooperation, love, and respect
6) Development of aesthetic sensitivity to appreciate and create sublime arts, to enjoy the beauty of nature, and to utilize leisure effectively for cheerful and harmonious life

The goal statements appear to represent an effort to blend modern concepts of education with traditionally approved social values. Ideas such as participation in the advancement of world peace, contribution toward the creation of world culture, scientific thinking and creative activity, love of freedom and well-harmonized community life, and effective utilization of leisure can be considered modern. On the other hand, concepts such as indomitable spirit, patriotism, enhancement of national culture, and faithfulness are traditional. Byung Hun Nam[12] saw this combination as reflecting a typical Korean syncretism which allows democratic education to be pursued without abandoning century-old ideals and traditions contradictory to democratic development.

The Education Law also states more specific objectives for each level of schooling. The goal of elementary education is to provide every child with the basic information essential to national life. There are seven objectives:
1) Building an ability to use and understand the mother tongue in everyday use
2) Cultivating an understanding of the relations among the individual, the community, and the state, and an understanding of past and present life of the local community and nation
3) Training scientific observation of natural phenomena
4) Developing sufficient mathematical ability for economic problems in everyday life
5) Cultivation of a proper concept of labor and good taste in food, clothing, and housing
6) Cultivation of basic understandings and skills in music, art, and literature

7) Teaching the importance of health and hygiene and help-
ing develop sanitary habits

The goal of education in the middle school is to continue the
liberal and general education of the pupils upon the foundation
laid by primary education. More specifically:

1) Extension of the objectives of the elementary school,
   including the knowledge and habits needed by a responsible
   member of society
2) Teaching basic knowledge and skills common to all occupations and improving the ability of the student to choose a
   vocation suited to his individuality
3) Improvement of the student's self-discipline, both in and
   out of the school, and development of an even-handed
   critical ability
4) Improvement of the student's physical well-being

The educational goal of the high school is to give advanced
general and technical education of the students on the basis of
prior achievement in the middle school. The specific objectives
can be summarized as follows:

1) Improvement and extension of the results of middle school
   education in order to develop the character and technique
   needed by a responsible member of society
2) Improvement of the student's capacity to understand and
   to form judgments about the nation and society
3) Improvement of the student's physical well-being and
   ability to plan and manage his own life

The nature of education in the junior (technical) colleges is
virtually an extension of the vocational education in high
schools, aiming to teach semi-professional knowledge and skills
for an occupation rather than academic knowledge in a
specialized subject.

On the other hand, the goal of education in the college and
university is to teach and help to investigate deeper theories of
learning and the vast, precise methods for their application
which are necessary to national and world welfare, and to
cultivate the virtue of leadership.

As a professional type of education, the junior teachers' college and the college of education have a rather specialized goal to train competent teachers by:

1) Improvement of the national character and competence, with special emphasis on diligence, cooperation, and sound critical judgment
2) Instruction in the theory and practical methods of national education
3) Instruction in the professional devotion and philosophy of the teacher

Since its promulgation in 1949, the Education Law has been revised at least fifteen times. Despite these changes, and despite a savage war, a military coup, and an economic boom, the statements of general goals and specific objectives have remained unchanged. One implication is that these statements have little to do with actual practice; they may serve only to maintain certain myths about education's role.

CHANGES IN POLICY AND PRACTICE

Major reforms of education were begun under the Rhee Government in 1955, and under the Park Military Government in 1961. But while both governments engaged in planning, neither provided the financial base to support its educational plans. Even after the economic "take-off" began in the early 1960s, there were shortages of teachers and facilities because required funds had not been appropriated. At one point, "the proposed educational plans were so financially limited that they . . . were kept confidential from the public."[13] Statements of policy, therefore, did not bear a direct relationship to government actions in education, and for that reason are not always faithful guides to the functioning of the educational system. What government ministers stated were the objectives of education did not always match either what actually was taught in schools or what people learned.

POLICIES EXPRESSED BY THE PRESIDENTS

If one takes public statements of the Presidents as an indicator of public policy in education, the following differences between the Rhee and Park Governments can be seen.[14] First, education has been more important to the Park Government. During an equivalent time period, Park mentioned education more frequently than did Rhee, 30 times compared to 19 (in major addresses). Attention to education by the President might also be reflected in the more rapid turnover of ministers under Park as compared to Rhee. The average term of office for a Minister of Education under Rhee was 23.7 months, compared to 13.5 months under Park.

Table 12 provides a breakdown of the policy orientations given to education in major addresses by the two presidents.

TABLE 12 Educational Policy Orientations in Major Addresses of President Rhee and President Park

	Rhee		Park	
Policy Orientation	%	Rank	%	Rank
National Defense and Spirit	36.7	1	20.0	2
Educational Quality	21.1	2	10.0	6
Individual Development	15.8	3	16.7	3
Socio-economic Development	10.5	4.5	26.7	1
Administrative Improvement	10.5	4.5	13.3	4.5
Cultural Development	5.3	6	13.3	4.5

Source: Jin Eun Kim, "Analyses of The National Planning Process," p. 108.

Under Rhee, Ministers of Education were concerned with individual knowledge and moral development, and especially anti-Communist education. In contrast, Park's government "gave first priority for education to exemplify socio-economic development, with concentration on educational productivity and technical education."[15] The efficiency of education became a major concern, as planners recognized the dangers of overproduction at the secondary and higher levels and sought ways to reduce unemployment among the educated. Vocational education was to be given major emphasis with the objective of reaching a 70-30 split of enrollments between vocational and academic high schools by 1980.[16]

The planning strategy of the Park Government was couched in terms of maximizing educational investments through reduction of illiteracy, and improvement of both the quantity and quality of graduates of primary education, since persons at this level were seen by planners as critical to an economic development strategy based on intermediate technologies. In short, where the Rhee regime had allowed education to develop without control in response to unbridled social demand, the new government would organize education to meet development needs.

Implementation of the plan was to be mandatory. In the fervor of the first days of the Park Military Government and the National Reconstruction Movement (the early 1960s) this meant an effort to weed out corruption, impose discipline, and establish a means for choosing and encouraging students most likely to contribute to development. With regard to the campaign against corruption, "the Ministry called on schools to rigidly observe regulations on enrollment capacity and dismiss incompetent, draft-dodging or concubine-keeping educators."[17] The new discipline involved uniforms for college students, including caps and badges, and "coeds were seen without high heels, parasols, manicured finger-nails or fancy coiffures."[18] Examinations given by each of the universities were replaced with a single state examination for entrance into the university, and a system of scholarships was created to make it possible for more bright, low-income students to attend.

It is not clear whether these policy statements actually resulted in a permanent major shift of educational priorities. The growth of higher education stopped until 1967 but since that time has increased at almost the same rate as secondary education. Vocational education does not yet enroll half of all students in secondary schools. Expenditures on primary education are still lower than in other countries (including those at the same GNP level), and relatively low compared to expenditures (by the state) on higher education. Class sizes in primary education *grew* between 1961 and 1965, and began to decline only as enrollments leveled off and began to decline. Class sizes for all other levels increased, suggesting no additional inputs to improve educational *quality*. In short, there seems to have been a lack of fit between presidential objective and implementation. Perhaps this can be understood better by a review of the development of educational planning in Korea.

EDUCATIONAL PLANNING

The major effort of the U.S. Military Government during 1945–1948 was to expand educational opportunities and train enough Korean teachers so that the system could be run by them. The lofty objectives of the National Committee on Educational Planning were seen to represent three major interests: "In 1947 all the primary schools ... had three slogans ... : 1) the development of patriotism; 2) the development of scientific education ... ; and 3) the development of the body."[19] This new educational philosophy was labeled the New Education Movement. Its roots were in the progressive education philosophy of American educators who attempted to realize in Korea what had become conventional wisdom in the United States: "New Education focused on subject-centered learning according to individual interest and capacity; the motto was experiential learning. Teaching methods and processes were important in order to train the individual toward creative and effective ways of thinking, thus creating a foundation for the reconstruction of the social order into a *progressive* cultural identity."[20]

American educators in Korea attempted to develop initiative in students, to encourage participation in classes, to stimulate an active, discovery method of learning. This included questioning (including of the teacher) in the classroom, flexibility in planning and scheduling, the introduction of materials from the outside (including field trips and visits of outsiders to the school), attention to individual differences, group work, and a variety of other techniques. Students were to be taught that there is no one right answer to most social questions, that what *works* is generally what is best, and that change is to be seen as desirable.

Ross Harold Cole in his study of Korean elementary education claims that the "new philosophy of education" was in sharp conflict with traditional values of Korean society and Korean educators, in part because of American ignorance about the Korean reality:

> The American educational advisors who suggested programs of educational reform in South Korea from 1945–1955 seem to have been poor examples of what educational advisors ought to have been. The programs that were suggested during the decade following World War II would condemn American educational advisors for ethnocentricity and for not regarding the needs of the Korean Government. Few, if any, American advisors understood what had been taught or what was then taught in Korean schools; even fewer, it seems, had working use of the language. One wonders if any American advisor understood the Korean culture values and systems of formal and informal behavior.[21]

Formal educational planning in Korea did not begin until after the war, when the most acute problem facing education was the restoration of heavy losses in facilities and in teaching personnel. As an energetic rehabilitation program, the Ministry of Education prepared the Compulsory Education Accomplishment Plan, 1954–1959, with the support from the United Nations Korea Reconstruction Agency (Ministry of Education, 1953). The plan aimed at achieving a 96-percent level of enrollment of school-age population by the end of the plan period, to be accomplished by building an additional 30,000 classrooms. The plan also estimated financial resource requirements. The plan was deficient in funding from the beginning year, however, and secured only 38 percent of the requested amount.[22] Thus, the enrollment ratio remained around 80 percent throughout the planning period.

Under the Park Military Government in 1961, the Ministry of Education prepared a Five-Year Educational Reconstruction Plan (1962–1966) for the purpose of integrating educational policies into the First Five-Year Economic Development Plan.[23] Covering secondary and higher education levels as well as compulsory education, the plan represented the first comprehensive attempt at educational planning in Korea. Special consideration was given to the problem of educated unemployment. In 1960, it was estimated that almost 60 percent of 15,000 college graduates failed to find employment within three months after leaving school. The plan fixed promotion rates to higher school levels, and allowed for only a natural increase of enrollments resulting from expansion of school-age population. A curtailment of college enrollment specifically was planned to maintain a balance with manpower needs.

During the First Five-Year-Plan period, high school enrollments were in excess of predictions by almost 30 percent and college enrollments by an average of 38 percent. A study at that time described the circumstances as follows:

> The military government adopted a policy orientation of decreasing the numbers of colleges and their authorized students in 1961. Five years later, after six ministers changed the position, colleges increased 90% and students 40% over the respective numbers in 1960.[24]

Planning seems to have had greater success in increasing enrollments than in curtailing them. In conjunction with the Second Five-Year Economic Development Plan (1967–1971), a primary education plan focused on facility expansion to solve the problem of "double-shift" use of classrooms. The investment plan for classroom construction was incorporated into the Economic Development Plan and the enrollment ratio climbed above the target of 95 percent, reaching 98.1 percent in 1971. The secondary education plan attempted to increase promotion rates to 51 percent for primary school graduates and to 75 percent for middle school graduates. Because of the abolition of middle school entrance examinations, however, the enrollment increase exceeded the targets. Unfortunately, perhaps, the increase in numbers of students was not followed by a corresponding increase in teachers and facilities.

In 1969, the National Council for Long-Term Educational Planning (CLEP) was established under the chairmanship of the Prime Minister. This council produced a draft 15-year plan that included an analysis of natural development trends and their implications for education, as well as current educational problems. The plan made quantitative projections of enrollments, demand for teachers, and physical and financial requirements at minimum and maximum levels. Priority was given to expansion and development of secondary and higher education including innovative expansion of graduate education.

Despite two years' work by 550 participants, the plan has had a mixed history. The new Minister of Education in 1971 decided to replace the National Council for Long-Term Educational Planning with an Educational Policies Council. This council, established as an advisory body for the Minister, has emphasized relatively short-term policies. With CLEP abolished, interest in continuous long-term planning has declined. Inadequate financial support from the budget agency also has been a serious constraint to implementing educational policies as well as plans. An ex-Minister of Education recalled such difficulties as follows: "Most of the matters on educational policies, which were submitted to the Cabinet meeting . . . passed through. But the particular matters on financial or personnel requirements were defeated by the economy and financial ministers who underestimated the socio-economic value of education."[25] Chong Ch'ol Kim, a key member of the Council for Long-Term Education Planning, commented: "The only long-range planning that has been implemented in Korea would be economic development plans in the practical sense, despite the fact that many long-range plans have been developed and are now being developed. Strictly speaking, the long-range educational plan also seems to fare the same as many other plans of the government."[26]

IMPLEMENTATION OF REFORMS
AT THE CLASSROOM LEVEL

There also have been difficulties in translating educational policies enunciated at the highest levels of government into instructional programs at the classroom level. Data to support this statement are based on an examination of government-published textbooks used in primary schools (where the government has invested most attention and capital).

An examination of textbook contents, as an indicator of curricular emphases, seems particularly relevant in Korea, given the heavy dependence on the text as a source of material to be used by teachers. Textbook content is carefully controlled by the government, which not only publishes all primary texts, the Korean language and moral education texts for middle and senior high schools, the books for vocational middle schools, and most texts for the vocational high schools, but also reviews the content of all other books. ("The government publishing system for textbooks is often considered to be like systems adopted under dictatorships where the government controls everything.")[27]

Textbooks have been rewritten after each of the educational reforms of 1953, 1961, and 1973. Apparently none of the reforms had as its major objective improvements in the teaching and content of technical subjects (science and mathematics) in primary and secondary schools. That does not mean that there have not been systematic improvements in these areas, with educators returning from abroad with advanced training, and in-service training within the Ministry of Education and the universities,[28] but only that reform of science and mathematics education has not been the central focus of attention.[29] Therefore almost all of what is reported below refers to changes in educational objectives as seen in the content of basic readers, and in texts in citizenship and moral education.

An examination of textbook contents and analysis of their themes suggest, in general, that there has been a steady trend away from emphasis on individuals and toward emphasis on the nation. In moral education texts published in 1957, emphasis was on individual behavior. In 1965, the emphasis of texts was on social ethics and problems of getting along in groups. In texts published in 1974, major emphasis was placed on the individual's contribution to the welfare of the nation. Similar trends are found in analyses of social studies and Korean texts.[30]

One way to examine the values communicated in textbooks written for young children is to catalog the "heroes" presented to them. The trend from 1955 on has been for heroes to represent increasingly nationalist values, as Table 13 demonstrates. Cole attributes the high proportion of foreign heroes in

TABLE 13 Themes of Hero Lessons According to Nationality of Hero in Primary Social Studies, Korean, and Moral Education

	1957		1965		1974	
	Foreign	Korean	Foreign	Korean	Foreign	Korean
Service to mankind	23	2	8	0	14	1
Study and dedication	16	9	6	9	11	13
Personal valor and patriotism	6	22	3	24	8	49
TOTAL	45	33	17	33	33	63

Source: Ross Harold Cole, p. 283.

the 1957 textbooks to the influence of American advisors during the 1945–1955 period. He points out that previously (given prohibitions by the Japanese and the distraction of the Korean War) little research had been done by Koreans into their own history. As democracy was a foreign import, educators could not easily identify Korean exemplars. Even in 1965, there was a strong emphasis on foreigners. Biographies are the most common type of material among the 189 units in the Korean texts published in 1965; of the 93 non-fictional people mentioned 47 are Westerners.[31] And, as the table shows, in 1974 foreigners, more often than Koreans, were cited as examples of service to mankind. "It was noted that most foreign heroes portrayed virtues in areas in which Korean heroes were lacking. For example, foreign heroes dominated the philanthropist, explorer and scientist-inventor categories which had no Korean hero representation."[37]

The table also shows that, over time, the textbooks increasingly hold up as models to young Korean children national heroes who demonstrate personal valor and patriotism. Included in this category are Admiral Sun-sin Yi, whose "turtle" ship destroyed the Japanese flotilla in the 1590s, and Kwan-sun Yu, a girl killed in the March 1st Independence Movement in 1919. Half the Korean heroes are military men. The 1974 moral education textbooks include ten lessons detailing aspects of the Korean army's involvement in the Vietnam War. Only three Asians (other than Koreans) were mentioned in the 1957 texts, and only one in 1965 and 1974.

In the most recent textbooks, nearly half the Korean heroes and all the foreign models were apparently chosen to encourage "creativity" among Korean youth. By creativity is meant the power that individuals acquire when they link themselves with the corporate will of the state. "By identifying with those sagacious Korean ancestors who established cultural traditions and exemplified the 'spirit' of the Korean race, . . . the student will 'discover what it meant to be a Korean'."[33] Korean heroes who exemplify creativity stress the need for intellectual development, and demonstrate the practice of virtues such as perseverance, prudence, living within one's means, and respect for labor. Foreign heroes are used to illustrate "the arduous struggle one had to endure in order to achieve success." The foreign heroes included in the texts include men such as Thomas Edison, Frederic Chopin, Jean François Millet, Louis Braille, Alfred Nobel, Alexander Graham Bell, Albert Schweitzer, and René Laennec. Cole comments:

Whether or not the Westerner accepts those values listed . . . as being indicative of lessons which foster development of the spirit of creativity makes little difference to the Korean educators who promulgated the curriculum in 1973. The fact is that the Korean educators have deliberately planned lessons that will foster what they consider to be the spirit of creativity . . . It is significant, indeed, that the development of personal qualities, skills and knowledge is funneled into the realm of national subjectivity—imposing the will of the state upon the individual—which contributes to the maintenance of the socially cooperative welfare state of South Korea.[34]

Although public policy addresses in the mid-1960s promised a reorganization of education to promote economic development, primary school textbooks did not change in that direction. The proportion of lesson themes mentioning or promoting economic development held relatively constant over the period, as can be seen in Table 14. Those stressing personal responsibility and independence declined in frequency of appearance, while those stressing creativity increased. The total of the three categories showed little change between 1957 and 1974. The most common theme included under the rubric Economic Productivity was: "Serve in community projects" followed by "Be frugal and economical." Personal Responsibility and Independence included themes such as "Be prudent in the face of emergencies," and "Know how to buy things in society." The most common theme included under Creativity was "Contribute to the progress of our country," followed by "Economize, be frugal, and live within your means."

Another analysis of textbooks has found no significant change in development values in textbooks for Korean, comparing 1966 and 1973 versions. Hong Yung Kim coded 15 stories from 1966 texts and 22 from 1973 books, using measures of achievement motivation, statements of man over nature, future orientation, activist personality, and individualistic human relationships. Kim reports no differences on scores on any of the five measures.

Similar findings were obtained by Cole. Table 14 indicates a

TABLE 14 Distribution of Lesson Themes in Social Studies,
Korean, and Moral Education Textbooks for
Primary Schools, 1957, 1965, 1974
(%)

Theme	1957	1965	1974
Economic Productivity	21.0	21.0	19.7
Personal Responsibility and Independence	17.0	13.2	13.2
Personal Development (Creativity)	17.7	17.4	22.9
Social Cooperation	9.5	10.6	7.2
Obedience to Social Rules and Regulations	5.5	7.3	5.4
Development of Positive Social Relationships	21.7	26.0	15.8
Anti-Communism	9.8	14.5	21.5
Nationalism and Patriotism	19.1	16.6	29.3

Source: Ross Harold Cole. Columns add to more than 100% as themes may be
included in more than one category.

decline in the frequency of themes dealing with either vertical
or horizontal social relationships. The Social Cooperation rubric
includes themes such as "Be cooperative with public works and
serve willingly," while Obedience to Social Rules includes
"Observe public morality." The most frequent theme in the
category Development of Positive Social Relationships urged
students to "Have an attitude of respect for those who work for
public good."

The decline in lessons stressing social relationships was filled
by an increase of lesson themes dealing with Anti-Communism
and Nationalism and Patriotism. The most common theme in the
first category was "Remember the 6.25 [June 25th] invasion;
hate communism," a reference to the anniversary of the invasion
of the country by North Korea. Nationalism and Patriotism
themes included "Contribute to the progress of the country," and
"Revere the spirit of patriotic ancestors who brought peace."

In summary, it would appear that the educational system in Korea has not grown consistently in response to planning to meet economic needs. The rapid growth of private education has pushed the total system in ways that do not always match what the economic planners would have desired. In addition, the content of education also has not changed in a direction that would seem consistent with modern values. Those values are present, but the trend has been as much or more toward anti-communism and acceptance of an authoritarian state as it has been toward individual initiative and entrepreneurship.

INCREASES IN RESOURCE
INPUTS TO EDUCATION

Does the weakness of planning mean that educational quality has suffered? Or is Korean education, despite the trends noted above, unique in both the quality of its inputs, and of its outputs?

Changes in educational policy and curriculum *have* been accompanied by changes in resources available to the educational endeavor. Table 15 compares the size of the total government budget with that for the Ministry of Education (excluding Seoul National University) from 1948 to 1975. After declining during the Korean War period, resources allocated to education increased both in total amount and as a proportion of the national budget, reaching a peak in 1971 when they totaled 19 percent of the national budget. In general, the Ministry budget has been a greater proportion of the national budget since 1961, when the present regime came to power.

Opportunities for education have increased dramatically during the past thirty years. First, as Table 16 shows, enrollments in formal educational institutions have expanded from 5.7 percent of the total population in 1945 to 28.8 percent in 1975. While in 1953 less than 60 percent of the corresponding age group was enrolled in middle school, all of the age group was enrolled by 1970. (Percentages greater than 100 reflect the presence of students older than the corresponding age group.)

TABLE 15 Ministry of Education Budget as Proportion
of Total Government Budget, 1948–1976

Year	Government Budget (million wŏn)	MOE Budget (million wŏn)	MOE/ Govt. X100
1948	19.5	1.7	8.7
1949	91.1	10.4	11.4
1950	243.0	13.8	5.7
1951	617.9	16.0	2.6
1952	2151.7	42.9	2.0
1953	6068.3	159.3	2.6
1954	14239.2	597.2	4.2
1955–1956	28143.9	2663.3	9.5
1957	35003.4	3283.1	9.4
1958	41097.0	4458.0	10.8
1959	40002.4	5986.4	15.0
1960	41995.5	6381.3	15.2
1961	61422.9	7598.2	12.4
1962	69481.2	10367.6	14.9
1963	76322.6	10916.1	14.3
1964	75396.2	12226.6	16.2
1965	94652.3	15331.2	16.2
1966	141629.0	25203.3	17.8
1967	181076.5	32085.9	17.7
1968	265719.5	45301.8	17.0
1969	370882.3	59579.5	16.1
1970	446273.3	78476.2	17.6
1971	524247.8	99508.4	19.0
1972	709335.7	119782.0	16.9
1973	659371.6	118431.7	18.0
1974	1038256.9	153858.4	14.8
1975	1291957.4	206987.9	16.0

Source: Ministry of Education, *Statistical Yearbook of Education, 1975.*

TABLE 16 School Enrollment as Percentage
of Corresponding Age Group, 1945–1975

Type of School	1945	1953	1955	1960	1965	1970	1975
Elementary (ages 6–11)	—	59.6	77.4	86.2	91.6	102.8	107.6
Middle (ages 12–14)	—	21.1	30.9	33.3	39.4	53.3	74.0
High School (ages 15–17)	—	12.4	17.8	19.9	27.0	29.3	40.5
College (ages 18–21)	—	3.1	5.0	6.4	6.9	9.3	8.6
% of total to the total population	5.7	13.3	17.2	18.5	22.0	25.3	28.8

Sources: For the statistics of the 1950s, see UNESCO, *Republic of Korea*, p. 9. For the 1960s, see Taehan Sanggon Hoeŭiso, *Kyŏngje kaebal kwa kyoyuk t'uja* (Seoul, 1973), Chapter 2. For the 1970s, see Han'guk Kyoyuk Yŏn'guwŏn, *Kyoyuk Kyehoek e kwanhan kich'o t'onggye charyo* (Seoul, 1975), p. 41.

In 1953, only 21 percent of the age group was enrolled in middle school, as compared with 74 percent in 1975. Only 12 of every 100 high school age students were enrolled in 1953, as compared with 4 in 10 in 1975. Opportunities for education have therefore increased significantly between 1945 and 1975.

Some results of this expansion of educational opportunity are shown in Table 17. In 1945, it was estimated that 78 percent of the adult population could not read or write Korean; by 1970, that figure had been reduced to less than 12 percent. By 1970, the average adult in Korea had completed almost six years of schooling.

Most of the increment in public sector resources allocated to education has gone into improving the quality of compulsory (or elementary) education. The evidence for this takes various forms. First, the share of the Ministry budget assigned to compulsory education has, since 1954, dropped below 70 percent only once, in 1974, when it went to 69.6 percent of the total. As Table 2 demonstrated, enrollments in elementary

TABLE 17 Educational Attainment Level of Total Population

	1945	1960	1966	1970
Illiteracy rates[a] (%)				
M	–	15.8	6.9	5.3
F	–	39.8	22.2	17.8
TOTAL	78	27.9	14.7	11.6
Average years of schooling[b]				
M	–	–	6.0 yrs.	6.9 yrs.
F	–	–	3.9 yrs.	4.7 yrs.
TOTAL	–	–	4.9 yrs.	5.7 yrs.

Notes: [a]Calculated from the census reports of the corresponding years.
[b]Weighted means of schooling years.

education have been declining since 1970, while increases have been recorded in middle and high schools. A constant share of the budget allocated to elementary education means, therefore, an increase in the per-pupil expenditure on elementary education as compared to that of other levels.

An examination of changes in class size also supports the argument. As Table 18 shows, class sizes (number of students per teacher in a classroom) for elementary schools have varied considerably since 1952 and are now declining. Class sizes in middle schools have remained fairly constant with a recent increase. Academic and vocational high school class sizes have definitely increased.

Furthermore, although class sizes in elementary schools have not been reduced dramatically, there has been a considerable decline in double- and triple-shift use of school buildings. Figure 2 shows the gap between the number of classes actually given and classrooms available from 1952 through 1974. More classes than classrooms necessarily means that some schools are used for two or three sessions a day, which in turn generally means shorter sessions and inconvenient scheduling. Thanks to massive

TABLE 18 Number of Students per Class, 1945–1975

Type of School	1945	1952	1956	1960	1965	1970	1975
Elementary	54.0	62.6	55.5	57.4	65.4	62.1	56.7
Middle		60.6	65.9	48.3	60.7	62.0	64.5
Academic High	55.3	34.8	46.3	45.7	59.8	60.1	58.1
Vocational High	49.6	45.9	44.9	33.8	53.5	56.1	57.0

Source: Ministry of Education, *Statistical Yearbooks of Education.*

efforts in elementary school construction, the gap generated by the ravages of the Korean War has been almost completely eliminated.[37]

At the same time, school buildings have been increased in size, principally by the addition of classrooms to existing facilities, and secondarily by the construction of larger new schools. In general, schools in Korea are much larger than those in most countries, including the United States. The figures in Table 19 are averages including small rural schools. In some urban elementary schools there are as many as 5,000 children in one building. Increments in size have been largest for elementary and middle schools, where the government has invested proportionately more resources (see Table 3).

The creation of larger schools makes possible the assignment of special teachers in fields such as music, physical education, moral education, health and hygiene, and other subjects not taught every day. The result is an enriched educational program. As Table 20 shows, student-teacher ratios have changed considerably over the years in elementary education. Increased unit expenditures have gone, in part, into providing elementary school children with a wider variety of special instructors.

Increased expenditures have also been required as the level of preparation of the teaching force has increased. In contrast with many developing countries, in which most teachers have had little more training than the students under their tutelage, Korea has employed a relatively well trained instructional force.

FIGURE 2 The Gap Between Classes and Classrooms
in Elementary Schools, 1945–1974

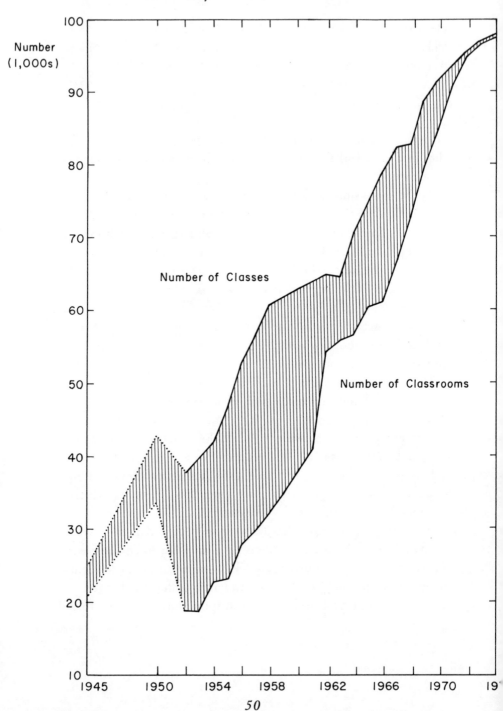

TABLE 19 Trend of School Size, 1945–1975
(classrooms per school)

Type of School	1945	1952	1956	1960	1965	1970	1975
Elementary	7.3	4.8	6.6	8.5	11.6	14.3	15.3
Middle	–	5.8	6.8	9.5	9.6	13.1	16.0
Academic High	–	15.3	8.4	11.2	13.2	12.6	16.5
Vocational High	–	7.5	7.3	10.8	13.2	9.8	14.9

TABLE 20 Students per Teacher, 1945–1975

Type of School	1945	1952	1956	1960	1965	1970	1975
Elementary	69.3	66.5	61.2	58.6	62.4	56.9	51.8
Middle		37.4	44.8	40.7	39.3	42.3	43.2
High	25.9	27.3	38.1	27.2	30.2	29.8	31.4
College	5.2	26.7	32.5	25.7	20.8	19.4	19.5

Table 21 shows the distribution of teachers by level of formal education, beginning in 1952. All elementary school teachers at that time had completed at least high school, a level considered adequate in most developing countries. Most middle and high school teachers had completed some higher education.

These high levels of teacher training have improved since 1952. Now most middle and high school teachers have completed a four-year college program, and almost half the elementary school teachers have gone through a two-year post-secondary training program. If increased training is reflected in improved instruction, then Korea has improved quality by spending its resources on training and hiring better teachers.

CHANGES IN INTERNAL EFFICIENCY

Increased inputs to education should have some impact on the efficiency of the system in meeting its objectives. Most educators agree that schools should carry students to some meaningful level of achievement and, therefore, that early leaving or

TABLE 21 Educational Attainment Levels of Teachers,
1952–1975

	1952	*1964*	*1970*	*1975*
Elementary teachers (persons)	36,100	75,455	101,095	108,126
Secondary education	98.4%	84.1%	59.4%	50.5%
Junior college	1.5	12.1	32.0	44.1
College	0.1	3.7	8.3	5.1
Graduate school	–	0.1	0.3	0.3
Middle school teachers	7,817	17,339	31,207	46,917
Secondary education	36.7%	7.6%	6.3%	3.8%
Junior college	42.7	37.7	24.5	15.4
College	20.6	53.0	65.5	78.3
Graduate school	–	1.7	3.7	2.5
High school teachers	4,931	13,036	19,854	35,755
Secondary education	25.3%	3.3%	7.3%	4.4%
Junior college	51.0	13.8	8.4	5.1
College	23.7	79.3	78.8	85.6
Graduate school	–	3.6	5.5	4.9
Total	48,848	105,830	152,156	190,798
Secondary education	81.1%	61.6%	41.7%	30.3%
Junior college	13.1	16.5	27.4	29.7
College	5.8	21.1	29.2	38.2
Graduate school	–	0.8	1.7	1.8

Notes: Figures include all kinds of teachers.
Dropouts were regarded as graduates.

desertion or dropping out reflect negatively on the educational system.[38] A common assumption is that the cycles in the educational process are integral, that their objectives are not met adequately unless the entire cycle is completed. Therefore, leaving school before completing the 6th grade, for example, is treated as early leaving or desertion (even though the marginal return to one additional year of schooling might in fact be small). In almost all the developing countries of the world, desertion or dropout rates are high. It is common for more than half the students entering the 1st grade to have left school before completing the 6th grade. Desertion is most common in the 1st grade; in some countries more than half the children entering the 1st are never promoted to the 2nd. Desertion rates are usually lower in the upper grades, but increase again in high school as children approach the age at which their chances for employment increase. Rates of transition from one level of schooling to another are usually low, but often because the next level of the system imposes obstacles to the enrollment of children. For example, until 1969 an entrance examination restricted passage from the 6th to the 7th grade in Korea.

Most educators choose to assume that dropout rates can be reduced by increased inputs to education, that is, by raising the quality of the education provided children. The assumption entails a belief that children leave school because they are unable to match the academic requirements objectively imposed, and that this inability can be overcome by increasing teaching and learning capacity, for example, by training teachers or providing more instructional materials. We might expect, therefore, that increased inputs to education in Korea should have affected rates of promotion in the system. Table 22 presents flow rates of school enrollments for grades 1–12 for various years. These rates were computed by comparing the enrollment in grade j at time t with the enrollment in grade j–1 at time t–1. The smaller the ratio, the greater the number of children not passing from one grade to the next highest, either because of failure (and repetition of the grade) or because of leaving the system (dropping out). The ratios can be greater than 1.0 because some children leave the system in one year and return later, or because repeating rates may be excessively high in a given year. As one can see, however, flow rates for Korea computed in this fashion are stable over time, and consistent from grade to grade. There have been only small changes in the rate of flow through the system from 1956 to 1974, at the primary, middle, and high school levels. At all levels, almost all children beginning school finish within the specified time periods. There are very few dropouts, and very few repeaters.

The transition from grade 6 to 7, and from 9 to 10, has improved over time. In large measure this is a result of policy, that is, a function of the space and budget available in the next

TABLE 22 Flow Rates of School Enrollments

Grades	1956–1957	1959–1960	1964–1965	1969–1970	1974–1975
1–2	.999	.950	.950	.967	.978
2–3	.996	.972	.975	.986	.989
3–4	.957	.964	.970	.992	.992
4–5	.977	.962	.992	.989	.992
5–6	.968	.954	.957	.987	.989
6–7[a]	.448	.397	.454	.621	.747
7–8	.938	1.000	1.000	.962	.978
8–9	.924	.937	.947	.995	.970
9–10[b]	.646	.733	.751	.698	.711
10–11	.949	.954	.966	.932	.939
11–12	.906	.956	.963	.989	.945

Source: Shin-Bok Kim, "A Systematic Sub-Optimization Model for Educational Planning with Application to Korea," unpublished PhD dissertation, University of Pittsburgh, 1973.

Notes: [a]Proportion of elementary school graduates going on to middle school.
[b]Proportion of middle school graduates going on to high school.

level, rather than of the quality of applicants. By 1980 the government hopes to admit all children to middle school, so that the transition rate will approach 1.000.

Unlike most developing countries, beginning with the Japanese colonial period Korea has maintained a policy of automatic promotion within each level. It is expected that all children will pass to the next higher level; teachers are not supposed to screen out the least capable, or to fail those at the lower end of an ability distribution. High promotion and low desertion rates in Korea are therefore a result of a policy decision to maintain all children in school irrespective of their abilities. Changes in school resources would not show up in the internal efficiency of the educational system.

CHANGES IN EXTERNAL EFFICIENCY

Increased inputs to education could result in improved external effectiveness or outputs of education. Possible indicators of improved quality of the educational product are variables such as public testimony about education, higher rates of employment of graduates, or higher salaries of graduates.

The difficulty with these kinds of indicators is that they are subject to a much broader set of influences than those stemming just from the quality of education. Man-on-the-street evaluations of the quality of graduates are influenced by expectations that may well be unrealistic. Employment rates and salaries of graduates reflect the state of the general economy and competing occupations and industries more than the attributes of trained people in a given sector. For these reasons we may expect, therefore, that it will not be possible to show that over time the quality of education in Korea has improved with increased inputs.

As in most countries, the expansion of education in Korea has been accompanied by a generalized belief that the quality of education in Korea has declined. In most likelihood this is a misperception prompted by the changes in qualities of *incoming* students as rural and working-class students once denied admission make their presence felt. While these students may or may not be less capable of learning when they arrive, they certainly are likely to have different skills and abilities than students whose families have always been able to provide them with the cultural accoutrements associated with wealth and privilege. Because schools in Korea do not make children over completely, any more than do schools in other countries, working-class graduates are likely to maintain many of the cultural and intellectual qualities with which they began school, as are children from bourgeois families. The increasing proportion of working-class graduates could create the impression of declining quality for persons who emphasize bourgeois values and manners.

Typical of comments by educators and other observers on the declining quality of Korean education is that of Myung Han Kim, who explains the decline on the basis of the quantitative expansion.

This accelerated growth of Korean education has been achieved at
the cost of quality; physical facilities became increasingly inadequate;
and many schools suffered from a limited number of competent
teachers and limited financial resources. In spite of the continued
increase of government expenditures for education over the past
decade, they could hardly meet the financial demand of the rapidly
increasing school population. Under such circumstances, the quality
of education suffered markedly.[39]

Kim's observations would appear to be correct only for the
period immediately following the end of World War II, when
the U.S. Military Government attempted to enroll every child in
school, no matter what the facility or quality of teachers, and
during and immediately after the Korean War, when many
teachers were killed or injured and facilities destroyed. The
information presented earlier would suggest that per-student
resources available to education have increased since 1955; there
is no evidence that resources have been inadequate to meet the
requirements of students admitted to public schools, although,
as Table 3 indicated, the expansion of public education did not
satisfy the total demand for education.

Another source of evidence as to quality of outputs is
information on employment of graduates. The Ministry of
Education collects, in March of the year following the December
graduation from a given level of school, information on the
employment or student status of graduates. Although the
results are incomplete (the status of a large percentage of
students is listed as unknown), they serve as a crude index of the
ease of finding employment for various kinds of graduates.
Table 23 presents results of these surveys for 1965, 1970, and
1975. The data are organized according to level of school, with
elementary school not included, since employment opportunities for young children are limited. The table indicates the
number of graduates for the year, the percentage of those
graduates admitted to the next level in the system, and the
percentage of those not going on who are either employed or
not employed. The employed category includes all students who

TABLE 23 Status of Graduates of Educational Programs in March of Year Following Graduation

	Year Graduated	Number of Graduates	Percent of Graduates Admitted to Next Level	Percent of Those not Going On	
				Employed	Not Employed
Middle School	1964	189,726	69.1	38.1	41.2
	1969	312,814	70.1	15.9	42.6
	1974	568,648	74.7	20.4	44.8
Academic High School	1964	68,487	43.0	31.3	31.1
	1969	82,208	40.2	17.1	35.3
	1974	137,228	41.5	16.7	44.0
Vocational High School	1964	47,289	16.7	42.4	34.4
	1969	62,854	9.6	55.6	21.1
	1974	126,141	8.8	55.1	22.1
Junior Technical College	1964	461	8.5	51.2	13.3
	1969	2,909	10.1	74.6	7.5
	1974	12,323	6.7	48.3	12.2
Junior College	1964	7,830	17.0	49.8	11.1
	1969	4,038	23.5	48.9	13.4
	1974	1,538	20.3	50.6	14.5
College and University	1964	36,180	2.9	35.8	15.2
	1969	23,515	4.6	61.3	11.9
	1974	33,610	6.5	62.4	9.8

Source: Ministry of Education, *Statistical Yearbook of Education 1965, 1970, 1975.*

said they were working at the time of the survey. The not-employed group consists of those persons listed in the Ministry's report as "unemployed," which includes those not actually looking for work. Not included in either category are those students who enlisted in the military, who died, or whose status is unknown. Enlistments and deaths are a small portion of the remainder category. As can be seen from examination of the last two columns, the status of a large number of graduates, sometimes as much as 40 percent, is unknown.

If one assumes that all of the unknown are actually employed, then the Not-Employed column serves as an indicator of the maximal unemployment level of graduates. Using these figures, we can estimate that unemployment increased slightly for middle school graduates from 1965 to 1975, although the proportion of students going on increased. This finding is consistent with an assumption that employment opportunities for relatively untrained youth have declined as the economy has modernized. Similarly, unemployment of academic high school graduates increased from 1965 to 1975, which could reflect either a reduced need by the economy for graduates with no specific skill training or an increase in requirements for employment because of an overall increase in education levels of those looking for work.

Fewer graduates of vocational high schools are likely to go on to higher education, and their unemployment rate three months after graduation appears to have declined, a pair of findings consistent with government policy and projections. Less clear are the outcomes facing graduates from junior technical colleges. Unemployment seems to have been higher in 1975 than in 1970, and the number of graduates going on to four-year colleges was smaller. The employment situation for junior college graduates has not improved significantly. Considerable improvement has been made, however, in the short-term employment status of college and university graduates.

In summary, the data suggest that the employability of graduates of some of the programs of the educational system has improved considerably between 1965 and 1975, while that of graduates of other programs has not improved, or has become worse. Given that educational planners have focused specifically on vocational education and the problem of unemployment among college graduates, these data would suggest that the Korean system *is* capable of articulating education with demands of the economy, so long as the government is willing to make difficult political decisions (such as reducing numbers of students admitted to the university).

But other information reviewed in this chapter suggests that the government has, over the past thirty years, been inconsistent in its degree of support of and intervention in the educational system. Planning is relatively new and still weak. Much of the financing of education has been left to the private sector. Educational policies have varied considerably from government to government. How has it been possible, therefore, for education to grow so rapidly? And is it reasonable to believe, as many claim, that education has made a critical contribution to the economic growth of Korea?

TWO

An Evaluation of the Uniqueness
of Education Growth in Korea

The conception of education as a critical factor in the development of nations is not new in the history of the world. His Republic would prosper, Plato argued, to the extent that the proper kind of education was provided. International donor agencies have for twenty years argued for the development of human resources as critical in the struggle for growth, and since 1945 many governments have preached the expansion of educational opportunity as a means for building the nation.

But as we know, few of those nations that raised the banner of modernization after 1945 have in fact achieved notable success in improvement of the political, economic, or social conditions of their citizenry.[1] The flag was waved, but in many cases the battle lost, or won only at such great cost that there now appears little strength left to continue the fight. Most countries in Latin America, for example, created national planning agencies,

adopted development as their objective, and made large investments in health, education, and physical infrastructure. Today
few of those countries are held up as models for development.
And many countries find themselves carrying heavy burdens of
social overhead that make difficult new efforts to generate
growth.[2]

How has Korea managed to avoid these problems? How has it
been possible to expand education rapidly, despite the ravages
of the Korean War, and yet also expand investment in other,
especially income-producing, sectors? What are the unique
features of education in Korea that explain its apparently singu-
lar rate of expansion?

IS THE EDUCATIONAL SYSTEM
OF KOREA UNIQUE?

A common preface to the argument that education and human
resource development were major contributors to the modernization of Korea is recognition that human resources there *are*
exceptionally well developed. Not only is the Korean population almost completely literate, but *all* children complete
elementary education, and an impressively large proportion of
the relevant age groups are enrolled in secondary schools and
colleges and universities.

The standard of comparison for these assertions of advanced
development is not, of course, the advanced economies, but
those nations with a similar level of income per capita. It is in
comparison with other countries with relatively low per capita
GNPs that Korea is said to have achieved such an impressive
record in education. For example, in a graph plotting a human
resources development index (based on proportion of age group
enrolled in secondary and tertiary level institutions) against
GNP, Harbison and Myers showed Korea furthest from the
regression line of all the 73 nations compared, in the direction
of more education than would be expected given GNP.[3] Cole

and Lyman combined the original Harbison and Myers statistics with more recent numbers to compare Korea's 1960 and 1965 levels of enrollment with those of countries at various levels of per capita GNP. With a per capita income of $90, "Korea stood fairly close to the normal pattern of human resource development for a country with a mean per capita GNP of nearly $200."[4] In 1965, with a per capita income of $107, Korea's pattern of human resource development was equivalent to that of countries with a GNP per capita of $380.

In 1960, the average country with a per capita income of about $90 could be expected to enroll only 22 percent of the 5- to 14-year-old age group in primary schools, while Korea's primary enrollment was 59 percent of the age group. In 1965, countries with an average per capita income of $380 enrolled only 62 percent of the 5- to 14-year-old cohort in primary schools, while Korea enrolled 82 percent (and had an average per capita income of $107). Differences at the secondary and tertiary levels are even more impressive. In 1960 and 1965, enrollments in secondary schools were about 27 percent of the 15- to 19-year-old group, which is as high as the average proportion enrolled in countries with per capita incomes of $380. Korea's enrollments in higher education were also high, equivalent to countries with per capita incomes three or four times as large, such as Chile, Hungary, Venezuela, and Italy.

Such relatively large proportions of enrollments have encouraged some to see in education a major antecedent or determinant of Korea's rapid economic growth, as though the economy was somehow driven to achieve a balance with a high level of educational attainment. What can be said about that? First, the argument will have more weight to the extent that it can be shown that the achievements of the educational system in Korea have been truly unique. Accordingly, this section looks at international comparisons in more detail.

EDUCATION AND GNP

The original Harbison and Myers human resources index has been recalculated to take into account differences among countries in the length of schooling and the expected entrance age. These adjusted data are presented by Harbison, Maruhnic, and Resnick for 112 countries, including Korea, for 1960 and 1965.[5] The same general picture emerges. Korea is classified as a Level III, or semi-advanced country (along with Hungary, Greece, Italy, Spain, Peru, and India) in terms of the human resources index, although its per capita GNP is lower than any other in that category (except India) and at $106 is only $7 higher than the average for less developed countries in Level I.

For both 1960 and 1965 Korea has an overall high level of educational attainment, although other countries are higher on one or the other of the three measures. That is, Korea is not the highest in terms of proportion of age group enrolled in primary, or secondary, or higher education, but it is higher than any of the Level I or II countries, and only a bit under the median for the Level III countries. The same is true in 1965. And a composite index of human resources development, based on proportions of age group enrolled in secondary and tertiary education, indicates a higher level of attainment for Korea than countries with comparable levels of national income.

In relative terms, Korea lost some of its distinctiveness between 1960 and 1965.[6] Half the 73 countries rated increased their third-level ratio more than Korea did between 1960 and 1965, and half also increased their second-level enrollments more than Korea. Many of these countries had per capita incomes lower than Korea's, and larger population growth rates. There was not much overlap between the two sets of countries, however, and Korea slipped only from 27th to 30th place in the composite index rating. All five countries overtaking Korea (Peru, Iraq, Lebanon, Venezuela, and Hungary) were also rated as Level III countries in 1960, and all had higher per capita incomes, although in the case of Peru and Iraq the differences were not outstanding.

A further comparison between the educational achievements of Korea and other nations can be gained from an examination of Table 24, which compares gross domestic product (GDP), and proportions enrolled in each of the three levels, between

TABLE 24 Comparisons Among Countries of GDP
and Educational Effort

| | | GDP | Population 1,000s | % Age Group Enrolled | | | | | |
| | | | | 1st Level | | 2nd Level | | 3rd Level | |
				MF	F	MF	F	MF	F
Korea	1960	155		96	91	27	14	4.7	1.6
	1965			100	97	34	25	6.2	3.2
	1970			104	102	41	34	7.5	3.8
	1972	378[a]	31,465[b]	105	103	47	38	8.1	4.4
Egypt	1960	129		66	52	16	9	4.7	1.6
	1965			75	60	26	15	6.8	2.8
	1970			68	53	32	21	7.9	4.3
	1972	225[c]	30,075[d]	70	54	36	24	9.8	5.7
Paraguay	1960	164		101	95	10	11	2.6	1.6
	1965			103	98	13	13	3.4	2.8
	1970			107	101	17	17	3.8	3.3
	1972	373[a]	2,354	—	—	—	—	—	—
Morocco	1960	164		49	28	5	2	.5	.1
	1965			39[e]	24[e]	24	11	.8	.2
	1970			55	38	12	7	1.2	.4
	1972	306[a]	15,379[c]	55	39	13	7	1.6	.5
Turkey	1960	190		75	58	14	8	2.9	1.2
	1965			101	83	16	9	4.4	2.0
	1970			111	96	28	17	5.6	2.3
	1972	546[a]	35,667[b]	105	93	32	19	—	—
Peru	1960	208		87	74	18	13	4.1	2.4
	1965			102	93	29	23	8.0	5.6
	1970			107	100	35	24	10.6	7.4
	1972	379	13,572	132	—	46	—	11.1	7.4
Ecuador	1960	216		83	79	12	10	2.6	1.0
	1965			91	88	17	15	3.3	1.4
	1970			95	93	26	24	7.6	4.6
	1972	386[a]	6,501[f]	96	94	25	24	—	—
Iraq	1960	245		65	36	19	8	2.0	.9
	1965			72[e]	43[e]	28	13	4.0	2.2
	1970			67	39	24	14	5.0	2.3
	1972	429[c]	8,047[g]	73	44	26	15	6.3	2.7
Spain	1960	341		—	—	24	—	4.0	1.9
	1965			116	115	38	29	5.6	2.5
	1970			131	133	57	49	8.5	4.7
	1972	1751[a]	30,041[b]	119	119	71	—	14.3	9.0
Venezuela	1960	1043		100	100	23	21	4.0	2.6
	1965			95	95	30	29	6.3	4.2
	1970			100	100	41	42	9.9	8.2
	1972	1579	10,721[c]	101	102	47	48	12.6	10.2

1960 and 1972. The countries presented were chosen as examples of nations with similar GDPs either at the beginning or the end of the period, or with a similar composite index of education, and a fairly large population.

With respect, first, to enrollments in primary school, between 1960 and 1972 Korea managed to achieve universal enrollment. The enrollments in excess of the population age group are explained by over-aged students who either entered late (perhaps because earlier there were not sufficient facilities) or by students repeating. By the end of the period, primary enrollments had already begun to decline. Total enrollments in secondary and tertiary-level institutions almost doubled, and they tripled for women.

Other countries, however, experienced equally high rates of educational growth. For example, Egypt increased its enrollment in post-secondary institutions from 4.7 percent of the age group to 9.8 percent, more than Korea, with a proportionately larger increment in women's enrollments. Enrollments in secondary-level institutions more than doubled but started from a smaller base. Paraguay and Turkey expanded enrollments in primary schools more rapidly than Korea. Peru improved its enrollments at all three levels to a greater extent than Korea, reaching levels higher than those of Korea by 1972, though starting from a less developed position in 1960. Ecuador's rate of growth in human resources is not quite as impressive, but still matches that of Korea. The expansion of education in Spain is spectacularly

---

TABLE 24 (continued)

Sources: UN and UNESCO *Statistical Yearbooks, 1974.*

Notes: [a]1973
[b]1970
[c]1971
[d]1966
[e]different age range used in this year.
[f]1974
[g]1965

explosive, although so is its rate of economic growth for the period.

The purpose of this review of the accomplishments of other countries is not to diminish the importance of educational growth in Korea, but merely to provide some standards of comparison for evaluating what has taken place. Other countries (although not a great many) have reached universal primary enrollments at about the same level of development, but without expanding secondary and higher education as much as Korea. Or, some countries have rapidly expanded secondary and higher education without first approaching universal primary enrollments. The few countries that have done both had higher levels of GNP than Korea. In summary, Korea's rate of educational expansion is not unique in comparison to other countries. Nor does Korea currently enjoy a uniquely high level of human resources. What is unique about Korean development from 1945 is that a high level of human resources was developed early and despite low per capita income. The explanation of how this was possible may contribute to our understanding of the contributions of education to Korean society and the relationship of education to economic development.

UNIQUE FEATURES OF THE
KOREAN EDUCATIONAL SYSTEM

A number of unique attributes of education in Korea may have contributed to the system's capacity for rapid expansion after 1945 despite low levels of national income. They all turn on a very high social demand for education, best explained by a centuries-old tradition of respect for the educated man combined with a recognition that both social and economic position in the modern Korea were closely linked, for most persons, with level of educational attainment.[7]

The expansion of education that has occurred in Korea since 1945 probably could not have been realized had the state assumed the entire burden of financing education. A number of developing countries today find themselves at an impasse, unable to expand primary educational opportunity to attain universal enrollment because the expense of education already seriously strains the national budget. Table 25 allows some comparisons of unit costs, by level and as a function of GNP, for 1965, using the countries considered in Table 24. Several conclusions can be drawn. First, unit costs in Korea are much lower than those in other countries, despite similar levels of per capita income. Second, with the exception of Paraguay, public recurrent expenditures on education are a smaller fraction of total GNP in Korea than in the other countries. Third, for all countries, higher education is much more costly per student to the government than is primary or secondary education. In Korea the per-unit cost of level-three education is more than 20 times that of level-one education.

TABLE 25 Recurrent Public Costs of Education, 1965
(U.S. dollars)

	Per Student			As % of GNP
	Level 1	Level 2	Level 3	
Korea	7	18	152	1.8
Paraguay	11	69	307	1.8
Morocco	50	154	515	3.9
Turkey	31	97	295	3.1
Peru	24	65	224	3.0
Eduador	19	97	861	3.1
Iraq	81	98	608	6.7

Source: Harbison, Maruhnic, and Resnick, Appendix 5.

Data for 1973 show the same kinds of relationships. Korea spent in that year a lower proportion of its GNP on education than 40 of 70 countries studied. In the Asia region, Korea spent less of its GNP on education than Malaysia, Papua New Guinea, the Philippines, and Sri Lanka, and more than Nepal, Indonesia, Burma, Singapore, Thailand, and Pakistan. Korea's per-student expenditures on elementary education were lower than 52 of the 70 countries. Expenditures on secondary and higher education were even lower by comparison but, because enrollment ratios in those levels are proportionately higher in Korea than in many other countries, relatively more (as percent of GNP) was spent on the upper education levels.[8]

The conclusion to be drawn from these figures is that the public education system of Korea is more cost-effective than those with which it has been compared. There has been some rise through time in public per-pupil expenditures on education. In 1948 the public subsidy for primary schooling (including capital costs) amounted only to about $2 per pupil,[9] but by 1969 the unit public cost at the primary level had increased to $31,[10] and in 1974 it was about $40. Despite these increments, education in 1974 absorbed less than 15 percent of the national budget, down from a high of 19.9 percent in 1971 and much less than the fractions spent by other developing countries at a similar stage of development.

THE ROLE OF FOREIGN AID

The low *public* cost of education in Korea can be explained as a result of several factors. Perhaps the *least* important of these is foreign aid to education. Between 1945 and 1948 the U.S. Military Government in Korea faced a high demand for education unsatisfied under the Japanese, and delayed in the terminal years of World War II. Enrollments in primary education increased about 800,000 in the three years following the end of the war. The number of students in secondary schools increased from 44,000 in 1943 to 114,000 in 1948 to 194,000 in 1950. Enrollments in higher education grew from 3,000 students in May 1945 to 19,000 in September 1947, and continued growing at a rapid rate.

Details of the U.S. Military Government's expenditures on education are not available. Apparently many of the needed educational facilities were provided by local communities rather than constructed by the central government. These facilities may have been adequate school buildings, unused rooms in houses, or the out-of-doors in clement weather. About two-thirds of the operational costs of running the primary schools was financed by the U.S. Military Government; about 38 percent of the school revenue at this level was raised through monthly dues levied on members of the Parent-Teacher Association for each school. Byung Hun Nam describes the problem as follows:

> Due to the constant increase in the number of schools and in enroll-ment, the government was not able to provide adequate school finance. Thus, in most cases, the principals of the schools took matters into their own hands. There were two common practices for meeting the financial shortages in both elementary and secondary schools. The first practice was to assess parents a certain amount of "contribution" before the child was accepted by the school. This assessment was supposedly voluntary but in actual fact a child whose parents were unwilling or unable to make the contribution would not be admitted to the school. The second practice was to collect regular monthly dues from members of the Parents' Association.[11]

About 54 percent of the revenue for secondary schools came from "voluntary" contributions of this kind. If we accept Nam's estimate of a per-pupil government subsidy of $2 for primary school students, then the U.S. Military Government was expend-ing about $5 million per year. To this figure we might also add equipment, materials, and labor donated by U.S. military forces in Korea.

Between 1952 and 1966 foreign aid to Korea for education totaled about $100 million. This sum was spent on classroom construction,[12] secondary and vocational education, higher education, and teacher training. A later section will evaluate the impact of technical assistance on the process and content of Korean education; for the moment our attention is given to the extent to which that contribution may have made a significant contribution to the expansion of the system.

About half of the $100 million was spent on classroom con-struction for primary and secondary schools and could therefore be considered to have facilitated directly the expansion of education. Primary school enrollments went from about 2.4 million in 1952 to 4.4 million in 1963. Secondary school enrollments went from 325,000 to 1 million for the same period. On the average, technical assistance provided about $14 per student over the twelve-year period, or a little bit more than $1 per student per year, in capital expenditures. The figures in Table 24 on recurrent costs per student in 1965, provide some standard of comparison of the relative importance of this capital assistance. U.S. capital assistance to school construction in Korea could be regarded as making it possible for the government to raise per-student public expenditure in primary school at least 16 percent, from $6 per student per year to $7 per student per year.

What *is* clear is that foreign assistance made it possible to build a great many classrooms (23,000 either new or rebuilt) specifically intended for instruction that probably would not have been constructed at such a rapid rate without the availability of capital and materials. Assuming half the classrooms built to be available for the entire period, and an average annual occupancy of 120 students (a combination of large classes and double-shift use of the facility) one could calculate quickly that the school construction program provided facilities for an additional 1.4 million children, a not insignificant number. As was the case during the period of the U.S. Military Government, an unmeasured amount of assistance to education also was provided through non-recorded labor of U.S. personnel and donations of equipment and supplies.

PRIVATE SUPPORT OF EDUCATION

An additional explanation for the low public cost of education in Korea is that parents are expected to contribute to the support of schools and teachers over and above their contribution through taxes. An earlier section described the situation immediately after World War II.[13] Patterns of financing begun at that time apparently still persist. A UNESCO report published in

1974 asserts that 1970 data show that direct *private* expenditure on education is 35 percent of the national expenditure. Grant indicates that student fees sometimes amount to as much as U.S. $1,000 per year.[14] Morgan and Chadwick's report estimates that private expenditures on education could amount to as much as 50 percent of total expenditure.[15] The Ministry of Education's *Education in Korea 1973*[16] presents the total educational budget at 118.4 billion wŏn, 17.9 percent of the total government budget. The same report mentions Yuksŏnghoe (voluntary parent-teacher association) fees of 38.8 billion wŏn. The 1974 budget of 133.9 billion wŏn (15.2 percent of total government expenditures) included Yuksŏnghoe fees of 37.5 billion wŏn.

Korea subsidizes the costs of secondary and higher education much less than other developing countries do, and part of the figures indicated above reflects private contributions to the higher levels of education, likely to be reached more often by students from higher-income families. It is also the case, however, that only 28 percent of the primary school children in Korea receive free textbooks, and the free meal service reaches only 1.65 (of the 5.5) million children enrolled in primary schools. In addition to costs of books and meals, parents also provide uniforms, transportation, and equipment and meet other expenses. The assumption of these costs by the people relieves the government of a considerable recurrent cost burden. An increasing private share of enrollments in middle and high schools (and universities), from 31 and 26 percent respectively in 1953, to 49 and 55 percent in 1970, indicates the extent to which the government has "saved" on education.[17]

LOW UNIT COST OF EDUCATION

As suggested earlier, the public cost of education provided is lower in Korea than in comparable countries. In 1970 the public unit costs of the three levels of education were estimated as follows: primary, $40; middle, $77; high, $97. Low costs are realized in two major ways. First, teachers are paid relatively low salaries and, second, class sizes are very large, distributing the costs of instruction over more students.

Estimates of teachers' incomes are risky because of the custom of asking parents to provide additional subsidies, either directly as part of Yuksŏnghoe, or indirectly through tutoring fees for instruction by the teacher outside school hours. In rural areas, teachers' incomes are sometimes supplemented through free housing or food provided by local residents. What is clear is that official salaries paid to teachers are lower than those received by other persons with equivalent levels of education and training. Civil service salary schedules for April 1946, as cited by Byung Hun Nam, established a range of W3,120 to W6,960 for primary school teachers, W5,100 to W6,000 for military sergeants, W5,100 to W7,920 for junior administrative officers, and W9,300 to W14,700 for section heads. Even most teachers at the primary level were high school graduates, which suggests that salaries for teachers were low compared to those received by others in government civil service.

In 1965, official teacher salaries were W6,220 per month for elementary teachers, W7,690 for middle school teachers, and W8,860 for high school teachers. Yong Hwan Chung reports that the average living expenditure for a family of five living in Seoul was W12,270 per month (exchange rate of W250 = $1).[18] All primary teachers were at least high school graduates; 72 percent of the middle school teachers and 82 percent of the senior high school teachers had graduated from college. In 1975, with even higher levels of education among teachers, the same salary disparities continued to exist. What is striking is that Korea has been able to provide a well-trained teaching force at relatively low cost.

In addition, low-cost teachers have faced relatively large numbers of students. As Table 18 shows, class sizes were very large after the Korean War, as might be expected. The construction of classrooms between 1953 and 1963 apparently helped to reduce class sizes considerably. Since that time, however, there has been a steady growth in size of classes for all except primary school, in which enrollments peaked in 1970 and are now declining. An average class size of 50 or 60 combines a number of large classes with small ones. For example, in 1965, 11 percent of the primary school classrooms held more than 90 students, and another 26 percent had between 81 and 90 students.[19] Professional educators in the United States regard 35 students as a large class, and 25 an ideal size. Many countries have attempted to limit official enrollments to a maximum of 50 in a class, expecting that poor attendance and dropouts will reduce class size during the course of the year. Those phenomena do not operate to the same degree in Korea. Attendance is higher and few students drop out. Most impressive, perhaps, are the large class sizes in vocational high schools. The nature of the vocational school curriculum, with its use of tools and machinery and emphasis on close instruction, usually argues for class sizes of 10 or 15 students.

AUTOMATIC PROMOTION OF STUDENTS

As mentioned in Chapter 1, Korea is one of the few developing countries that has implemented a policy of automatic promotion at all levels. Typical in most countries is a pattern of late entry, failure, and repetition, leading either to high dropout rates (usually mistakenly ascribed to lack of interest of parents in their children's education) or to a high percentage of children who are several years older than would be expected for their grade level. In the upper primary grades in many elementary schools it is not uncommon to find that most children are older than the age expected for those grades. Because most failure and repetition takes place in the early grades, enrollments in 1st and 2nd grades often are more than 20 percent of the total enrollment, and enrollments in the 6th grade 10 percent or less of the total.[20]

As indicated in Table 26, that is not the situation in Korea.

TABLE 26 Elementary School Enrollments by Age and Grade, 1974

Grade	Enrollment as % of Total	% Children of Expected Age
1st	16.5	96.0[a]
2nd	16.7	91.8[b]
3rd	16.1	89.7[c]
4th	16.5	84.5[d]
5th	17.4	91.2[e]
6th	16.8	91.1[f]

Source: Ministry of Education, *Statistical Yearbook of Education 1974.*

Notes: [a]6–7 years of age
[b]7–8
[c]8–9
[d]9–10
[e]10–11
[f]11–12

Enrollments in elementary schools are almost equally distributed across the six grades. Most children are of the correct age for their grade.

Beginning in 1971, the examination limiting admission to the middle school from the elementary school was eliminated. In effect, students were automatically promoted from 6th to 7th grade. Not all students applied for entrance to middle schools, however, perhaps because of higher fees or higher opportunity costs. But the proportion of students going on to middle school is much higher than that found in almost any developing country, and equivalent to the transition rates of more economically advanced countries. Between 1964 and 1971, Shin-Bok Kim reports, 75.6 percent of the males and 55.8 percent of the females went on to middle school.[21] In 1974 the figures were 83.0 and 67.1 percent respectively.[22] These rates are practically equivalent to automatic promotion, and are consistent with the announced intention of the government to make middle school compulsory by 1981.

CURRICULUM, TEACHING, AND EVALUATION

How is automatic promotion maintained? Educators in many countries justify high rates of failure in terms of the inability of students to master the material presented to them, material necessary for success at higher levels in the system and, supposedly, for performance as a productive member of society. Failing less able students allows teachers to focus on those with more ability, to operate with smaller classes, and, in general, to maintain a high standard of educational input. Korea, on the other hand, not only keeps all children in school through the 6th grade and most through the 9th, but also does so with very large classes. One might expect, therefore, that the content of what is taught in Korean schools and the method of teaching used would differ considerably from what is taught in other countries' schools.

One area in which Korean schools do differ (in comparison with systems such as those described above) is in terms of emphasis on health and physical education, music, vocational education, and moral education. These four subjects account for one-third of the class hours per week in both elementary and middle school. They are activities in which it is possible for all children to experience success.

But the major difference is in terms of how hard students work. All students pass in Korea, but grades are still used as diagnostic information by parents concerned about the long-run educational future of their children. Because all students are seen as capable of passing, poor performance in the classroom is viewed more as evidence of inadequate application by the student than as an indication of low ability, and is likely to result in increased pressure from the parents concerned to assure that their children reach the higher educational levels.

Students work primarily to prepare themselves for the external examination. The examination limiting entrance to high school tests on every subject taught in middle school (Korean, English, math, physics, biology, commerce, industry, music, morals, civics, physical skills, and so on).[23] Effects of the exam are felt even in elementary schools, because middle school teachers orient their teaching to fit the demands of the examination, and elementary school teachers in turn articulate *their* curriculum with the expectations of middle school teachers.

The effect of the exam on learning goes beyond the school. Given automatic promotion and large classes, ambitious parents eager to guarantee admittance of their children into high school seek additional examination preparation after hours. Children not only must attend long hours of school during the regular day but are expected to sit with a tutor in the evening hours, preparing for the examination.

The financial sacrifices made in preparation for examinations are equaled only by the payment of Yuksŏnghoe fees as an indicator of the overwhelming social significance of education in Korea.

> The *Dong-A Ilbo*, a prominent newspaper, has shown that the direct contribution collected from parents for examination prepared after school ranged from 2,000 wŏn to 26,000 wŏn per month for a child in a middle school, while the average salary for an employee in a company is not more than 20,000 wŏn per month, 360 wŏn to the dollar . . . Half of the seventh grade children were presently engaged in the extra-examination preparation for an A-class high school with assessments levied against the home for each student ranging from 2,000 to 5,000 wŏn. Two-thirds of the eighth-grade children were engaged in this activity, spending 2,000 to 8,000 wŏn, and most of the ninth-grade children were levied amounts from 8,000 to 26,000 wŏn because the entrance examination to high school was coming near at this stage.[24]

The "examination hell" of Seoul has been likened to that in Japan. Efforts have been made in recent years to reduce pressures on children, first by eliminating the entry examination into middle school, and more recently by randomizing admission to high schools so that high scorers are not automatically assigned to elite schools. Entrance into the elite universities, however, is still a function of scores on college entrance examinations.

The presence of a parallel education system that prepares

children for examinations may account for the success of automatic promotion in Korea. Pressures on teachers to favor some students over others, or to teach to the brightest students, are reduced when bright students with affluent parents can receive additional attention outside school hours. (Ironically, the child's school teacher may also be employed as his tutor for the examinations.)

What most distinguishes the content and method of instruction in Korean schools from that of many other developing countries is that the curriculum tends to reinforce social integration rather than to weaken it, as all students are treated equally, and while within the school enjoy or suffer the same destiny.[25] Less clear is the extent to which students in Korea learn more or less about those things that might be considered important for economic development. We will return to that question later. It also is clear that a curriculum based on the lecture method of instruction and rote memorization by students, combined with preparation for an eventual examination, enhances the legitimacy of the teacher, and facilitates the handling of large classes. Classes of 50 or 60 students would be impossible in elementary schools were teachers obliged to work with each student individually or were students encouraged to pursue their own interests and to challenge the teacher as the sole source of knowledge.

SUMMARY

The following seem to be the major features that distinguish the Korean education system from systems in most developing countries, in terms of possible links with economic and socio-political development. For one thing, it experienced rapid growth, in enrollments and in accompanying facilities and teachers. This growth occurred not only in the primary grades but also in middle school, academic and vocational secondary school, and at the level of higher education. The rate of growth was as high or higher than that in most countries for all levels.

This growth was possible despite a low level of national income. Several factors were critical. First, per-student public expenditures on education in Korea are lower than those in most developing countries, even those with similar levels of GNP.

A second factor that made rapid growth possible is that, even if low unit expenditures are taken into account, the government's share of the educational burden in Korea is less than in most other developing countries. High parental demand for education of children, coupled with a governmental inability or unwillingness to provide educational facilities and teachers and the encouragement of the U.S. Military Government to decentralize educational decision-making, resulted in private contributions to the maintenance of public education, sometimes amounting to almost 50 percent of the total educational expenditure. In recent years, unmet social demand for education has resulted in the development of a large private educational system at the secondary and tertiary levels. (This system is private in the sense that it is not financed with public funds. The government, however, maintains tight control over institution size and curriculum.)

The low unit cost of education has been possible because of the willingness of teachers to work for wages lower than those paid persons of equivalent training in other developing countries. There are several explanations for this. First, the profession of teacher is highly respected in Korea and must therefore provide considerable psychic benefit. Second, teachers could expect to receive some financial and material rewards over and above those included in official reports of costs, chiefly through working as examination tutors after school hours. Third, especially between the early 1950s and late 1960s, the overproduction of high school and college graduates unable to obtain employment in more remunerative professions made available a pool of low-cost labor for education. Teacher training programs for high school and college graduates were of relatively short duration and low cost.

The use of relatively quickly trained teachers in schools in Korea is facilitated by the existence of strong traditions of respect for the teacher and strict discipline in the classroom. Both male and female students wear uniforms. Students usually greet their teachers by bowing, and considerable deference is paid to teachers and principals in the classroom and outside. Teachers employ lecture and recitation techniques of instruction requiring relatively less professional training than discovery and participation methods. The legitimacy of automatic promotion and the stress on preparation for critical transition examinations help maintain order.[26]

These factors in the aggregate permit teachers to manage classes that average 60 or more students in attendance—a feat equaled in very few other countries—which contributes to the maintenance of low unit cost of education.

Finally, the rapid expansion of education in Korea during a critical period of economic development (1952-1963) was assisted by the contribution of more than $100 million in capital assistance. This amount can be compared with the almost $3 billion total of capital aid provided to Korea during the same period.

In sum, the expansion of education in Korea could occur at low levels of per capita income because of the maintenance of education at a level of quality commensurate with the per capita income level of the society (accompanied by some foreign capital). That is, in contrast with many other developing countries, Korea chose to emphasize quantity rather than quality, especially at the lower levels of the system. Not all observers of this phenomenon agreed with these policies:

> From the first American advisor to Korean education in 1945 through to the American education team in 1955, a consistent call was made to Korea to revise and reorganize both the method and content of her total curriculum . . . in all areas and at all levels of education . . . As seen through foreign eyes, the Korean education system was highly inadequate in almost every aspect of its structure and program. With the exception of the eagerness for learning on the part of students and teachers, and the affection of elementary school teachers for children, Korean education was weighed and found woefully wanting.[27]

Thinking, reasoning, critical abilities, insight and creativity are the concern of only a few teachers and parents. A child spends his day in the packed classroom forced to rote-memorize everything; at home, parents watch that he does his assignments and prepares for tomorrow's tests. Late in the evening, many are sent to private tutors. The student is sandwiched in between the teacher's demand for school expenses and the parents' reluctance and inability to pay them.[28]

FOREIGN CONTRIBUTIONS
TO EDUCATION IN KOREA

An understanding of the unique characteristics of education in Korea necessarily requires a consideration of history. Occupied by Japan for more than thirty years, and by a caretaker U.S. Military Government for three, Korea did not begin to develop its own system of education until 1948. That process was shortlived, and an American presence was soon prevalent again as a result of the Korean War. One could expect, therefore, that at least vestiges of the Japanese colonial experience and the two periods of U.S. involvement in Korea remain and influence the course of education.

This section is less a review of what took place under the Japanese and under the Americans than it is a consideration of what features of the current educational system are *not* autochthonous. All countries borrow some features of their educational system from other countries; there are no surprises in that. But to the extent that the borrowed elements bear a strong relationship to the special achievements of the system, then those achievements take on a different importance than if the principal determinants of the achievements were generated totally within the culture.

In the Korean case, the question is whether those elements of the educational system that are supposed to have contributed to modernization are unique to Korea or found elsewhere. If the elements are common in other educational systems, if they occur in countries without high rates of growth, then the argument that they were critical for modernization is weakened. Similarly, if education's contribution to modernization occurred principally during the Japanese or American periods, then currently unique features of the system are of little explanatory value.

WHAT DID THE JAPANESE LEAVE BEHIND?

Most descriptions of the Japanese colonial rule of Korea call attention to the active efforts made by the Japanese to use education to obliterate the Korean nationality and to replace it with a new Japonized man. Korea was defined as part of Japan, and Koreans as (albeit inferior) Japanese who would learn Japanese as their national language, use Japanese family names, render homage to the emperor, and adopt the practices of Shintoism. Schools played an important role in the implementation of these policies.

Beginning in 1919, a serious effort was made to eliminate all private education, especially that offered by Christian missionary groups. Primary education was made obligatory, and public schools expanded rapidly. All instruction was given in Japanese, and children were forbidden to speak Korean to each other during school hours. Texts were rewritten to provide a Japanese perspective on Korean history, and the Imperial Rescript (which commanded filial piety and obedience to the emperor) was introduced into the daily ritual of the school.

While the Japanese sought to enroll as many children as possible into the primary grades, very few Koreans were allowed to enroll in secondary school or to go on to the university. Criticisms of the Japanese contribution to education in Korea concentrate on the wide disparities of educational opportunity available to Japanese living in Korea, as compared to Koreans. In 1939, for example, there were 143 Japanese students enrolled in primary schools for every 1,000 Japanese living in Korea, while there were only 55 Korean primary students for every 1,000 Koreans.

Inequalities were greater at the upper levels of the system. There were only 1.3 Korean students in high schools for every

1,000 Koreans, compared to 32.7 Japanese students for every 1,000 Japanese. The Korean fraction in colleges and universities was even smaller.[29]

On the other hand, by 1945 almost 45 percent of the Korean youth of school age were enrolled in primary school.[30] Under the Japanese, the Koreans achieved a higher level of educational attainment than many other colonized countries. In this sense, Korea's educational uniqueness was greater in 1945, immediately at the end of thirty years of Japanese colonial rule, than it was ten (or twenty) years later (by which time other developing countries had expanded their national educational systems).

Instruction in primary schools run by the Japanese was apparently of relatively high quality.[31] Most schools had textbooks, most teachers were specifically trained in normal schools,[32] and costs of education were borne principally by the government rather than by parents. Some appreciation for the quality of the system maintained by the Japanese can be gained by recognizing both the seriousness of the Japanese intention to make over Korea as an extension of the fatherland, and in the severe shortage of books (in Korean) and teachers (who were not Japanese or Japanese-trained) after Liberation.

Although Japanese-run schools set political socialization as their primary objective, they also were oriented toward development. This was especially true for schools located in rural areas. The Japanese rural school of the 1930s, for example, had many similarities with the Saemaul Undong (New Community Movement) education program begun by the Park Government in the late 1960s. Secondary schools in rural areas provided service activities, loaned new farming tools, helped farmers evaluate products, constructed family kitchens and gardens, distributed special eggs and chickens, and instructed in farming skills. "It was the (Gani) semi-school that played an important role in enlightenment and education. This school ... was built on behalf of ... vocational training for community life."[33]

The Japanese also made an important contribution to the training of skilled workers, not only through on-the-job training provided in industries and factories (albeit for war purposes) located in Korea, but also through more formal vocational training. "Industrial and vocational training received an impetus in Korea under Japanese guidance that may be regarded as a great advantage to the country."[34] Enrollments in technical and industrial schools had reached 34,743 by 1943, a number almost as large as that of enrollments in academic secondary schools,[35] and much higher than commonly found in developing countries at a similar stage of development.

To Koreans trained in South Korea under the Japanese should be added those persons who migrated to South Korea at the time of Liberation, who also had received education from the Japanese. These included 1,100,000 Koreans from Japan, and 800,000 persons from North Korea. Most studies on migration indicate that migrants generally have higher levels of education than persons who remain behind. Migrants from North Korea included a disproportionately large number of Christian Koreans exposed to a set of ideas and perspectives more "modernizing" than those experienced by non-Christians.

Finally, although the Japanese provided very few opportunities for Koreans to attend the university in Korea, the physical facilities built by them (for Japanese students) were left intact at the time of Liberation and facilitated a rapid start of the new national university system. An American advisor participating in the transformation of the Imperial University of Korea to Seoul National University in August 1946 reported:

> An inspection of the buildings and equipment of the various schools and colleges reveals a vast physical plant and a fine assortment of equipment. Physical care of the plant and facilities is another thing. But it is noteworthy that there are ample buildings and facilities. The library contains over 500,000 volumes and is probably the repository of the best single collection of books on most Oriental questions. They have most of the bound volumes of scientific and literary magazines and periodicals as well as newspapers for most countries in the world up to 1940.[36]

The Japanese left behind not only books, but also a set of academic traditions and practices that today form an integral part of the Korean educational system. Many of the unique features of Korean education described earlier originated with the Japanese Colonial Government, and still are found today in Japanese schools. These characteristics include large class sizes, heavy academic emphasis, moral education, deep respect for the authority of the teacher, and the examination system for entrance into high schools and the university.[37] The following two observations are included as a reminder of the persistence of social forms even when nations strive for a unique political orientation:

> Almost immediately following the Japanese departure in 1945 the Japanese language, the pictures of the Mikado, and the Imperial Rescript disappeared from schools and Shinto shrines from the face of the countryside. But "moral education" and rituals did not. The schools continued their mass morning exercises. Students marched onto the bare playfields in formation to the blare of military music, lined up in rigid rows, bowed to the principal, and listened in cathedral silence to his morning moral talk. Moreover, it did not take long after the Republic of Korea was duly constituted for Syngman Rhee's picture to appear in every school in the nation.[38]

> Certain features of the characteristic life of Korean secondary school in 1952 are worth mentioning. Every morning, students gathered on the parade or playground and assembled in military formation to salute the Korean flag and hear a brief speech by the school principal. After this daily ceremony they were marched into classrooms under the command of their student platoon and company leaders. Girls and boys were in black Japanese-style uniforms.[39]

The uniforms are (in 1976) no longer black, but many students still march in formation, and para-military organization of the student body is found in most secondary schools and in all universities. Just as "the whole Japanese system was characterized by rigid control of everything by the government,"[40] so schools are controlled today.

To look for origins of aspects of the Korean educational

system in the Japanese colonial period does not, of course, take away anything from the achievements of the present system. Nor does calling attention to the advanced state of elementary education in Korea under the Japanese demean Korea's current advanced position vis-à-vis other developing nations. What it does do, however, is provide some basis for an argument that Korea's achievements in education are to some extent a result of thirty years of colonial rule by a nation also renowned in the history of development, not only for rapid advancement in education, but also for unprecedented rates of economic growth. It may be unreasonable, therefore, to generalize from the Korean experience to other developing countries that have not had the same colonial experience.

THE IMPACT OF
THE AMERICAN PRESENCE IN KOREA

Another unique contribution to the shaping of education and economic development in Korea was the intense involvement of the United States in the liberation, reorganization, and defense of South Korea. The objective of this section is to review the various inputs to education that resulted from the American presence in Korea, to assess the extent to which the unique educational achievements of the nation can be attributed to that presence, and to evaluate the assistance provided by the American government and private sector to the development of Korean education. In all of this, the underlying concern will be to provide a framework for analyzing the possible linkages between the expansion of education and political and economic development in the nation.

U.S. presence in Korea since 1945 can be divided into three distinct periods: occupation of Korea by the U.S. Military Government from 1945 to 1948; United States participation in the Korean War from 1950 to 1953; and United States participation in Reconstruction from 1953 to 1962. The first and third periods will be the main focus of attention, given the chaotic educational situation that persisted during the Korean War.

The contributions of the United States to educational development in Korea from 1945 through 1948 have been reviewed and summarized by Adams,[41] Sung-hwa Lee,[42] Won-Sul Lee,[43] Byung Hun Nam,[44] and Hyung Koo Pak[45] among others, and evaluated by Koh.[46] This last is an excellent summary piece. The U.S. Military Government determined to use education in Korea as a major vehicle for the democratization of society. For this to be accomplished, three principal efforts were necessary: the extension of educational opportunity to all Koreans; the inclusion of democratic values and practices in the curriculum; and the creation of an infrastructure and educational administration that would maintain democratic practices.

The U.S. Military Government found itself short of trained teachers, especially as Japanese teachers were repatriated; with practically no teaching materials in the Korean language; and with strong traditions acting against the democratic practices endorsed by American educators. Efforts of the U.S. Military Government received strong support, however, from Korean educators and the public in general. The following actions were taken:

1) Some 1.7 million textbooks were printed and distributed by April 1946; by 1948 the total had risen to 15 million books.
2) Efforts were made to eliminate Chinese characters in favor of Han'gŭl, the Korean alphabet.
3) Local education committees were created to supervise schools.
4) All schools were made coeducational.
5) Education was made compulsory through the 9th grade, and a three-year middle school separate from high school was created.
6) Four-year colleges were created, and Seoul National University was founded.
7) More Koreans were trained as teachers.
8) More than one million adults were enrolled by 1948 in "civic schools" for literacy and basic education. Illiteracy among adults over 19 years of age was reduced from 78

percent in 1945 to 41 percent in 1948 (and to 10 percent in 1954) according to Sung-hwa Lee.[47]

9) By 1948, 2.3 million children were enrolled in elementary schools, more than 100,000 in secondary schools, and almost 90,000 in technical/industrial schools.

10) A national youth movement, which reached an audited membership of 1,154,821 in 1948, was created. The movement contributed approximately 12 million 8-hour workdays to community development projects, as well as enrolling 80,000 youth in skill-training programs and training 100,000 leaders.[48]

Harold Koh sums up the record as follows:

> In the three-year period ... the number of elementary pupils increased by 82 percent, the number of secondary pupils by 184 percent, and the number of available teachers for each level increased by 55 percent, 569 percent and 268 percent respectively ... largely as a result of the vigorous teacher training programs ... Decentralization seemed to have been effectively accomplished by introduction of "local control" of education through popularly elected school boards.[49]

But not all of the proposed changes survived the institution of the Rhee regime in 1948. Coeducation was universal only in primary schools. The nation could not afford compulsory education through the 9th grade, and universal primary education was not attained until the late 1950s. Local control of education was abandoned in favor of the strong central Ministry that persists today. The youth movement became highly politicized and had to be abandoned. Koh observes:

> Whether the American Military Government succeeded in its aim to "democratize the spirit" of the educational system ... is open to debate. Even today, the pattern of student-as-passive-observer is prevalent in Korean schools, showing perhaps that merely restructuring the educational system does not guarantee ready acceptance of a foreign concept.[50]

Byung Hun Nam faults the U.S. Military Government's relative lack of attention to higher education:

> Inasmuch as a nation depends on its colleges and universities for its enlightened leadership, it may be questioned whether the concentration of the Military Government upon elementary and secondary education was wise.[51]

We will have more to say about higher education later.

The significance of the expansion of enrollments under the U.S. Military Government can be evaluated also by reference to the experiences of other countries. An earlier section discussed rates of growth of educational systems in several developing nations. Another comparison is between the rate of expansion of the system under the Japanese and that during the period of heavy U.S. technical assistance. From 1930 to 1945 enrollments in primary education grew from 450,000 to 1,500,000, while from 1945 to 1960 they grew from 1,500,000 to 3,600,000. During the period of American influence, there was thus a lower rate of growth, but from a larger base.

Finally, growth of education in the Republic of Korea under American influence can be compared with the growth of education in North Korea. Enrollments in schools in the Republic grew more slowly than those in North Korea. The north attained universal primary enrollment several years before the Republic. Universal enrollment in middle school was reached by the north in 1967, while South Korea has not reached this level yet. In 1973 the North Koreans made education compulsory through 10 years. In addition, almost all children are enrolled in preschool programs (practically unknown in the Republic of Korea). Enrollments in higher education are as large in North Korea as in the Republic, although the population of South Korea is almost twice that of North Korea. All (including higher) education is free in the north.[52]

In short, the accomplishments of the U.S. Military Government during the period 1945 to 1948 were considerable, especially in terms of the quantitative expansion of the educational system, but do not represent a unique occurrence in the annals of history. And history writes with an ironic pen. Much of what had been built during that halcyon period of 1945 to 1948 was destroyed between 1950 and 1953. Not only were thousands of physical facilities demolished, but much of the human capital of teachers and administrators trained in new educational principles and procedures was lost in the tragedy of the war.

The task facing the Republic of Korea and its allies in 1953 was, consequently, as large as that facing the U.S. Military Government in 1945. But this time American assistance focused, at the primary and secondary level, on the provision of material aid rather than on reforms of curriculum or other attempts directly to influence the content of education. Much greater investments were made in the expansion of higher education.

AN EVALUATION OF AID FROM 1952 TO 1963

Between 1952 and 1963, about $100 million of aid was provided to education by the U.S. Government. Additional assistance came from private foundations. Most aid went to classroom construction, secondary and vocational education equipment, higher education, and teacher training.

Over the period, about 23,000 classrooms were put into service, either newly built or repaired. The total dollar value of this effort is calculated (by Dodge[53]) at about $70 million, including $48 million in capital grants from the U.S. Government, and the rest in donated labor and materials from the U.S. Armed Forces and local communities. The construction included 14 model schools intended to serve as architectural guides for future school construction. The largest single effort was made in 1955, at the beginning of the program.

Dodge reports a number of difficulties in arranging for counterpart funds to match U.S. dollars, and in supervising the expenditure of the funds. The United States had limited control over the actual use of the funds, and there were many competing demands:

In the years 1956 to 1959, the spread of construction projects over the country seemed designed to promote the political fortunes of the party in power. It is probably more than coincidental that a national election took place in October 1963 just at the time when the construction of 4,778 classrooms under the fiscal year 1962 programs was being completed.[54]

Dodge goes on to observe that equipment and material are not a substitute for "know-how," by which he means that the United States did not provide enough in the way of supervision and demonstration for the Koreans to make the best use of the materials and equipment provided. The problem was most acute in the case of classroom construction (and vocational education), where it was difficult to find Koreans who could speak English, or American technicians who could speak Korean. In any event, a number of classrooms were built, sufficient to lower class sizes briefly, as shown in Table 18. The rate of construction of classrooms declined after that period and class sizes increased again.

Another $7.8 million was provided by the United States for materials and equipment for secondary-level education. Almost 90 percent of these funds went to improving vocational education facilities, through purchase of equipment and tools, construction of shop facilities, and some technical assistance. The amount includes the organization of two vocational teacher training departments at Seoul National University, the training of 82 teachers outside of Korea, the development of two comprehensive high schools (with students taking both academic and vocational subjects in the same building), and some aid to science instruction improvement. Seoul Technical High School was strengthened as a model facility.[55]

Some special comments may be made here about contributions to the development of vocational/technical education in Korea. The first four years of technical assistance (1952–1956) were, according to Dodge, extremely difficult ones, for these reasons. First, the Ministry of Education found it difficult to provide the needed leadership. It shared control of the 49 technical high schools in the country with the provincial governments through the Ministry of Home Affairs. Second, it was difficult (as it is most everywhere in the world) to recruit teachers from industry, especially because in Korea the Ministry required teachers to have an academic degree. Third, there were no instructional materials in Korean for technical subjects. Finally, technical schools are much more expensive than ordinary secondary schools, and the limited funds available did not go far.

The first full-time foreign advisor in technical education did not arrive until 1958. Through fiscal year 1961 a total of $5 million was spent on vocational technical education, including commodities, U.S. technicians, and 59 Koreans sent abroad. The first teacher training programs in vocational education were not in operation until 1963, at the Colleges of Engineering and of Agriculture of Seoul National University.

Finally, these critical comments on vocational education in Korea deserve some attention:

> The major part of the [vocational high schools] were vocational in name only as they lacked both equipment and the instructors qualified to demonstrate practical work skills. As a result, these schools became a refuge for students unable to pass examinations for the academic schools, or who lacked funds.[56]

Approximately $19 million was spent during the period for higher education. Most ($17 million) of this went to Seoul National University, where the objective was to upgrade the faculties "to the point where the programs there would compare favorably to those of high-ranking universities anywhere in the world."[57] The largest single technical assistance grant was to the University of Minnesota, for staff training in Korea and the United States, the formation of a Graduate School of Public Administration, and the upgrading of the faculties of Medicine, Agriculture, and Engineering. The project provided for 300 person-years of staff training, with 226 Koreans going abroad and 56 members of the Faculty of the University of Minnesota coming to Korea.

Assistance to higher education also included $1 million to rebuild the Merchant Marine Academy, $1 million to create a program in business adminsitration modeled on U.S. offerings, and additional funds to send Koreans to the United States (and other countries) for study. By 1956–1957, the third largest foreign student enrollment in the United States was from Korea, behind only Canada and Taiwan. One in every 20 foreign college students in the United States was a Korean, many of whom majored in Social Sciences (29.4 percent) or Humanities (17.9 percent). Enrollments in Natural Sciences and Engineering were proportionately lower than those for other foreign students.[58]

Finally, almost $9 million was expended on the development of a teacher education program in Korea, with 65 person-years of technical assistance provided by George Peabody College of Teachers. In addition to Seoul National University, this program benefited several other universities, the 18 normal schools of Korea, junior colleges, specific high schools and middle schools, and some preschool programs. Between 1956 and 1962, technical assistance was provided in the fields of textbook preparation, science education, early childhood education, educational research, library science, the teaching of English as a second language, and in-service teacher training.

The experiences of the programs described above have been evaluated in studies by Williams and Dodge. Several of their criticisms of the programs have been anticipated. First, to the extent that not all educational goals were reached (for example, universal middle school) the amount of aid could be considered to have been insufficient. On the other hand, it could be argued that the large lump of U.S. capital made it possible for the Korean government to keep its contribution to education below that spent by most countries on public education. Education averaged about 15 percent of the national budget, while many other countries were spending up to 20 and 25 percent of their budgets in an attempt to provide free education to all. The counter to this argument is that in fact only 3 percent of capital aid went to education, a helpful but not overwhelmingly significant contribution.

A second criticism argues that U.S. aid had relatively little impact on the content of education in Korea, and therefore failed to contribute to attaining goals of educating a democratic Korean person. Technical assistance takes knocks from two directions. Dodge first criticizes U.S. advisors for insensitivity to Korean culture (and ignorance of the language and customs):

> Should it not have been recognized during the U.S. effort to rebuild and upgrade education that Korean culture should still be the core and Western culture the supplementary element to make the core culture functional? With the exception of some work under the Peabody program there is little evidence that the United States effort to upgrade Korean education did much to address this problem.[59]

On the other hand, Dodge reports criticisms by Koreans of the Peabody technical advisors, who were active in developing curriculum materials and techniques to be used in the lower grades, relying on Korean materials. The criticisms seem to turn mostly on the success that the Peabody people had in encouraging Korean teachers to begin to develop their own innovative styles in the classroom. Finally, Dodge criticizes the U.S. program for failing to make maximum use of the leverage that $100 million of aid should have given it, noting that, especially in the later years, little attention was given to fundamental changes in the system.

U.S. technical assistance during the period 1952–1963 might also be faulted for overemphasis on higher education. Sizable expenditures on universities at a time when there were not enough buildings for (especially rural) children to attend primary school could be considered to favor the already economically privileged strata of society. Even if all the approximately $70 million of construction had gone into primary education (which it did not), then only about 5 million children would have been benefited; in other words, aid amounted to $14 per child. The $17 million for Seoul National University, on the other hand, had at the most benefited directly only 132,000 students in all universities (about $130 each) and probably only 17,000 Seoul National students (for about $1,000 each). Especially as the government was already spending more than 13 times as much on a university student as on a primary student[60] and access to the university was limited for working class students (given class-biased examinations and the high private cost of education), the U.S. contribution to higher education could be seen as tending to redistribute wealth upwards.

The justification for investment in higher education went as follows:

> Of the large number of Korean institutions of higher education, only a few could claim to be institutions of higher learning by the standards of advanced countries. The Republic of Korea was unable to devote sufficient budgetary support for higher education. Consequently there were very wide qualitative disparities in the system. An important deficiency of Korea's higher education was the absence of centers of advanced teaching and research. Korea needed such centers to provide high-level manpower over a broad professional and disciplinary spectrum. The availability of advanced, high-quality centers would reduce the outflow of talented students seeking training in foreign universities and lower the risk of losing them to the "brain drain." They might also draw back to Korea outstanding scholars who had settled abroad.[61]

Hindsight allows us to see some of the errors in this reasoning. First, the provision of centers of excellence for high-level training may have *exaggerated* the brain-drain problem, as Koreans highly trained (in technologies abundant in more advanced countries but not yet established in Korea) found it easier to migrate abroad, especially given changes in the immigration laws of the United States.[62] Second, the cost of training high-level manpower for other countries (or for Korea) would be borne principally by Korea under the policies recommended. Third, the recommendations were made in apparent ignorance of the real demand for high-level manpower within the Korean economy.

In fact, perhaps as early as 1953 there had begun to be a surplus of university graduates. While the ravages of war closed many primary and secondary schools and enrollments plummeted, the number of students pursuing higher education increased dramatically between 1950 and 1953, since for a period university students were exempt from the draft.[63] University enrollments mushroomed, as private colleges sprang up over the countryside.[64] By 1955 there were 15 universities, 30 independent colleges, 6 junior colleges, and 20 other third-level schools. Enrollments went from 34,000 in 1952 to 66,000 in 1954 to 97,000 in 1956 to 146,000 by 1961.

It is likely, of course, that the quality of education provided in these institutions was low, especially as enrollments grew far more rapidly than the supply of trained teachers. But diplomas granted at these institutions were officially recognized, and graduates expected employment. Data on numbers of graduates are not available. But, if even only half graduated (a low figure for Korea, given policies of social promotion even at the university), then the number of college graduates entering the labor force in this period increased much more rapidly than the expansion of the labor force, or even the demand for high-level manpower. Jin Eun Kim reports that, by 1960, 9,000 of 15,000 college graduates were unable to find employment.[65] Underwood describes the situation this way: "Recent studies show that over 50 percent of the college students are in the wrong department . . . ten years after graduation over 70 percent of college graduates are working in fields not directly related to their college department."[66] Quee-Young Kim and others suggest that the lack of employment opportunities for college graduates contributed to political unrest and the eventual student revolt against the Rhee Government.[67] The Revolutionary Park Military Government in 1961 made strenuous efforts to curtail enrollments in higher education, and in fact enrollments declined by about 10 percent for two years before beginning to climb again.[68]

When serious attention to planning began with the Park Government in 1963, it was discovered that Korea had an excess of high-level manpower. The Economic Planning Board's 1964 data reported a demand of 31,408 and a stock of 56,842 technicians and skilled workers, with an annual supply of 13,395. A study by the UNKRA and FAO[69] showed that the colleges and universities were producing 19 times more agricultural technicians than were needed. The USOM recommended reducing enrollments in civil engineering, electricity, mechanics, and chemistry. The EPB stated an oversupply of law graduates by a factor of 21. A good supply of MDs was being generated by the university, but there were too many pharmacists (about one-fourth were out of work). On the other hand, teachers, especially for primary schools, were in short supply.[70] For the 1960s, Korea was described as an exporter of trained manpower:

> ... there is now emerging, in one less developed country after another, a substantial oversupply of medical and engineering personnel, i.e., an oversupply in relation to effective demand ... The oversupply becomes manifest in the form of underemployment, changes in occupation, or emigration ... The major losers to date in terms of numbers have been India, Iran, Turkey, Pakistan, the Philippines, Taiwan, Korea.[71]

> The excess was in those areas encouraged by AID. The total projected professional and technical manpower requirements against supply over the period 1967 to 1971 shows that only the technician category is expected to be short, whereas for scientists, engineers and professionals, and craftsmen, supply will exceed demand by about 55 percent and 35 percent respectively.[72]

The Park Government again in 1968 made serious efforts to curtail university enrollments with some slight effect, but rates of growth soon went back to more than 10 percent per year. At present, no new university can be created, nor can any existing college or university offer a new program without government approval, and enrollments in all programs are fixed by the government. Apparently, the problem of overproduction of university graduates continues, as a 1974 UNESCO report indicated that in 1972 only 60 percent of graduates in engineering and related sciences found employment, and long-range forecasts by Shin-Bok Kim[73] indicated continued oversupply.

SUMMARY

Foreign assistance to education in Korea would appear to have had mixed outcomes. On the one hand, U.S. foreign aid and technical assistance were critical for the rapid expansion of educational opportunity at the primary (and secondary) level, both at the end of World War II and at the end of the Korean War. The provision of massive amounts of aid and materials freed up for the Korean government a considerable lump of capital that could be put toward investments with more rapid returns.[74]

On the other hand, technical assistance and capital aid to secondary and higher education no doubt contributed toward increasing the public subsidization of the relatively few students able to reach higher education at that period in Korean history. By overshooting the requirements for trained manpower, foreign aid wasted valuable resources.

Overall, the rapid expansion of educational opportunity at all levels—primary, secondary and university—no doubt enhanced real, and greatly promoted subjective, mobility, perhaps of vital importance to the maintenance of political stability in a regime committed to asking its populace to sacrifice in order to promote economic development. This point will be dealt with in a later chapter. At the same time, expansion of higher education may have countered other tendencies in society toward a more equitable distribution of income. This point will be discussed in Chapter 4 on equity issues in education.

The failures of American aid and technical assistance in education could be attributed either to the inadequacy of the conventional wisdom about development strategies that prevailed around the world in the late 1950s and early 1960s, or to ignorance of the real problems of Korea. Programs in higher education made sense according to a development strategy based on high-level manpower development. But they were the wrong strategies for a country whose rapid economic growth would be achieved through emphasis on use of intermediate technologies and labor- instead of capital-intensive ventures. The mistake may have been made because it was easier to provide technical assistance to higher rather than lower levels of education, through scholarships for Koreans to come to the United States or grants to American professors to lecture in Seoul universities. Language barriers were lower in universities than in primary or even secondary schools and one could more safely assume similarity in cultural backgrounds. Aid to higher education made few demands on the U.S. advisor—but it also may have failed to meet Korea's more pressing needs.

THREE

Education and the Growth of the Economy

Korea has experienced not only a rapidly growing educational system during the past thirty years but also a rapidly growing economy. In fact, some might want to argue that the high and sustained levels of economic growth in the Republic of Korea during the past decade are truly outstanding. These rates of growth have been equaled by few other countries, and are even more impressive than achievements in education.

For many observers there is a relationship between the two. They see in the historical contiguity of economic and educational growth an association that is more than merely chance. Korea's economic modernization and growth were possible, those people say, only because human resources existed in abundance: without a large supply of educated people, the economic policies pursued would have failed:

... Korea can achieve high rates of growth and ... given its human resources capabilities, it should probably be at a considerably higher level of self-development and real income than it is.[1]

... the high rate of economic growth was the consequence of a constellation of policies designed to utilize with maximum effectiveness the country's wealth of human resources.[2]

The remarkable and rapid economic growth that has occurred in Korea over the last decade has been based to a large degree on human resources, and education has assisted in the production of a literate and industrious people.[3]

The concept of "human resources" is a broad one; it contains a variety of meanings. For example, growth of both economy and education could be attributed to the passive presence of a large body of trained labor, merely awaiting the arrival of technology and organization to be employed productively. Or education could be said to contribute actively to economic growth by fostering increased entrepreneurial activity, innovation, development of technologies, high labor mobility, and other behaviors which result in increased rates of growth. It also is possible that both education and the economy of Korea grew because vast amounts of capital were pumped in by foreign donors. Or that education grew because of the growth in the economy and not the other way around.

In this chapter we review evidence for differing views of the possible relationships between education and economic growth. We have grouped these into two outstanding perspectives. The first is the better known, and considerable work has been done to marshall evidence to support it. The second perspective uses the same facts about growth but makes different assumptions as to the ways in which education and the economy are linked. In both cases the intent is to explain the association at the societal level.

THE HUMAN-CAPITAL PERSPECTIVE

Education has been said to contribute to national economic progress in such ways as:

1) improving the quality of labor through increased skills, efficiency, and work knowledge
2) increasing labor mobility, promoting division of labor and increased labor force participation
3) increasing scientific and technical knowledge to promote technical progress through invention, discovery, and swift adaptation
4) increasing entrepreneurial ability to improve management and allocation of factors of production
5) making people more responsive to economic change, removing social and institutional barriers to economic growth [4]

In most cases, the impact of education on the economy is achieved through the improvement of the quality of the labor force, which is why this theory has been labeled the "human-capital" approach. Education possessed by the worker is treated as analogous to physical capital, that is, as a factor of production. Central to the theory is the assumption of a competitive labor market which rewards increments of production contributed by the more productive types of labor at the market value of those increments.

In all countries, people with more education tend to earn higher incomes than people with less education. Figures 3 and 4 provide limited evidence that Korea is no exception to the universal tendency. The graphs show that increasing years of education are associated with earnings differentials which widen from age 25 on. The evidence is considered limited in this case because the graphs refer only to the earnings of regular, full-time industrial workers. This is a relatively homogeneous group; if data were available for a broader range of workers (including, say, government workers, farmers, and fishermen) the range of

FIGURE 3 Average Monthly Earnings in Industry by Age
and Education, Males, 1972

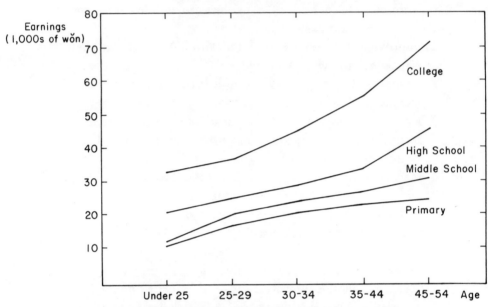

FIGURE 4 Average Monthly Earnings in Industry by Age
and Education, Females, 1972

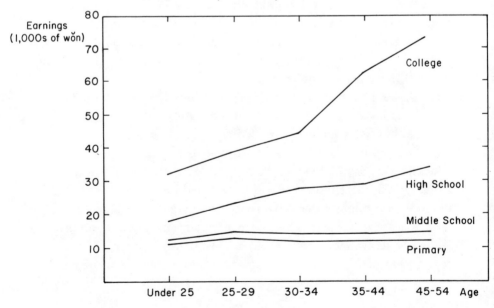

Source: Based on Office of Labor Affairs, *Wage and Employment Survey* (Seoul, 1972).

earnings associated with different levels of educational attainment probably would be wider still.

The human-capital theory asserts that the higher incomes of more educated workers result because they are more productive, and that their higher productivity is recognized in a competitive labor market. The returns to education are known to the public; individuals, their families, and society as a whole forego consumption to meet the direct and indirect costs of education, and are rewarded by a higher earnings stream during the working life of the educated individual.[5] Employers rely on educational credentials as important (and, the theory asserts, valid) proofs that an individual possesses the skills and knowledge necessary for economic production (or, in a more recent version, the ability to learn how to be productive once employed).[6]

Educational requirements for employment tend to rise in society because technological change creates a need for more highly skilled workers. The expansion of education is a response to these demands made by the modernizing society in which not only economic, but also familial, social, and political roles become increasingly complex.[7]

The above assumptions allow several (not always consistent) hypotheses. The theory is a bit vague on the sequence of events in the relationship between education and economy. Does education supply needed skills only as those become necessary (for example, once new technologies have been introduced)? If this were the case, then one should find increments in education, especially those kinds of education thought to provide the skills presumed needed, following an economic take-off. An economy based on labor-intensive or low-technology efforts would require more persons with relatively *low* levels of education. A development process including advanced technologies, on the other hand, would argue for increased graduates from *higher* levels of the system, especially graduates trained in technical subjects.

An equally plausible hypothesis is that education provides the skills necessary for an economic take-off, that is, that the skills must already be present in the society when technologies are introduced. In this case, changes in the structure of education should precede the take-off period, with sufficient lead time to anticipate changes in technology. Increments in lower-level enrollments would have to occur several years earlier than increments in secondary and higher education enrollments, since the lower levels feed the upper levels. Given the operation of a competitive labor market, the supply of trained manpower would match (that is, neither exceed nor fall short of) the demand for it.

The human-capital approach also would hypothesize, for the Korean case, that schooling provided either the specific skills and knowledges required for changes in technology, or the kinds of learning skills required to acquire new technological abilities.[8] That is, changes in curricular offerings of Korean schools should match (either leading or lagging) changes in the structure of the economy.

TREND OF ECONOMIC GROWTH
AND HUMAN RESOURCES DEVELOPMENT

The historical development of education in Korea since Liberation has already been described (Chapter 1). Our purpose here is to relate that development to the economic growth that occurred during the same period. The post-1948 era can usefully be divided into three sub-periods based on growth trends: 1) economic instability and destruction during 1945–1953; 2) reconstruction and expansion of the economy during 1954–1961; and 3) accelerated economic growth after 1962 (see Table 27). Although efforts were made to activate the disorganized economy during the post-World War II period, and production capacity was expanded continuously throughout the 1950s, only after 1962 were there significant increases in real per capita GNP.

The first period, 1945–1953, shows discontinuities in economic progress caused by social and political instability, such as economic disorganization after the Liberation and partition of the country, slow recovery and high inflation in the late 1940s, and the Korean War destruction of production facilities. The Liberation that brought partition of the country left the Republic of Korea with 48 percent of the Korean land mass, 66 percent of the population, 60 percent of the agricultural production, and 42 percent of the mining and manufacturing production.[9] During this period, production never regained pre-Liberation levels. Lack of managerial and technical manpower, shortages of raw materials, inflation, and unstable social and political environments are among the possible explanations. It has been estimated that in 1948 manufacturing output for the Republic of Korea was only 15 percent of the 1939 level. At the same time, the Seoul wholesale price index increased about 16 times during the last five months in 1945 and about 18 times between the fourth quarters of 1945 and 1949.[10]

The economy, which started a slow recovery from 1947, was seriously damaged by the Korean War. Statistical sources indicate that the loss of manufacturing facilities due to the war was equivalent to 42 to 44 percent of the pre-war facilities.[11] Production recovered sharply in 1953 to exceed the 1949 level, but the Seoul wholesale price index rose by more than 15 times in the meantime. As compared to the 1939/1940 level, the net value of commodity-products in the Republic increased by 16 percent, and population by 30 percent in 1953, resulting in an 11 percent decrease of per capita net commodity-production.

During the second period, 1954–1961, the economy managed to grow modestly, with continuous expansion of the mining and manufacturing sector. GNP grew at an annual average rate of 4.3 percent, while mining and manufacturing production increased by 11.3 percent per annum. Economic growth in this period, however, was not steady and effective. The annual growth rate of GNP fluctuated between 0.4 percent in 1956 and 7.7 percent in 1957, depending upon performance of the dominant agricultural sector. The growth rate of per capita GNP averaged 1.5 percent per annum during the period.

The Korean industrial structure changed gradually during this

TABLE 27 Major Indicators of Korean Economic Growth
%

	1939/40–1953	1954–1961	1962–1975
Annual Growth Rates			
Population	2.12	2.64	2.11
Per Capita GNP	–0.87[a]	1.58	7.51
GNP	1.11[a]	4.34	9.78
Agriculture, Forestry, Fishery	1.88	3.42	4.75
Mining and Manufacturing	–1.67	11.94	17.57
Social Overhead	–	8.18	15.88
Service	–	3.35	6.85
Composition of GNP[b]			
Agriculture, Forestry, Fishery	47.3	40.2	25.7
Mining and Manufacturing	10.0	15.2	29.1
Social Overhead & Service	42.7	44.6	45.2

Sources: BOK, *National Income in Korea, 1975* (Seoul); BOK, *Economic Statistics Yearbook 1975* (Seoul); and Kim and Roemer.

Notes: [a]Growth rates of net value of commodity-products for the Republic of Korea.

[b]As of the end of each period.

period as the share of the mining and manufacturing production in GNP increased from 10.0 percent in 1953 to 15.2 percent in 1961. Economic growth during the period might be attributable principally to foreign aid, which supplied most raw materials, intermediate goods, and capital goods. Kim and Roemer indicate that foreign savings financed 81.3 percent of the total capital formation during the 1953–1960 period, and foreign aid accounted for 94.7 percent of the foreign savings.

The economy grew steadily until 1958 as the large-scale influx of foreign aid promoted development of the import-substituting non-durable consumer goods industries. But inflation was continuous, increasing the wholesale price index more than three times during the 1954–1958 period. In the later period, 1959–1962, the economic growth rate declined to 3.4 percent per annum accompanied by decreasing aid and political unrest.

The third period, beginning in 1962, has witnessed a rapid transformation of the economy and accelerated economic growth. Nearly every aspect of the economy has experienced quantitative expansion and structural transformation. The annual growth rate of GNP averaged 9.8 percent during the period 1962–1975, and that of mining and manufacturing production 17.6 percent. With population growth rate declining, the rate of growth per capita GNP increased to an average of 7.5 percent per annum. The accelerated trend of economic growth has been accompanied by dramatic increases in the levels of investment, domestic savings, exports, and imports.

Growth began to accelerate with the inauguration of a formal development effort in 1962. The government formulated three Five-Year Economic Development Plans aimed at structural improvement of the economy and high economic growth through export promotion, and made subsequent institutional reforms. The annual growth rate of GNP was raised to 7.8 percent during the First Five-Year Plan period (1962–1966), and increased to 10.5 percent in the Second Five-Year Plan period (1967–1971). Despite the adverse world economic environment of the early 1970s, rapid growth continued during the four years of the Third Five-Year Plan (1972–1975), averaging 10.0 percent per annum.

Economic growth during this period was led by the mining and manufacturing sector, which grew nearly twice as fast as the economy as a whole. The proportion of mining and manufacturing value added in GNP rose from 15.2 percent in 1962 to 29.1 percent in 1975. Rapid industrialization, in turn, was largely a result of export promotion. Exports increased by more than 40 percent per annum to raise the value of exports on a customs clearance basis from $41 million in 1961 to $5,081 million in 1975. Meanwhile, the rate of inflation was reduced to about 14 percent a year.

It can be argued that the success of this process depended on such factors as political leadership, social environment, administrative efficiency, and entrepreneurship. Economic development appears to have resulted from an outward-looking development strategy that established a comparative advantage in labor-intensive industries. The human-capital approach would say that those industries capitalized on the abundance of relatively well educated people.

Korea today has relatively abundant and well-developed human resources. According to one estimate, the amount of education embodied in employed persons in 1970 was valued at 2,122 billion wǒn or $5.7 billion in 1970 prices, and the value per employed person had increased by 5.9 percent per annum since 1960.[12] Another estimate indicated that the value of the nation's human capital stock, measured by educational investment, was equivalent to 125 percent of the value of physical capital.[13]

But these resources were not always present. The enrollment expansions described in Chapter 1 led to the rapid increases in the educational attainments of the adult population which are shown in Figure 5 and Table 28. At the time of Liberation, the general level of education of the Korean people was low; 86 percent of the population aged above 15 had received no formal education. After Liberation, many industrial plants stopped production activities, mainly because of the evacuation of Japanese entrepreneurs, managers, engineers, and technicians. The Japanese owned about 94 percent of the business establishments in 1940, and Korean engineers and technicians employed in manufacturing, construction, and utilities in 1944 were only about 2.0 percent of the total technical manpower.[14] The 1944 population census also shows that only 2 percent of the population aged above 15 had received secondary education or more. A shortage of highly educated manpower could have prolonged the disorganized economic state during the pre-Korean War period.

During the second period (1954–1961), education developed

TABLE 28 Population, Aged 14 and Over, by Educational Attainments, 1944–1974[a]
(1,000s)

			None	1–6	7–9	10–12	13–14	15 & over	Unknown
1944[b]	Total	14,189	12,303	1,608[c]	248	22	8		
	Male	6,950	5,440	1,282[c]	202	19	7		
	Female	7,239	6,863	326[c]	46	4			
1960	Total	14,831	6,468	5,347	1,428	1,134	175	207	72
	Male	7,300	2,321	2,762	998	854	149	184	32
	Female	7,530	4,147	2,584	430	280	26	23	41
1966	Total	17,134	5,271	6,848	1,903	2,332	211	568	1
	Male	8,457	1,822	3,184	1,171	1,641	176	463	
	Female	8,677	3,449	3,663	732	691	35	105	1
1970	Total	18,943	4,444	7,433	3,396	2,621	361	687	1
	Male	9,313	1,470	3,251	2,011	1,754	280	548	
	Female	9,630	2,974	4,182	1,386	868	81	139	
1974	Total	20,872	4,234	7,513	4,347	3,586		1,193	
	Male	10,116	1,376	3,208	2,401	2,222		909	
	Female	10,758	2,859	4,305	1,946	1,364		284	

Source: Yung Bong Kim, "Education and Economic Growth," p. 11.

Notes: [a]Minor discrepancies are attributable to rounding.
[b]Figures of 1944 include population, ages 15 and over, for the whole of Korea.
[c]Includes secondary school dropouts (7–11 years).

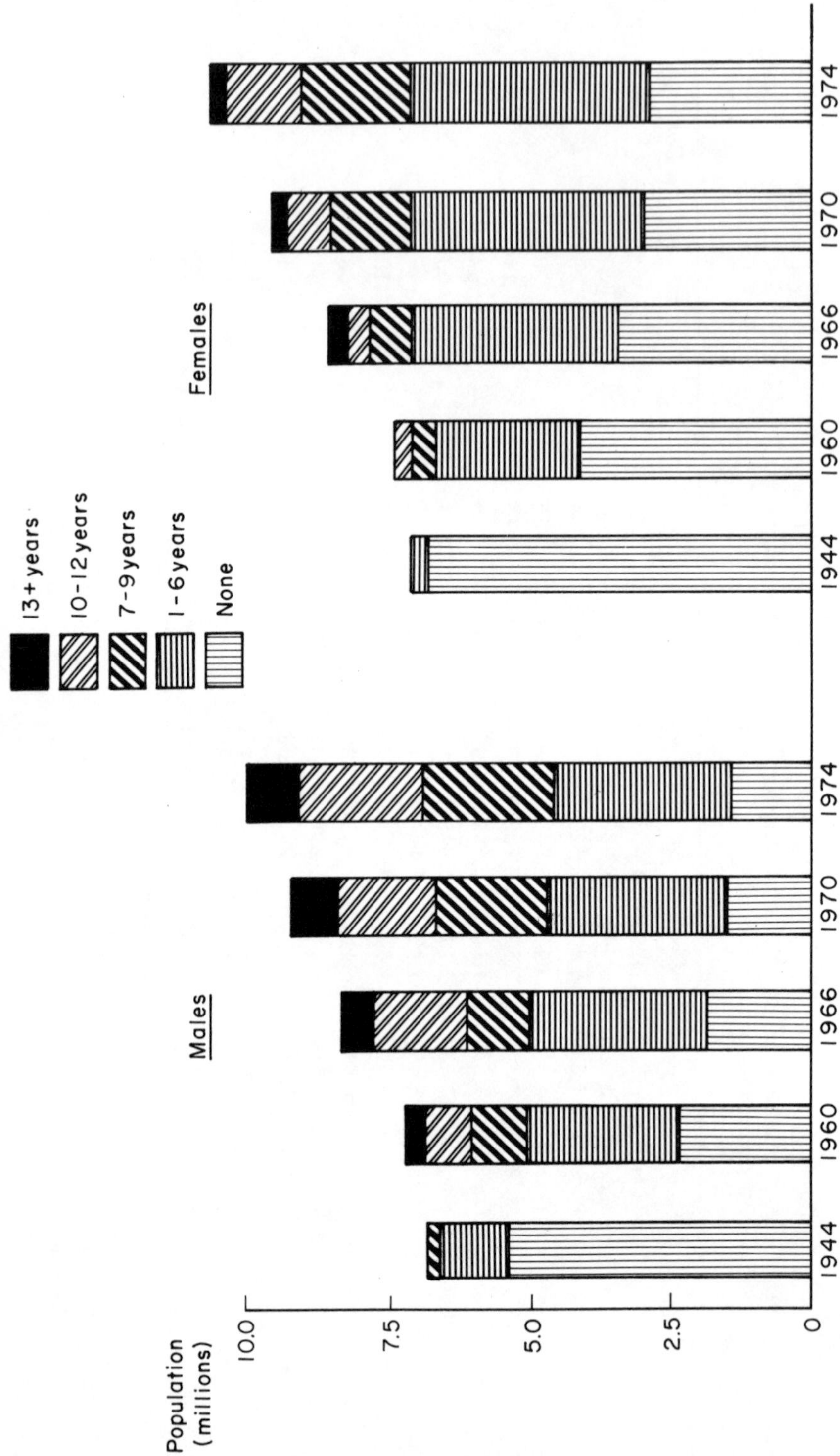

FIGURE 5 Educational Attainments of Population Aged 14 and Over, 1944–1974

far in advance of other productive resources. The moderate economic growth of the 1950s, based on import substitution in non-durable consumer goods industries, increased employment but failed to provide adequate job opportunities for the nation's rapidly growing stock of educated labor. According to the 1960 Population Census, 6.7 percent of the economically active population was unemployed and 15.4 percent worked less than 18 hours a week. The census also indicates that the illiteracy rate was cut in half, while the number of college graduates increased about 25 times as compared with the 1944 level.

The human-capital argument would go on to assert that the accumulation of educated manpower helped lay a foundation for the rapid economic growth which occured after 1962. The export-oriented pattern of economic growth during this period increased the demand for skilled laborers, technicians, engineers, managers, and entrepreneurs. Table 29 shows that educational expansion, especially at secondary and higher levels, had made these workers available. Accelerated economic growth effectively absorbed both the accumulated educated human resources as of 1962 and the post-1962 increments.[5] Effective utilization of human resources was reflected in the decline of the unemployment rate from 8.1 percent to 4.1 percent during the 1963–1975 period, the expansion of manufacturing employment from 8.0 percent of the total to 18.6 percent, and the increase in value added per worker at an average rate of 6.0 percent per annum during the period 1963–1975.

Tables 30 and 31 give some idea of the relationship of educational attainment to employment patterns in 1960 and 1970. (Unfortunately, neither the range of data available nor the period covered is as great as one would want.) Table 30, which shows the educational make-up of the labor force within broad occupational groups, reveals a dispersion of educated labor force within the economy in 1960 which is unusual for a country of Korea's income level at the time. By 1970 the economy was employing nearly 3.9 million more educated workers, as total employment rose by 3.1 million, and some

TABLE 29 Distribution of Persons Employed by Years of School Completed, 1960-1974
(1,000s)

	Total Persons Employed	Years of School Completed					
		0-5	6-8	9-11	12-15	16 or more	
Male							
1960	5,005 (100.0)	2,123 (42.4)	1,977 (39.5)	483 (9.6)	344 (6.9)	78 (1.6)	
1966	5,425 (100.0)	1,414 (26.1)	2,276 (42.0)	545 (10.0)	938 (17.3)	252 (4.6)	
1970	6,577 (100.0)	1,252 (19.0)	2,716 (41.3)	1,092 (16.6)	1,164 (17.7)	353 (5.4)	
1974	7,196 (100.0)	976 (13.6)	2,954 (41.0)	1,336 (18.6)	1,516 (21.1)	414 (5.7)	
Female							
1960	2,022 (100.0)	1,353 (66.9)	573 (28.3)	60 (3.0)	32 (1.6)	4 (0.2)	
1966	2,538 (100.0)	1,229 (48.4)	1,028 (40.5)	129 (5.1)	132 (5.2)	20 (0.8)	
1970	3,574 (100.0)	1,353 (37.8)	1,661 (46.5)	317 (8.9)	210 (5.9)	33 (0.9)	
1974	4,256 (100.0)	1,258 (29.6)	2,109 (49.5)	505 (11.9)	341 (8.0)	43 (1.0)	

TABLE 29 (continued)

Source: Yung Bong Kim, "Education and Economic Growth," p. 19.

Notes: Figures in parentheses denote the percentage distribution of persons employed by level of education in each period.
In the absence of information, adjustments were made subject to the following principles:
 1) unknowns are included in the group 0–5 years,
 2) those who enrolled in schools are equally divided in the groups 9–11 years and 12–15 years,
 3) graduates of the old system middle school (7–11 years) are treated as high school graduates,
 4) dropouts and school graduates unclearly classified in the employment data are divided proportionally according to the distribution of the population by level of education.

TABLE 30 Distribution of Employment by Education
Within Occupational Groups, 1960–1970

Occupational Group	Distribution by Years of Schooling (%)[a]					Mean Years of Schooling[b]
	0	1–6	7–12	13+	Total	
			1960			
Professional and technical	3	9	54	34	100	11
Administrative	15	37	37	11	100	7
Clerical	1	21	58	20	100	10
Sales	34	44	20	2	100	5
Production process workers	26	54	19	1	100	5
Service workers	23	47	26	4	100	6
Farmers and fishermen	56	37	7	–	100	3
Total (%)	45	39	13	2	100	4
Total (1,000s)[c]	3,127	2,764	942	166	7,028	
			1970			
Professional and technical	1	6	38	55	100	13
Administrative	1	15	45	40	100	12
Clerical	–	9	59	32	100	11
Sales	13	40	40	7	100	7
Production process workers	9	48	40	3	100	7
Service workers	10	51	36	4	100	7
Farmers and fishermen	39	49	11	1	100	4
Total (%)	24	44	26	6	100	6
Total (1,000s)[c]	2,414	4,430	2,684	622	10,153	

Source: Population Censuses.

Notes: [a]Workers whose educational attainment is unknown are excluded.

[b]A rough estimate, based on the following assumed group means: 1–6 years = 5; 7–12 years = 10; 13+ years = 16.

[c]Includes those whose occupation is unknown

TABLE 31 Distribution of Employment by Occupation
Within Educational Attainment Groups, 1960–1970

Occupational Group	Distribution by Years of Schooling (%)[a]				Total (%)	Total (1,000s)
	0	1-6	7-12	13+		
			1960			
Professional and technical	–	1	10	34	2	166
Administrative	–	1	4	6	1	90
Clerical	–	1	11	22	3	183
Sales	6	9	12	9	8	577
Production process workers	8	18	18	6	13	926
Service workers	3	7	11	10	6	414
Farmers and fishermen	82	62	33	12	66	4,613
Total	100	100	100	100	100	7,028[b]
			1970			
Professional and technical	–	–	5	30	3	323
Administrative	–	–	2	6	1	96
Clerical	–	1	13	31	6	593
Sales	6	9	16	12	10	1,028
Production process workers	8	24	33	11	22	2,198
Service workers	3	8	9	4	7	679
Farmers and fishermen	83	57	22	5	51	5,148
Total	100	100	100	100	100	10,153[b]

Source: Population Censuses.

Notes: [a]Workers whose educational attainment is unknown are excluded.
[b]Includes those whose occupation is unknown.

700,000 unschooled workers were replaced by those who had had at least some formal education. Educational standards rose within every occupational group during the decade, as a comparison of the upper and lower portions of the table reveals.

In Table 31 the same data are arranged in a different way to show the distribution of workers with particular educational attainments among occupational groups. The upper part of this table shows the typical less-developed country pattern, in which highly educated manpower is concentrated in professional and technical occupations (especially teaching and public administration), middle manpower is concentrated in lower-level white collar jobs, and uneducated labor is heavily centered in primary production, where it makes up the overwhelming bulk of the labor force. Again, however, the pattern is less pronounced than in many other countries. By 1970 (see the lower part of Table 31), educated labor is much more widely spread throughout the economy. Note the increasing importance of clerical, sales, and production-process work as outlets for workers with secondary or post-secondary schooling. The human-capital approach attributes changes like these to the introduction of more sophisticated technologies, or expects to find increased productivity in those sectors with no change in technology.

CONTRIBUTION OF EDUCATION
TO ECONOMIC GROWTH

Several attempts have been made to measure education's contribution to economic growth in Korea.[16] These efforts give different estimates of the magnitude of education's contribution, but they are consistent with the view that an important (although perhaps declining) proportion of economic growth after 1960 is attributable to growth in education.

In our attempt to estimate the contribution of education to economic growth, we have applied the procedure used by Denison[17] for measuring sources of economic growth to data for the period 1960–1974. The improvement of labor quality due to additional education is assessed by giving an appropriate weight to each level of education, with adjustments for the effects of differences in age, sex, native ability, and other related factors.

As discussed in the previous section, the effects of education are not confined to productivity increments of the labor force, but spread to other aspects of the economy. In *Why Growth Rates Differ*, Denison isolated every measurable source of output growth and credited the residual that remained unexplained to advances in society's stock of knowledge. Selowsky[18] has suggested that one can estimate "the part of the contribution of education that stems from maintaining the average level of schooling of the labor force." For the sake of simplicity, however, we deal only with the contribution to economic growth resulting from increases in the educational attainments of employed labor. The analysis is based on the following data conditions, methods, and assumptions.

1) The labor share:
Labor earnings are assumed to constitute 60 percent of value added in Korea. This figure reflects the labor share of value added in 1970, estimated by Wontack Hong.[19] Hong's estimate, based on input-output data, shows a decreasing labor share over time. For the whole economy, labor's share decreased to 54 percent in 1973, while in the manufacturing sector it fell from 45 percent in 1966 to 40 percent in 1973.

2) The distribution of employment by amount of education:
Employed workers are divided into five groups: college graduates, high school graduates, middle school graduates, primary school graduates, and those with less than an elementary education. (A more detailed breakdown would increase the accuracy of estimation, but we were limited by the availability of wage data.) The employment data were taken from the Population Census Reports of 1960, 1966, and 1970, and the Employment Survey of 1974 (Economic Planning Board, *Employment Statistics*). In order to fit the employment data

into the above categories, those who did not finish each level of education were considered as lower level graduates, and some adjustments were made as indicated in the notes to Table 29.

3) Qualitative and quantitative changes of education:
Education is assumed to have improved both in quantity and quality over time. For example, the days of school attended per year today are more than in the periods of World War II and the Korean War, during which more absenteeism and interruption occurred as a result of remoteness from school and mobilization of students for labor, combat, and air-raid drills. The quality of education should have improved significantly because of improvements in teacher training, teaching methods, facilities, and materials. The present stock of graduates contains more persons who attended school in recent years. Because of the unavailability of data, however, no adjustments were made to allow for these presumed improvements. Graduates of the old system middle school (11 years of education) were treated as receiving the same amount of education as those who graduated from the new high school (12 years of education).

4) Weights for education groups:
Wage differences by educational attainment are assumed in the Denison analysis to reflect the difference in productivity or the marginal value product of labor due to education. The computation of wage differences between education groups relied on the wage data provided in the Office of Labor Affairs' *Report of Occupational Wage Survey, 1972.* The weights for education groups are given for both sexes after taking necessary steps to eliminate the effects of other factors remaining in the wage differences. To eliminate the effects of age difference, and loss of work experience and benefit from education on income, the wage data were cross-classified by ages and years of education, mean wages were computed for each cell expressed as a percentage of the mean wage of the primary school graduates, and

averages of the percentages of each age group were obtained.[20] Of the resulting wage differences between education groups, three-fifths are assumed to represent differences in earnings due to differences in education as distinguished from native ability, family background, and other income-associated factors.

Two arbitrary assumptions underlie these weights. First, the average earnings of those with no education or less than complete elementary schooling are assumed to be 70 percent of the average earnings of the primary school graduates. Information on the wage level of those with less than 6 years of education is not available, since wage surveys focus on the graduates of each education level. It is, however, necessary to give a differential weight to this group because of the importance of its contribution (through its shrinkage) to improvement in the level of education of Korean workers during the period 1960–1974. The assumption is based on the relationship of the average wage earned by primary school graduates (6 years) to that of high school graduates (12 years), which is a little more than 70 percent for male workers.[21]

Second, it was assumed that education accounts for 60 percent of observed earnings differences among educational categories and that other income-related elements, such as ability, intelligence, family background, and so on, account for the remaining 40 percent. This assumption is the same as that adopted in Denison's analysis.[22]

Table 32 gives the resulting weights and wage differentials by years of education. The education weights for males are of a pattern similar to those derived by Denison for the United States. For females, wage differentials between education groups are much larger, which may result from the low wages paid to unskilled female workers in the light industries. It is, however, still possible that the differences in education's contribution to productivity are not fully accounted for by these weights since they are based on wage differentials instead of income differentials. Although we do not know whether the income differences of non-wage earners due to education are

Education and Economic Growth

TABLE 32 Weights and Wage Differentials by Years of School Completed, 1972

Years of School Completed	Weights for Education Groups	Mean Wages as Percentage of Mean Wages of Average Primary School Graduated by Age Group				
		Average	Below 25	25–34	35–44	45 and over
Male						
0–5[a]	76.0	60.0	60.0	60.0	60.0	60.0
6–8	100.0	100.0	100.0	100.0	100.0	100.0
9–11	110.9	118.1	118.7	111.9	115.9	126.5
12–15	135.0	158.3	185.9	135.1	141.1	177.2
16 or more	191.6	252.6	307.2	209.4	229.3	276.2
Female						
0–5[a]	76.0	60.0	60.0	60.0	60.0	60.0
6–8	100.0	100.0	100.0	100.0	100.0	100.0
9–11	113.6	122.7	110.8	120.8	130.7	132.3
12–15	178.5	230.8	174.7	198.2	255.9	303.5
16 or more	313.2	455.3	296.7	329.8	544.8	666.7

Source: Computed from Office of Labor Affairs, Report of Occupational Wage Survey, 1972. See also note 20.

Note: [a] Assumed.

larger than those of wage-earners, it would seem reasonable to expect that educated wage-earners could raise their productivities and incomes above their wages through utilization of unemployed time, better management of assets, and other means.

5) Weights for female workers:

A female worker is given 45.6 percent of the weight given to a male worker, which is the ratio of the female average wage to the male average wage in 1972. One of the most remarkable features in the employment pattern in the recent period is the steady increase in the ratio of female workers to male workers. As seen in Table 33, the number of female workers more than doubled during the period 1960–1974, raising the share of female workers in total employment from 29 percent to 37 percent. Reflecting the increase in this ratio, the weight for female workers in the construction of the quality of labor index due to education was increased from 15.6 percent in 1960 to 21.2 percent in 1974.

Based on the above data and assumptions, the quality indexes for education can be constructed for males, females, and all employed persons. Each index is the weighted sum of the proportion of labor inputs by each education group multiplied by the weights in Table 32, given the value of the index for 1960 as 100. The education quality index for Korea in the period 1960–1974 is the weighted average of the male and female indexes. The indexes, given in Table 34, suggest that education increased the productivity of labor by 17.9 percent during the period 1960–1974, and that the productivity increase was greater for female than for male workers.

Estimation of the contribution of education to economic growth is now possible. Education's contribution to growth was calculated by multiplying the annual average growth rate of the education quality index by the share of labor earnings in the total value added of Korea (assumed to be 60 percent). The growth contributions attributable to increases in fixed capital formation and employment were also estimated, so that their

TABLE 33 Labor Input by Sex, 1960–1974

	Number of Persons Employed (1,000s)		Composition (%)		Composition of Labor Inputs Weighted (%)[a]	
	Males	Females	Males	Females	Males	Females
1960	5,005	2,022	71.2	28.8	84.4	15.6
1966	5,425	2,538	68.1	31.9	82.4	17.6
1970	6,577	3,574	64.8	35.2	80.1	19.9
1974	7,196	4,256	62.8	37.2	78.7	21.3

Sources: Same as Table 29.

Note: [a]Weight of females is given by the ratio of the average wage of female workers to that of male workers, 0.456.

TABLE 34 Education Quality Indexes, 1960–1974

	Weighted Average	Males	Females
1960	100.0	100.0	100.0
1966	110.8	110.9	110.3
1970	114.5	114.4	114.7
1974	117.9	117.5	119.6

Sources: Derived from Tables 29, 32, and 33.

values could be compared with the contribution of education to the annual growth rate. Table 35 shows the annual growth rates of these inputs and their estimated contributions to economic growth.

TABLE 35   Growth Rates of Factor Inputs and Their
Contributions to Economic Growth

	1960–1974	*1960–1966*	*1966–1970*	*1970–1974*
Growth of inputs and output (annual percentages)				
GNP	9.07	7.25	10.78	10.14
Capital	7.19	3.75	10.43	9.27
Labor	3.55	2.11	6.26	3.06
Education	1.18	1.72	0.82	0.73
Percentage contribution of factor inputs to output growth rate				
Capital	2.88	1.50	4.17	3.71
Labor	2.13	1.27	3.76	1.84
Education	0.71	1.03	0.49	0.44
Others	3.35	3.45	2.36	4.15
Contribution of factor inputs to output growth rate (GNP growth=100)				
Capital	31.8	20.7	38.7	36.6
Labor	23.5	17.5	34.9	18.1
Education	7.8	14.2	4.5	4.3
Others	36.9	47.6	21.9	40.9

Sources: Computed from BOK, *National Income in Korea, 1975,* pp. 268–269; Tables 33 and 34; and Wontack Hong, Table A-27.

During the period 1960–1974, GNP grew by an average rate of 9.07 percent per annum, while fixed capital, employment, and the quality of labor due to education increased by 7.19 percent, 3.55 percent, and 1.18 percent, respectively. The increase in capital is estimated to have contributed 2.88 percentage points, or 31.8 percent, to the GNP growth rate, and the increase in labor 2.13 percentage points, or 23.5 percent. Of the remaining 4.06 points, 0.71 percentage points, or 7.8 percent of the GNP growth rate, was explained by the quality improvement of labor due to education.

The contribution of education to growth appears to have been more significant in the period 1960–1966 than in the later periods. As shown in Table 29, the increase in the education quality index during the period 1960–1966 was mainly due to the decline in the proportion of male workers with less than 6 years of education. This share dropped by 16.3 percentage points between 1960 and 1966 but fell by only 12.5 additional percentage points during the period 1966–1974. Meanwhile, the proportion of those workers with 12 or more years of education increased by only 4.9 percentage points during the later period as compared with the increase of 13.4 percentage points in the previous period. Compared with the accelerating trend of per capita GNP growth, the increase in utilization of educated manpower has been rather slow since 1966.

The estimated percentage that education contributed to output growth in Korea exceeds those estimated by Denison[23] for the United States and European countries. But it is far less than the estimates given by previous researchers.[24] Part of the difference is explained by extension of the period on which our estimate is based, since the apparent contribution of education has been relatively small in recent years. The remainder is attributable to differences in methodologies and assumptions.

The foregoing analysis contains several arbitrary elements which may lead to misstatement, most likely understatement, of education's true contribution to economic growth. Although there are also problems of data availability, the fundamental problem lies in the limitations of the Denison methodology. Three different methodological considerations lead to the suspicion that education's contribution to growth may be understated.

1) As noted earlier, the education quality index estimated here could have missed a considerable part of the quality improvement of labor attributable to education because it failed to take account of probable qualitative improvement in education through time and of income differences between education groups that are not reflected in their wage incomes.

2) It was also noted that the economic growth of Korea is often attributed to social and political stability, administrative efficiency, entrepreneurship, and the people's responsiveness to economic opportunity. The contribution of education to these factors is not fully reflected in the measured quality improvement of employed persons but may well account for part of the unexplained residuals.

3) More fundamentally, our analysis asks what the economic effects of increasing the educational attainment of the labor force over the 1960 level may have been. A more meaningful question might be: What would have happened to production if the education of Korean workers had remained at, say, 1930 levels? By 1960 much educational upgrading had already taken place, but it may be that, in the economic environment of that time, most educated workers were in occupations that made little use of their training, whereas by 1975 the need for education had increased to the point where lesser training on the part of educated workers would have led to a marked decline in productivity. This hypothesis[25] implies that wage differentials related to education in 1960 represented not so much differential productivity as differential economic power (the fact that the educated wage structure was dominated by government employment makes this more likely), while by 1975 wage differentials in the now-industrialized economy are much more closely aligned with economic productivity. This scenario, which is plausible although we can neither prove nor disprove it, suggests that education's contribution to productivity could have been much larger than indicated by the Denison approach.

Similarly, points which might lead to a downgrading of education's contribution to output growth would have to be directed at the fundamental methodology of the Denison approach. One has to question either the assumption that income or wage differentials *associated with* educational differences are in fact *caused by* education or the assumption that the nature of the causation, if its existence is conceded, is related to education's effect on productivity. We will deal with these points in the following section.

Concluding this section, however, we can state that the estimates based on the human-capital perspective that can be made with the available data suggest that education made a relatively small productive contribution to the growth of Korean GNP, especially after 1966. The smallness of the measured contribution is probably attributable in part to limitations in the methodology employed.

AN ALTERNATIVE PERSPECTIVE

Although the human-capital theory is the most elegant explanation of education's effect on income (and, for that reason, its contribution to economic growth), it is under heavy attack today. Sociologists[26] refer to the human-capital approach as a *technical-function* theory of education and offer as an alternative a *status-conflict* theory. Economists of education refer to "screening," "credentialism," and "socialization" theories. In both cases the argument is that the structure of employment and earnings opportunities is essentially given, independent of the supply of people with different levels of education, and that the function of schooling is to select people to fill pre-existing slots. Although education may have some technical function and probably makes some contribution to productivity, much of the expansion of education and its relationship with the social (and economic) status of an individual can be explained by taking into account the contribution of education to social status.

This approach has widespread support among sociologists and among economists who believe that labor markets are most often segmented and seldom if ever competitive. The theory asserts that a small number of status groups control hiring in most forms of employment and impose their criteria on the labor market in the selection of workers. As education has (in most countries and especially in Korea[28]) always been defined as an important criterion for elite status, it has always been used in the selection of new entrants to the ranks of the elites.[29]

Since many people want to occupy the few elite positions, education is eagerly sought:

> The existence of a relatively small group of experts in high status positions . . . can have important effects on the structure of competition for mobility chances. In the United States, where democratic decentralization favors the use of schools (as well as government employment) as a kind of patronage for voter interests, the existence of even a small number of elite jobs fosters demand for *large scale* opportunities to acquire these positions.[30]

In Korea, examinations based on formal academic study have been used since the tenth century to determine entrance to all-important government positions. Today examinations determine entrance to elite universities (for example, Seoul National University), which in turn practically guarantees entrance to a good government position. The educated man, so defined by his certificates, has traditionally been more highly respected than the person who is merely rich (that is, who obtained his wealth without education). But population tends to increase more rapidly than the number of elite positions. As a consequence, it is necessary, the status-conflict theory argues, to raise the levels of education required for entrance to certain positions so as to limit entrance into elite status. Schooling expands as the educational requirements of positions in society go up; requirements go up not because positions demand more skills, but because otherwise they would lose their elite status.

At each level of education, schools have certain functions of socialization into social membership assigned to possessors of that degree of educational attainment. Students from heterogeneous social backgrounds are socialized into a common social framework in the elementary grades. Examinations or other procedures select those likely to meet the criteria for the next level of socialization, at which training for more specialized social roles may take place. Elite formation, in an advanced society, is delayed to the upper grades unless it has been possible to establish a private, elite educational system parallel with the public system.

The association between individual incomes or wages and the level of education attained is less a function of differences in their relative contributions to productivity than it is a reflection of the way elites assign status. For that reason, the theory asserts, there is no reason to expect that growth in education in Korea has contributed greatly to economic growth.

There is no doubt that Korea has achieved a great expansion of its educational opportunities. The issue is whether that expansion is principally a response to a need for more highly trained persons in an expanding and increasingly modernizing economy, or whether the expansion of education can be attributed more to increased demand for education by parents and children faced with rising job requirements unrelated to real skill needs. In its baldest form, the first (or human-capital) argument says that education contributes to economic development by giving people skills needed for production. The second argument says that might be so, but that most important in determining how much education people demand are the artificial education requirements for employment set principally by those seeking to limit access to elite positions.

Both arguments are ambiguous as to the mechanism employed to link economic (or status-maintenance) requirements with educational offerings. Human-capital theorists most often refer to the market mechanism, but also may recommend planning and direct interventions in the educational system. Status-conflict theorists imply some direct control of education and the setting of requirements, but the mechanism is left unspecified.

What is certain is that in Korea there was a period of rapid educational expansion beginning in 1945, interrupted by the Korean War, and reaching its zenith for primary education about 1966. Secondary and higher educational enrollments continue to grow at a rapid rate. It is also the case that Korea's economy grew slowly (compared to other periods in its own history, but well compared to most developing nations) until 1962, when it began to experience the (nationally and internationally) unprecedented rates of economic growth which continue today. Major changes in the content of education have been effected at several points since 1945, but especially in 1946, 1955, 1962, and 1972.

EVALUATION OF THE TWO PERSPECTIVES

At its most simplistic level the human-capital theory would predict a mechanistic relationship between education and economy. Growth in education should be followed fairly immediately by economic growth.[31] The status-conflict explanation of educational growth, on the other hand, would predict a steady rise in enrollments at the upper levels, with no relationship to the behavior of the economy. Lower-level enrollments would grow first, as they provide the entrants to higher education, but barriers to higher-level education would slowly fall, as the point of final selection into the elite was moved higher and higher. Unit costs of higher education would become relatively greater than secondary or primary education to emphasize the elite nature of the university. Changes in curriculum would emphasize social cohesion and national unity at the lower levels (for those not expected to assume elite status), but creativity and initiative at the upper levels. In general, there would be more emphasis on skills and knowledge associated with status than on those associated with productivity.

Arguments for the status-conflict approach would seem most reasonable where it could be shown that elites did directly influence education. The Ministry of Education in Korea has done educational planning since 1963, and a Long-Range Comprehensive Educational Plan was published in 1972, covering all aspects of the educational system.[32] In fairness, however, this plan was intended as only an *indicative* plan which attempts to forecast what enrollments will be and to determine on that basis what facilities and teaching staff will be required.

As discussed earlier, growth in primary school enrollments would appear to have begun about 1919 under the Japanese and to have progressed continuously (slowing down during the Korean War) until about 1966, when demand began to slacken. Although there are not enough data points to be certain, it would appear that the rate of growth of primary enrollments between 1945 and 1950 was greater than at any period after that time. From 1955 on, until about 1966 or 1967, enrollments grew at an almost constant rate and several times faster than the population growth rate.

Figure 6 and Table 36 present enrollment data for all levels annually from 1945. The numbers for middle schools for the early part of the period are estimated; under the U.S. Military Government, no separation in statistics was made between middle and senior high school. The figure shows that enrollments grew rapidly until the war, declined, and then grew again until 1955. Another period of decline was experienced then, with enrollments actually shrinking (because of the reduced cohort of primary graduates caused by the war). After a brief period of increase, enrollments slowed in rate of growth again during 1962 to 1964. Since that time, the growth of enrollments in middle school has been exponential.

Enrollments in high school might be expected to lag slightly behind enrollments in middle school. Secondary enrollments declined during the Korean War but recovered a bit more slowly than middle school enrollments. Enrollments slackened in growth but did not decline in the 1955–1960 period, coterminous with the decline in middle school enrollments. Another leveling off of enrollment growth took place in 1965–1967, three years after a similar leveling off in middle school enrollments. The rate of growth of enrollments since

FIGURE 6 Enrollments in Primary, Middle, Secondary, and Higher Education, 1945–1975

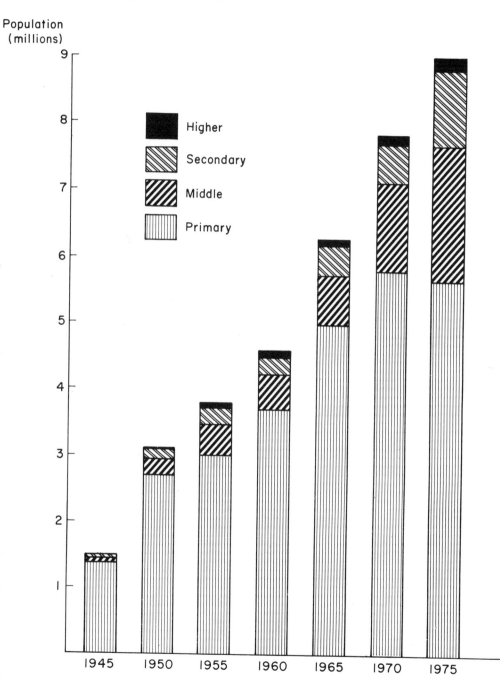

TABLE 36 Enrollments in Primary, Middle, and Secondary
Schools, Colleges and Universities, 1945–1974
(1,000s)

	Primary	Middle	Academic Secondary	Vocational Secondary	Colleges and Univeristies
1945	1366	53	16	12	8
1946	2159	81	25	19	10
1947	2183	129	40	29	14
1948	2426	181	56	41	
1949	2771	210	64	48	
1950	2658	249	76	57	
1951	2073	174	53	40	
1952	2369	312	59	74	31
1953	2259	324	86	93	38
1954	2679	420	113	111	63
1955	2947	475	142	123	78
1956	2997	459	154	135	90
1957	3171	440	156	128	84
1958	3316	398	159	120	74
1959	3558	472	161	110	76
1960	3662	529	164	99	93
1961	3855	621	180	102	134
1962	4089	655	199	124	116
1963	4422	666	214	150	105
1964	4726	667	237	163	113
1965	4941	751	254	172	106
1966	5165	822	260	175	131
1967	5383	912	259	183	124
1968	5549	1013	274	208	124
1969	5623	1147	294	236	133
1970	5749	1319	315	275	146
1971	5807	1530	337	310	155
1972	5776	1638	370	360	164
1973	5692	1832	411	428	178
1974	5619	1930	530	451	192
1975	5599	2027	648	475	209

Source: Ministry of Education.
   Note: As middle and high schools were combined between 1945 and 1951 enrollments were not reported separately. We distributed the total enrollment figures given
for 1945–1950: 65% middle school, 20% academic secondary, 15% vocational/
technical.

1967 has increased from year to year. Enrollments in vocational secondary schools have grown at about the same rate as those in academic secondary schools.

The growth of enrollments in colleges and universities has been more erratic. No data are available for the years 1948 through 1951. Enrollments grew from 1951 until 1956 when they declined for three years (like middle and high school enrollments). Enrollments declined again, in absolute numbers, from 1961 to 1966, and from 1966 to 1969. As noted above, despite government efforts to limit enrollments, the number of university students has increased steadily since that time.

How can these rates of growth be compared with the growth of the economy? Table 37 presents GNP in 1970 constant market prices. The growth rate of GNP was an almost perfect match of that for primary school enrollments, between 1954 and 1964. When the economy prospered, more schools were built and more children enrolled. When the economy slowed down, fewer schools were built. The argument would be that expansion of primary education was in response to the economic situation of the country, rather than one of its determinants. The leveling off of primary school enrollments after 1964 is unrelated to the growth of GNP; it was a function of having enrolled almost 100 percent of the age group in school.

The rate of growth of enrollments in middle schools was erratic until 1964, bearing no apparent relationship to the growth of the economy. Between 1964 and 1970 or 1971, middle school enrollments grew at the same rate as GNP. Again, it seems reasonable to explain this association on the basis of access to school being determined by the success of the economy. Once the government had provided capacity for all children in primary schools, it began to spend more on middle school construction. When the entrance examination to middle school was eliminated in 1971, enrollments grew faster than the GNP, perhaps because by this time changes in the occupational structure of the economy made primary school education insufficient for urban or modern-sector employment. It can be noted that middle

TABLE 37 Gross National Product in Constant 1970 wŏn
1953–1974
(billions)

Year	Wŏn	Year	Wŏn
1953	843.5	1964	1442.0
1954	890.2	1965	1529.7
1955	938.2	1966	1719.2
1956	942.2	1967	1853.0
1957	1014.4	1968	2087.1
1958	1067.2	1969	2400.5
1959	1108.3	1970	2589.3
1960	1129.7	1971	2826.8
1961	1184.5	1972	3023.6
1962	1221.0	1973	3522.7
1963	1328.3	1974	3810.4

Source: BOK, Economic Statistics Yearbook 1975.

school enrollments grew most rapidly long before the economic take-off of the 1960s, in 1945–1950 and 1952–1955. In other words, the provision of educated labor at that period of time can not be temporally associated with an improvement in the economy. Enrollments also grew rapidly between 1958 and 1961. If this increment in the education level of the potential labor force contributed to the growth of the economy in the 1960s, it was not a factor in the 1970s, as by that time the average worker in the modern sector already had more than 9 years of education.

Enrollments in academic secondary schools grew at essentially the same rate as the GNP between 1955 and 1965; they have grown more slowly since that time. Once again, the most rapid period of growth was prior to 1950, well before the takeoff. Inasmuch as most people in the labor force do not yet have complete secondary education, the conclusion could be drawn that changes in the economy since 1964 have not generated a need for relatively greater numbers of academic secondary school graduates. If one accepted that assertion, it would then seem appropriate to conclude that the provision of rapidly increasing numbers of academic secondary graduates prior to 1950 (or 1955) did not make a large contribution to increased productivity.

Enrollments in vocational secondary schools have increased *since* 1965, and those increases have matched the growth of the GNP.[33] It has been the government's intention since 1965 to emphasize vocational education over academic secondary, striving for a 60–40 (or 70–30) split of enrollments favoring vocational education. In an effort to overcome traditional resistance to vocational education, the Ministry of Education has offered special incentives to students, including handsome scholarships and promises of employment (and has allowed private schools to expand more rapidly than public). Vocational education has grown more rapidly than academic secondary, but has not reached the levels hoped for by planners. In the case of vocational education it could well be that the fit between education growth and GNP growth is a result of an intervention by the government (and not therefore a reflection of market demand).

As noted above, the growth of college and university enrollments was highly erratic until 1967. There is no obvious relationship between GNP growth and enrollment fluctuation. Enrollments in higher education are currently growing at a slower rate than GNP, and the fastest period of growth of enrollments was prior to 1957.

In summary, enrollments at all levels of education have grown either at the same rate or more slowly since 1964 (excepting an increment in middle schools since 1971). The fastest rates of growth in enrollments occurred generally before 1955, and enrollments grew relatively slowly (compared to earlier or later) between 1955 and 1964. In reference to our hypotheses, increments in education are not strongly associated with the economic take-off. If labor force skill requirements have changed after 1964, they have not yet required rapidly increasing numbers of educated manpower. Perhaps, as suggested earlier, they have fed on existing but previously underutilized stocks.

On the other hand, growth in education was most rapid more than ten years before the takeoff, a lag longer than would have been expected were the supply of skilled manpower the only (or major) factor associated with economic growth. A more plausible explanation is that social demand for education outstripped economic needs in the early 1950s, resulting in a period of underemployment of educated manpower. Only when the economy began to heat up and require larger numbers of workers, and the government gained some control over enrollments, was it possible to achieve some balance between GNP growth and growth in education.

CHANGES IN CURRICULUM AND TEACHING

The government *has* intervened directly to determine the content of education. This occurred under the U.S. Military Government in 1945–1948, and in 1955, 1962, and 1972 when the Ministry of Education carried out three major curriculum reforms. All four of these interventions were carried out with little local participation. Although some effort was made to involve educators and politicians at the provincial level, there was little or no contact with local teachers and none with the general populace. The curriculum reforms serve, then, as clear-cut examples of government objectives with respect to content of education.

The evidence presented in Chapters 1 and 2 with respect to changes in curriculum suggests that, while the quantity of teaching provided in schools may have improved over time, the content of instruction did not move in the direction usually thought to be associated with modernization and technical development. Neither with respect to specific skills taught nor to the values promoted officially does the Korean curriculum appear to distinguish itself from those of other countries as doing more to: increase skills efficiency and work knowledge; increase labor mobility and promote division of labor; increase scientific and technical knowledge to promote invention, discovery, and swift adaptation; increase entrepreneurial ability; or make people more responsive to social change. And from the evidence available, what is taught today does not appear to emphasize these objectives much more than what was taught twenty or thirty years ago.

The critical question, in terms of determining the nature of the contribution made by education and training institutions to the economic takeoff, turns on whether, by 1964, schools and training progress had produced a large number of skilled workers. Chapters 1 and 2 have described how most education was academic until 1961 or 1962. Most vocational/technical schools didn't function well before that time because the Ministry of Education lacked proper administrative controls, because it was difficult to recruit teachers from industry given the requirement of a formal degree, because there was a severe shortage of instructional materials in the Korean language, and because funds for operation were restricted (by the enormous demand on the government to expand primary and middle schools). As a result, "the major part [of the vocational high schools] were vocational in name only."[34] The first programs to develop technical education instructors were not begun until 1963. As a result, Bom Mo Chung concluded: "As far as technical training is concerned, training in developed countries or training under those who acquired skills in the developed countries has been the most predominant access for the Koreans to skill and technical know-how."[35] But most of those sent abroad were only beginning to return in the early 1960s.

Evidence for the non-modernizing character of Korean education is suggested in two studies.[36] Sung Chick Hong surveyed farmers, businessmen, and 4-year college professors in 1964. He found farmers to be most traditional, followed by professors, who on every item were more traditional than businessmen. The businessmen were less well educated than the professors. He concluded: "In view of the slow [sic] economic development in Korea, the traditional character of Korean values here seems to have a definite relevance in accounting for the Korean economy."[37] These values were, apparently, not affected by high levels of education. Sung-mo Huang, after commenting on the high levels of education of workers in industry (compared to the rest of the labor force), reports results of his survey in 1960 in mining, textiles, and chemicals that show workers to hold to traditional Confucian attitudes. Therefore, he suggests, "As Korean industrial laborers are not technically skilled laborers, they did not establish the labor value of their own as such . . . they cannot be regarded as a factor for modern social structure since they are still holding the agricultural outlook."[38]

If the contribution of education to rapid growth of the GNP is doubtful, or at least difficult to demonstrate, what can be said about the effects of rapid expansion of educational opportunity on the distribution of income? If it isn't clear that education fostered modern values, can we at least say that education fostered social mobility? Chapter 4 answers those questions.

FOUR

Education and Income Distribution

In addition to making a critical contribution to rapid economic growth, education in Korea also is credited[1] with having contributed to a more equitable distribution of income than is found in most countries. The rapid expansion of education is said to have generated considerable social mobility, favoring a more equitable society.

The claim merits examination for at least two reasons. First, of course, because the experience of Korea could be of interest to other countries concerned with achieving an equitable distribution of income while undergoing rapid economic growth. Education may have been a mechanism for achieving that objective. Several developing countries have experienced rapid economic growth but have seen their income distribution worsen in the process. Others have rapidly expanded their educational systems, but have been able to achieve neither rapid growth nor an equitable distribution of income.

The Korean case also has relevance for a more academic controversy. There is a growing chorus of critics who assert that an expansion of education not only will fail to improve the distribution of income but that it will tend to make worse an already inequitable system.[2] This group is linked with another that claims that education by itself makes little or no contribution to the social and economic status of the individual, over and above that which can be explained by taking into account the social origin (class) of the individual in question.[3] This chapter attempts to address some of those questions.

LEVELS AND TRENDS
IN INCOME INEQUALITY

The present situation with respect to our knowledge of income inequality in the Republic of Korea is somewhat paradoxical. A review of the literature suggests three generalizations:

1) Numerous observers[4] agree that the *level* of inequality in the size distribution of income is less in Korea than in virtually any other low-income country and comparable to levels pertaining in some industrialized countries; those who have examined *trends* in inequality have found that the distribution has improved,[5] or at least not worsened,[6] during the period of rapid rise in mean income since 1964.

2) A number of writers[7] cite a plausible list of reasons why income inequality should be low and either steady or decreasing.

3) Yet those analysts who have closely examined the statistical basis for these or other assertions about the size distribution of income[8] have found it to be very weak. Thus, the present situation can be characterized as an abundance of plausible explanations for a set of facts which is itself in some doubt.

Any discussion of income distribution in Korea must, uncomfortably, take this paradoxical state of affairs as its starting point. The problem is certainly not a lack of estimates of the size distribution of income. Jain[9] lists no fewer than 14 estimates of the national, urban, and rural size distributions for years between 1966 and 1971, and the list could have been longer, since the Annual (urban) Family Income and Expenditure Survey and Farm Household Survey can be pooled to provide an estimate, albeit a questionable one, of the national size distribution for any year since 1963. Instead, Korea's data problems are those common to countries that have made less statistical effort than Korea has: coverage exclusions, definitional inconsistencies and ambiguities, probable response biases.

Although neither the Gini concentration ratio nor any other single-valued measure provides an adequate expression of all significant dimensions of income inequality, the Gini ratio is the most commonly cited overall measure and provides a useful starting point for cross-section and intertemporal comparisons. Around the mid-1960s, when the first statistics on income distribution were collected, the value of the Gini ratio for Korea appears to have been in the low 0.30s.[10] This result (and associated measures such as decile shares in total income) firmly places Korea among the most egalitarian economies outside the centrally planned group and makes the country an especially notable outlier among countries at a similar level of GNP per capita.[11] Clearly, Korea was a land of unusually equal income distribution at the time it began its rapid growth spurt in 1964.[12] The next question is: What has happened to income inequality since that year?

The trend of inequality over the past decade or so is harder to define than Korea's position in an international comparison. Although Adelman characterizes the 1964–1970 period as showing "little change in the overall size distribution of income,"[13] Jain gives 0.37 and 0.38 as estimates of the Gini ratio of the distribution of income among households in 1970, suggesting some rise in inequality during the late 1960s.[14] There is reason to believe that this worsening of distribution may have been reversed in the early 1970s, for reasons which come to light when we decompose income inequality into: 1) inequality between the urban and rural sectors; and 2) inequality within each of these sectors. This kind of decomposition provides an attractive analytical approach in the Korean case because of the separate data sources for the two sectors, the largely different forces which determine their respective internal distributions, and the fact that, in the absence of other internal demarcations (for example ethnic groupings) which are important in some other countries, the rural-urban distinction is probably the most important one in Korea.

Observers agree that rural incomes and consumption declined significantly relative to urban incomes in 1964–1968.[15] Adelman states that the ratio of mean income in industry to mean income in agriculture increased from 1.4 to 2.0 in 1964–1970. After 1968 there was significant redressal of this disparity, to such an extent that Abraham reports a widespread belief that farmers are now actually better off than townspeople. Although this is unlikely to be true, for reasons stated by Abraham, it does seem likely that the ratio has declined to around 1.7. Since a ratio of 2.0 or more is common in developing countries, it appears that (except during the late 1960s) Korea has had a relatively low level of rural-urban income disparity.

The distribution of income *within* the rural sector has indisputably been relatively equal throughout the period since World War II. Although it is possible that there has been some increase in intra-rural inequality since 1964 (increases in farm income have been less equally distributed than past farm incomes, while off-farm incomes, on which poorer farm households are more dependent, have risen slowly), according to Abraham, the distribution in 1974 can still "be judged satisfactory by any relevant standard," with the poorest 40 percent of farm households receiving 19 percent of total income and the richest tenth about 25 percent; the Gini coefficient of the distribution is in the low 0.30s. Since the distribution of rural income among households is *positively* correlated with family size, inequality in the distribution of income among rural individuals must be even lower.

The distribution of *earnings* within the urban sector of the Korean economy is remarkable in that it is not only surprisingly even but has become strikingly more so since 1963. Income inequality as measured by the (urban) Family Income and Expenditure Survey is less than inequality in the rural sector and has actually fallen (from a Gini ratio of 0.27 in 1963 to 0.23 in 1972) during the period in which mean urban income has soared, declining both absolutely and relative to rural income.[16] Improvements in the incomes of households headed by blue-collar workers relative to those headed by salaried workers, and of those headed by daily laborers relative to all workers[17] provide clear evidence of reduced dispersion in earnings. That the dispersion of total incomes (as opposed to earnings) also has declined is less certain, since the survey has an upper cut-off point which excludes the higher urban incomes from its coverage.[18] Adelman reports that the relative share of property income, the most unequally distributed functional income component, rose sharply in 1964-1970; in addition, much of the de facto property income of wealthy Koreans may take the form of unrealized (and unrecorded) capital gains.

In summary, despite the many uncertainties about the statistics, it is clear that all four of the forms of income inequality we have examined (in the national distribution, between the rural and urban sectors, and within each of these sectors) were low by international standards on the eve of the period of rapid growth in 1963-1964. What has happened to them since 1964 is less clear-cut, but at least (with the exception of rural-urban inequality in the late 1960s and possibly of intra-urban income inequality for the whole period) they have not worsened dramatically. This in itself makes Korea outstanding among low-income countries, especially, perhaps, among those that have experienced significant economic growth.[19]

CAUSES OF INEQUALITY

We now turn from the question of what the levels and trends in income inequality have been to the question of why they have been what (we think) they have been. As noted above, there is, paradoxically, more agreement among analysts about the "whys" than about the "whats." For example, several writers have cited lists of reasons for expecting a low level of inequality around 1963-1964. Basically, these turn on the existence of an unusually even distribution of both physical and human capital.

The even distribution of physical capital which existed at the start of the period of rapid growth is attributable to a series of historical circumstances.[20] 1) Prior to World War II, the commanding heights of the Korean economy, including 90 percent of the capital invested in manufacturing and 27 percent of the area of large farms, were controlled by the Japanese.[21] After Japan's defeat in the war, these assets were redistributed, the manufacturing facilities primarily to the Korean governments (North and South) and the agricultural land (in the south) to individual Korean farmers. 2) Korean fortunes, which in any case were few because of the stifling Japanese dominance, suffered from the partition of the country and the other disruptions associated with the post-World War II period. 3) A second land reform, implemented in the early 1950s, broke up holdings (by Koreans) in excess of three chŏngbo[22] and distributed them to tenants. Tenancy, which had already fallen from 70 to 33 percent in the redistribution of Japanese-owned lands, was virtually eliminated.[23] 4) The Korean War destroyed the property of many well-off Koreans.[24]

The foregoing redistributions of physical capital have been characterized by Adelman as the "static asset redistribution phase" of Korean economic history. This phase ended with the 1953 Armistice. What happened to income distribution during the ensuing decade, 1953-1963, is less clear. There were no more dramatic asset redistributions and little economic growth. Adelman refers to this decade as a "dynamic redistribution phase," by which she means that it featured the extraordinary expansion and spread of education we have documented elsewhere. This, although it led in the short run mainly to widespread educated unemployment and discontent which contributed significantly to the 1961 revolt, is believed by Adelman to have contributed to the rapid development of the economy after 1963. By 1965, Korea's human resources development had exceeded the average level for countries with three times its GNP per capita, according to the Harbison and Myers scale,[25] and this, according to the factor analyses of Adelman and Morris,[26] was likely to have been a major contributing factor in the rapid growth that followed. We will return to the question of education's impact on economic equality in the next section.

After 1963, South Korea entered what Adelman calls a "redistribution-cum-asset-value-realization phase" of redistribution. We have seen that the facts to be explained for this period are none too clear. Nor, with one exception, are the main forces influencing income distribution. The period began with celebrated reforms of interest rates and foreign trade incentives in late 1964 and early 1965.[27] These reforms clearly increased the efficiency of the economy and made an important contribution (just *how* important has been debated) to the growth that followed. Their immediate effect on income inequality is less obvious, but they may have brought some redistribution away from special interest groups which had been growing rich by their ability to manipulate the pre-reform systems of credit and trade controls.

Over the longer run, the reforms undoubtedly had a major impact on income distribution through the pattern of development they fostered. Such economic growth as had occurred during the decade between the Korean War and the 1964–1965 reforms had been largely along the import-substitution lines then being pursued by most low-income countries. The trade reforms slanted incentives in favor of export expansion, and enhanced a tremendous capacity for the development of relatively labor-intensive manufactured exports. This, in turn, meant that industrialization in South Korea was not only rapid but was accompanied by far faster growth of manufacturing employment than occurred in other developing countries.[28] Between 1966 and 1970 nearly half of labor force growth was absorbed directly into export-related employment, while a further fraction was pulled into indirectly related activities.[29] This booming demand for labor kept wages rising and pulled large numbers of workers out of the less dynamic, Malthusian rural sector, thus at least preventing land pressure from worsening.[30] The one thing that is clearest about income distribution trends in the post-1963 period is that the high rate of labor absorption contributed significantly to the maintenance of relative distributive equality, preventing the emergence of a sharply delineated high-wage urban enclave such as emerged in many other countries. There *was* some widening of the rural-urban gap in the late 1960s, as we have seen, but this was attributable mainly to a policy of low rice prices, which was followed during those years in an attempt to hold back the rise in urban wages; the policy was subsequently reversed in an effort to improve farmers' incentives.

EDUCATION'S CONTRIBUTION
TO ECONOMIC INEQUALITY

We now turn to the question of education's impact upon economic inequality. We have seen that Korea experienced an unprecedented expansion of education at a low level of income. We have also seen that its distribution of income was unusually egalitarian before rapid growth began and has, in general, remained so. What connection is there between these two facts?

This is a question with which contemporary social science is poorly equipped to deal. A leading authority in the field comments that "the state of knowledge about the education-income connection in the developing countries is, to put it mildly, quite underdeveloped."[31] Nevertheless, we can perhaps increase the tractability of the question by breaking it up into parts, at least some of which may prove more manageable than the question as a whole. Accordingly, we propose to examine three sub-questions:

1) Who receives access to the different levels and types of education?
2) At what cost; that is, what are the terms of educational finance?[32]
3) What are the effects of education on the future incomes of those who receive it?

ACCESS TO EDUCATION

Compared to the complex issue of education's effect on incomes, which we will save for last, the question of who gains access to education is a straightforward one. Nevertheless, it is complex enough to benefit from being broken down into three components.

The first relates to the structure of educational opportunities provided. What is the shape of the "educational pyramid"? To how high a level is the school system universalistic? When it becomes selective, just how restrictive is it?

The second component of the access question concerns the selection criteria invoked when the system becomes selective. (Sometimes these criteria come into play even when it is supposed to be universalistic.) What devices are used to choose those who will be allowed to continue when social demand exceeds the supply of places?

Third is the issue of the end results of the selection process. Who in fact is permitted to continue? What is the impact of the first two factors on urban dwellers, rural residents, regions, social classes, the two sexes? Is the system relatively "meritocratic" (that is, blind to these distinctions and based on some concept of in-school performance) or does it discriminate systematically?

In this selection, therefore, we will ask *how many* are

selected, *how* the selection is carried out, and *who* is finally chosen. In dealing with these issues, the main tools of analysis used will be the enrollment ratio, that is, the percentage of the relevant age cohort enrolled in school, and the share of enrollments taken up by each of the groups in question.

The Educational Pyramid

The educational pyramid for 1960 is depicted in Figure 7. It shows a high degree of coverage (over 90 percent of the age cohort) for primary schooling (grades 1-6); a lower rate, especially for girls, in middle school (grades 7-9); and considerably lower rates yet for high school (grades 10-12) and post-secondary education.

These statistics gain meaning when we: 1) compare them with similar statistics for other countries; and 2) see how they have changed through time. Table 38 uses UNESCO data to compare the growth of enrollments in the Republic of Korea between 1950 and 1970 with enrollment growth in 18 other Asian countries. We see that Korea has consistently had a more extensive school system than most other Asian countries, falling into the group (along with the Philippines, South Vietnam, and Taiwan) that most closely followed Japan to the attainment of universal primary schooling. It has also been among the leaders in expansion of secondary enrollment. Finally, third-level enrollment has also grown relatively rapidly in Korea, but not at the rates attained by Japan, the Philippines, and Taiwan.

In evaluating these comparative rates of growth, it is important to take cognizance of the separate operation of demand and supply forces. Social demand for education in Korea has been stupendous. In the face of vigorous, buoyant demand for places in school, the government's policy regarding the expansion of system capacity can best be described as cautious. Although, as discussed in Chapter 2, (nearly) universal primary schooling was reached relatively early, the government has been slow to extend universal education from six to nine years and downright grudging in its provision of places in high school and post-secondary institutions. The result, as we saw earlier, has

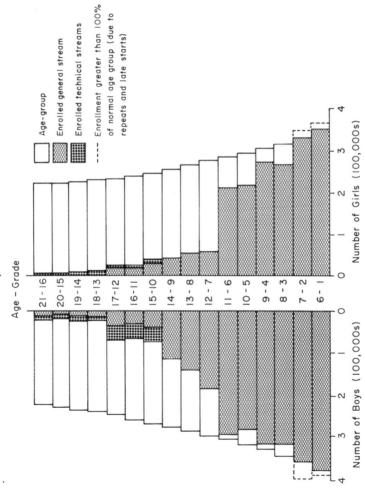

FIGURE 7 Enrollment in Korea by Grade and Sex, 1960

Source: UNESCO, *Long-term Projections for Education in the Republic of Korea*, 1965.

TABLE 38 Enrollment Ratios for Korea and Other Asian Countries 1950, 1960, 1970

Country	Total Enrollment as % of Population 5-24			First Level: % Enrolled			Second Level: % enrolled			Third Level Enrollment per 100,000 Population		
	1950	1960	1970	1950	1960	1970	1950	1960	1970	1950	1960	1970
Republic of Korea	35	44	53	83	96	104[c]	16	29	41	179	409	627
Afghanistan	2	3	9	5	8	22	[b]	1	5	3	12	44
Burma	5	20	36	22	72	94	7	10	19	18	60	169
Ceylon	40	52	48	77	86	89	12	28	31	56	68	117
India	15	25	33	44	61	79	8	17	23	118	253	469
Indonesia	17	24	28	46	60	69	3	6	12	8	113	187
Iran	11	25	37	26	39	62	4	11	24	37	92	243
Japan	54	59	56	100	102	100	69	79	90	289	761	1,656
Khmer	10	25	37	30	62	90	1	2	11	6	32	165
Laos	5	10	18	12	25	47	[b]	1	3	[a]	4	18
Malaysia	27	41	45	72	93	91	5	16	33	5	117	166
Mongolia	[a]	28	41	[a]	73	109	[a]	33	51	239	523	699
Nepal	2	8	12	6	20	31	2	4	8	11	55	156
Pakistan	13	15	20	39	34	45	9	9	13	91	149	350
Philippines	51	41	53	91	91	116	27	29	42	882	1,080	1,737
Singapore	31	52	54	80	111	105	8	33	45	181	629	650

TABLE 38 (continued)

Country	Total Enrollment as % of Population 5-24			First Level: % Enrolled			Second Level: % Enrolled			Third Level Enrollment per 100,000 Population		
	1950	1960	1970	1950	1960	1970	1950	1960	1970	1950	1960	1970
South Viet Nam	8	27	44	26	101	101	2	10	27	10	83	267
Taiwan	30	50	57	79	102	106	11	29	53	89	330	1,450
Thailand	31	37	37	84	84	81	6	13	16	111	192	196
Average:												
Unweighted	22	31	37	51	69	81	11	19	29	130	261	493
Weighted	21	28	35	51	64	78	13	21	28	134	282	548

Source: UNESCO, *Progress of Education in The Asian Region: Statistical Supplement* (Bangkok, 1972).

Notes: [a] not available
[b] insignificant

[c] These are crude enrollment ratios defined as first-level enrollment as a percentage of estimated total population in the customary age range for first-level schooling. The percentage can exceed 100 when children outside of the customary age range are enrolled, for example as a result of late entry or repetition.

been continuing heavy applicant pressure on existing institutions, accompanied by a rapid growth in private schooling. The private sector's share in total enrollments rises rapidly as one moves from lower to higher levels of schooling (Table 39), and private schools have provided an increasing share of post-primary places over time (for example, 57 percent of high school enrollments in 1973, compared to 37 percent in 1958). For these reasons, we conclude that a large share of the enrollment growth that has occurred since the end of the Korean War must be attributed to strong social demand backed by a willingness of families to pay a large share of the cost of education, rather than to the expansion of facilities by the government.

Figure 8 shows how enrollment ratios for four age groups have changed since 1953. Three characteristics of the graph are noteworthy:

1) The steady rise in the enrollment ratio for each group through time, the only exception being a slight fall in the percentage of 18–21-year-olds enrolled in the early 1970s.

2) The gradual flattening out of the curve as middle school enrollment has expanded and the screening process has become more continuous throughout the educational sequence, rather than being concentrated at the middle school entry level. This change can be seen also in Table 22, above.

3) The increasing steepness of the curve as time goes by; even though primary schooling reached universality in the 1960s, and despite higher rates of enrollment growth at the upper levels of schooling, the number of percentage points which must be shed from the enrollment ratio as a cohort ages increased steadily throughout the period.[33]

As a result of these trends, the Korean school system of today can be characterized as one in which primary schooling is universal, middle schooling widespread, and high school enrollment substantial but significantly less general, while access to college-level education is still quite drastically restricted. If the enrollment ratio structure remains as it was in 1975, more than

FIGURE 8 Enrollment Ratio by Age Group,
Whole Population, 1953–1975

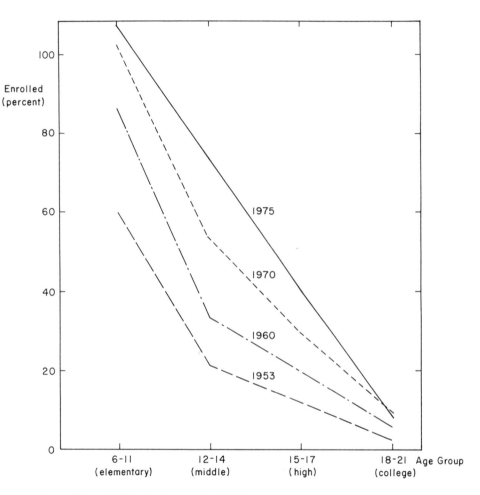

Source: Ministry of Education data, special tabulation.

153

TABLE 39 Enrollment in Public and Private Schools
as a Percentage of Total by Level of Education, 1973

	% of Total Enrollment	
Type of School	*Public*	*Private*
Primary	98.8	1.2
Middle	58.5	41.5
High	43.0	57.0
Colleges and Universities	26.9	73.1

Source: Ministry of Education, *Statistical Yearbook of Education 1973.*

90 percent of the pupils now enrolled in primary school will fail to gain admittance to college. Considerable interest, therefore, attaches to the question of how the comparatively small number of students who do reach college are picked out of the much larger number who do not.

The Selection Process
The Korean Constitution states, *inter alia*, that "all citizens shall have the right to receive equal education according to their ability" and "compulsory education shall be free."[34] How nearly are these ideals attained in practice?

Primary schooling has theoretically been compulsory, universal, and free since 1948. In fact, as we have seen earlier, enrollment ratios approached 100 percent only in the early 1960s, and there have always been some costs (significant by the standards of most Korean families) associated with attendance. Entry to middle school was by means of a national examination until 1969; the examination has been eliminated and enrollment is now being expanded, with the aim of making middle school attendance universal for 12–14 year-olds by 1980. High school and college continue to be entered by examination.

Thus, selection criteria for continuation are of three types:
1) Successful completion of the previous level of schooling
2) Performance in standard national examinations, when

imposed (that is, for middle school entry up to 1969, for high school and college throughout the period)

3) Willingness and ability to pay the private costs of education

Fees enter into the selection process in two different ways. First, as noted earlier, the majority of those who want to remain in school beyond the middle school level must meet the costs of private education. Second, even in public schools, and not excluding the "free" primary schools, there are significant money costs which must be covered by the student's family. As discussed in Chapter 1 and 2, these include:

1) "Voluntary" PTA contributions at all levels and in all types of schools (these fees were recognized by the government and standardized in amount in 1970, after numerous complaints about inequities)

2) School tuition fees applicable to virtually all post-primary education

3) Special tuition fees paid by many parents to coaches who prepare students for the standard examinations

4) Other costs, such as books and instructional materials, extra-curricular activity fees, and transportation costs

Together, these fees place a substantial burden on the finances of most Korean families. In 1963, according to UNESCO mission estimates,[35] these fees paid by households averaged (on a pupil-year basis):

Primary school	1,470 wŏn	($11.31)
Middle school	6,450 wŏn	($49.62)
High school	9,280 wŏn	($71.38)

Relative to a mean annual household income of about 62,000 wŏn in that year, a family with two children in school would have to pay between 5 and 30 percent of its income (depending on the levels of school attended) just as the private, explicit cost of education. This does not take account of either the implicit private cost of education (that is, the loss of earnings from keeping children in school) or of taxes paid to finance public education.

Has this financial burden grown or lessened over time? Trends in explicit educational costs assumed by households can be measured with reasonable accuracy only for the period since 1966. Using available data and employing conservative assumptions about the level and growth of out-of-school expenditures (about which less is known than about in-school expenditures), Yung Bong Kim has estimated that real per-pupil outlays by households rose little if at all at the primary, middle, and high school levels. But outlays increased by 41 percent in real terms for college and university students between 1966 and 1975. Because of the relative shift to higher (and more expensive) forms of schooling, the average outlay for all students rose by 48 percent in real terms during the period. Aggregate real outlays by households for education, taking into account enrollment increases, rose by 103 percent over the period. Since real disposable income (estimated by using official national accounts aggregates, deflated by the urban consumer price index) had already more than doubled its 1966 level by 1973, the relative financial burden of educational outlays on households appears to have lessened somewhat over the past decade. However, a constant proportion (about two-thirds) of direct educational costs has been borne consistently by households throughout the period.

The Results of Selection

Despite the Constitution's promise of equal educational opportunity based on merit, a promise that may derive from American educational ideals, one would expect the use of the three selection devices just enumerated (continuity in the system, examinations, and fees) to introduce biases which would be evident when the relevant enrollment ratios are compared. Accordingly, we have compiled data on comparative enrollment ratios for urban and rural areas, districts with different educational attainments and employment structures, students from different socio-economic backgrounds, the nine provinces and two major cities, and males and females.

Evidence on urban-rural access differentials is provided in

Table 40, which gives some crude enrollment ratios for Seoul, other urban areas, and the rural areas of the country in 1960. One can see limited urban-rural differentiation for the 13-years-and-under population, and sharper differentiation for the population over 13. By 1960, the country was approaching almost universal primary enrollment, which would necessarily mean that the 13-and-under category would show little difference among regions. The larger differentiation for the older group might be exaggerated by the fact that enrollments reported for urban areas include students from rural areas who have migrated to attend school or the university.

The enrollment ratio for the over-13 age group in Seoul is 2.2 times that in the rural areas, while the proportion enrolled in other urban areas is 1.8 times that of rural areas. How significant are these 1960 disparities? On the one hand, they indicate significantly greater access to education for urban as opposed to rural children. On the other, the disparities are smaller than those in many other countries. Charles Nam[36] has assembled roughly comparable data for some OECD member countries. These data show differentials in the late 1950s and early 1960s ranging from 2.8 to 5.5 (in countries such as Austria, Denmark, Greece, and the Netherlands), while France and the United States had differentials smaller than those of Korea.

Tables 41 and 42 provide enrollment ratios in the 175 counties of Korea in 1960.[37] These counties are classified in two ways: by the literacy rate of their adult population (Table 41) and by their occupational structure, crudely measured by the percentage of farmers and fishermen in total employment (Table 42). In both cases, we find enrollment ratio differentials generally in the expected directions. For the 13-and-under cohort, these differentials are rather mild and in fact are really only evident at the extremes of the distribution (that is, in the comparatively small number of counties in which literacy was below 60 percent on the one hand, or above 85 percent on the other). For the over-13 cohort, variation is more continuous and wider in range, although, as in Table 41, the comparison is biased to some degree by the location patterns of educational institutions.[38]

Next in Figures 9 through 12, we examine enrollment ratios for 1970 classified by the educational attainment (Figures 9 and 10) and occupational category (Figures 11 and 12) of the head of the household from which the school-age person comes. These

TABLE 40 Enrollment Ratios for Seoul, Other Urban Areas, and Rural Areas, 1960[a]

	13-and-Under (% of Population Ages 0–13)	*Over-13 (% of Population Ages 14–59)*
Seoul	0.331	0.210
Other Urban Areas	0.337	0.169
Rural Areas	0.298	0.095
Republic of Korea	0.307	0.121

Source: 1960 Population Census.

Note: [a]Urban areas are defined on an administrative basis to include Seoul City and all si (cities) and ku (boroughs); rural areas include all kun (counties).

TABLE 41 Enrollment Ratios for Si (Cities), Ku (Boroughs), and Kun (Counties) Grouped by Literacy Rates, 1960

		Average enrollment ratio	
% Literate in Population Age 13+	*Number of Units*	*13 and Under (% of Population Ages 0–13)*	*Over 13 (% of Population Ages 14–59)*
Less than 60%	12	0.269	0.086
60–65%	37	0.299	0.091
65–70%	35	0.305	0.096
70–75%	38	0.300	0.098
75–80%	26	0.300	0.121
80–85%	16	0.301	0.142
More than 85%	11	0.338	0.199
Republic of Korea	175	0.307	0.121

Source: 1960 Population Census.

again show differentials in the expected directions. It can be seen that: 1) the amount of relative dispersion of enrollment ratios by both father's education and father's occupation is greater for females than for males; and 2) variation in the father's educational attainment seems to create wider dispersion in the enrollment ratios of males, while variations in the father's occupational status lead to greater differences for females. In fact, there is still considerable discrimination on socio-economic grounds in the higher reaches of the Korean educational system. According to the data depicted in Figure 11, the son of a professional, technical, or managerial worker is 3.5 times as likely to be enrolled as the son of a farmer and 2.6 times as likely as the son of a laborer. For daughters, these ratios are even higher, 7.4 and 4.2 to 1.0, respectively.

Differences in access to education can also be seen across the provinces of Korea. Table 43 displays the provincial share of persons in each category as a proportion of the total numbers in

TABLE 42 Enrollment Ratios for Si (Cities), Ku (Boroughs), and Kun (Counties) Grouped by Occupational Structure, 1960

Farmers and Fishermen as % of of Total Employment	Number of Units	*Average enrollment ratio*	
		13 and Under (% of Population Ages 0–13)	*Over 13 (% of Population Ages 14–59)*
Over 90%	10	0.293	0.089
85–90%	24	0.297	0.091
80–85%	53	0.299	0.093
75–80%	22	0.298	0.090
65–75%	14	0.300	0.102
55–65%	9	0.282	0.091
15–55%	20	0.299	0.130
5–15%	11	0.332	0.171
Under 5%	12	0.336	0.198
Republic of Korea	175	0.307	0.121

Source: 1960 Population Census.

FIGURE 9 Male Enrollment Ratios by Educational
Attainment of Household Head, 1970

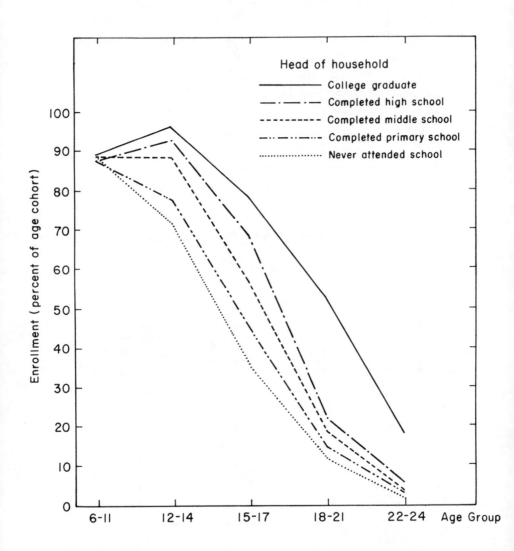

Source: Special processing of 1% sample data from 1970 Population Census.

FIGURE 10   Female Enrollment Ratios by Educational
Attainment of Household Head, 1970

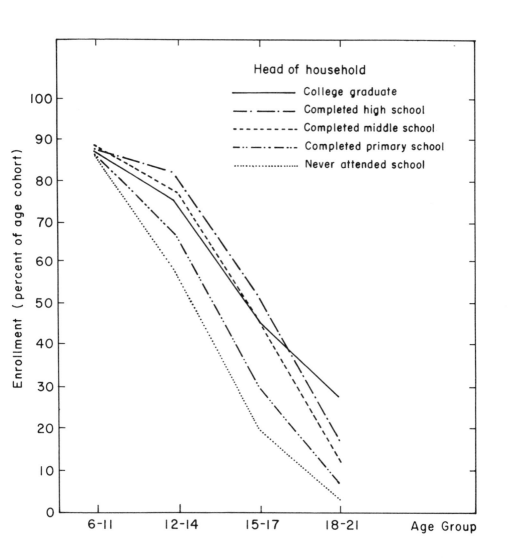

Source: Special processing of 1% sample data from 1970 Population Census.

FIGURE 11 Male Enrollment Ratios by Occupational
Category of Household Head, 1970

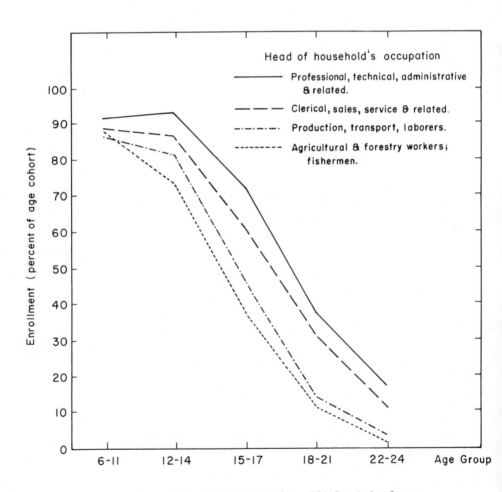

Source: Special processing of 1% sample data from 1970 Population Census.

FIGURE 12 Female Enrollment Ratios by Occupational
Category of Household Head, 1970

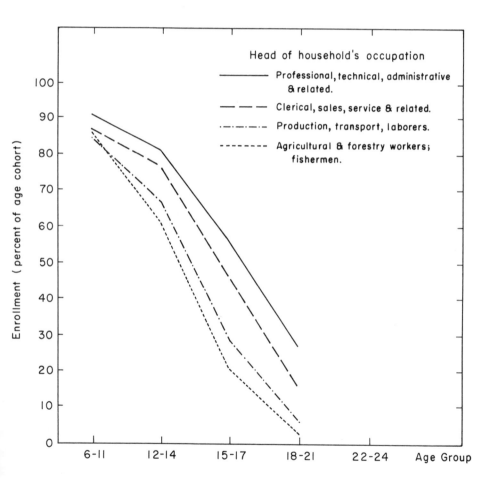

Source: Special processing of 1% sample data from 1970 Population Census.

that category. In 1965, for example, graduates of primary schools in Seoul were 12.0 percent of Korean students graduating from primary that year. In 1975 Seoul had 16.3 percent of the primary school graduates. The proportions of primary school graduates can be used as base numbers for comparing each province's share at other levels in the system. To some extent, these proportions change over time as a result of migration. Seoul has today a larger share of the nation's total population than it had in 1965. Migratory patterns should show in the 1965 to 1975 comparisons of the same level.

It is also possible that, to some extent, differences between levels within the same year reflect the impact of inter-provincial migration. For example, Seoul had 26.6 percent of entering high school students in 1965, compared to only 12.0 percent of primary school graduates. That difference could be a function of students migrating to Seoul immediately after primary school graduation, or sometime during the three-year period of middle school. The first possibility is not supported by Ministry of Education reports on applications to middle, high school, and post-secondary institutions, which indicate that only a small fraction of graduates apply outside their province.[39]

An alternative explanation of differences between Seoul's proportion of new high school students and its share of primary school graduates in the same year is that more students go on in Seoul than in the rest of the country as a whole. Table 43 presents some data that allow one to assess the possible impact of migration on provincial share of enrollments, as compared to disparities in educational opportunity. The table can be read as follows: In December 1964 Seoul had 12.0 percent of primary school graduates. Of that same group, 16.1 percent went on to middle school in Seoul in March 1965. South Chŏlla province, on the other hand, with 12.3 percent of 1964 primary graduates, had only 10.5 percent entering middle school in 1965. Seoul gained about 25 percent between December 1964 and March 1965, while South Chŏlla province lost about 15 percent. This seems too large a difference to be explained solely by migration.

TABLE 43 Provincial Share of Students at Various Levels in the Educational System

		Primary Graduates	Entering Middle	Graduating Middle	Applying to High School	Entering Acad. High	Graduating Acad. High	Applying Higher Ed.	Graduating Higher Ed.
					Province's Share of Students Who Are				
Seoul	1965	12.0	16.1	19.2	22.2	26.6	35.5	38.4	44.2
	1975	16.3	19.0	20.0	23.2	24.4	34.2	38.3	42.5
Pusan	1965	5.3	6.0	7.6	8.5	8.8	9.2	9.6	10.4
	1975	5.6	6.4	6.7	7.7	8.3	8.2	9.9	9.4
Provinces:									
Kyŏnggi	1965	11.1	10.9	9.5	9.6	8.1	6.7	6.8	4.8
	1975	10.5	10.9	10.2	10.2	10.4	5.0	4.4	3.7
Kangwŏn	1965	6.0	5.2	3.8	3.5	3.2	2.7	2.8	1.8
	1975	6.0	5.1	4.8	4.5	4.5	3.5	3.3	3.6
N. Ch'ungch'ŏng	1965	5.8	5.1	4.3	3.7	3.3	3.6	3.3	3.0
	1975	4.9	4.5	4.6	4.4	4.0	2.8	2.8	2.7
S. Ch'ungch'ŏng	1965	10.2	9.6	9.6	8.7	8.3	6.1	4.8	4.9
	1975	9.6	9.2	9.1	8.5	8.0	8.1	6.4	5.6
N. Chŏlla	1965	7.8	8.3	8.8	8.3	8.7	5.9	6.4	4.6
	1975	8.0	7.3	6.8	6.5	6.4	7.7	7.4	6.3
S. Chŏlla	1965	12.3	10.5	9.5	10.5	10.4	8.9	8.2	9.0
	1975	13.9	11.7	11.1	10.1	9.9	8.2	7.9	8.0
N. Kyŏngsang	1965	16.0	15.3	14.2	12.7	13.0	14.2	13.4	12.7
	1975	14.4	14.6	14.6	14.0	13.6	13.7	13.0	12.5
S. Kyŏngsang	1965	12.4	11.8	12.1	11.1	8.2	5.7	5.1	4.1
	1975	9.8	10.1	10.8	9.4	9.1	7.2	5.5	5.0
Cheju Island	1965	1.0	1.2	1.5	1.2	1.4	1.4	0.8	0.9
	1975	1.2	1.3	1.3	1.3	1.3	1.3	1.1	0.9
National Total	1965	617,554	193,333	189,726	156,318	79,275	68,487	65,638	29,459
	1975	924,727	714,079	568,648	476,735	250,438	137,228	99,694	57,007

For several reasons, it is probable that a primary school graduate living in Seoul is more likely to continue in school than is a primary graduate living in South Chŏlla province.

Seoul's share of students also increases between middle school entrants and middle school graduates. In this case, we are not dealing with the same cohort, but with cohorts separated by three years. The rate of growth is about 6 percent per year, not too far from Seoul's overall rate of population growth. Given high promotion rates (and low dropout rates) throughout the country, it seems more feasible to attribute this difference to migration than to inequalities in educational opportunity. (On the other hand, Ministry figures show very low rates of transfer out of schools *during* the school year.)

Migration does not seem to explain the next pair of figures, however. In December 1964 Seoul graduated 19.2 percent of all middle school graduates in the country. Its share of graduates applying to high school (the same cohort) was 22.2 percent, and in March 1965 Seoul had 26.6 percent of all new high school students. North Kyŏngsang province, on the other hand, which had 16.0 percent of primary school graduates in 1964, and 14.2 percent of middle school graduates, had only 13.0 percent of students acutally entering high school. The proportional growth in high school enrollments in Seoul means either that students migrate there to go to high school (because of better quality perhaps) or that more Seoul middle school graduates go on to high school than do graduates in the rest of the nation.

Entrance to high school is controlled by an examination. These data could be interpreted to mean that Seoul middle school graduates have a greater chance of passing the examination than students in the rest of the nation. Or it may mean that proportionately more students are admitted in Seoul (independent of their examination scores) than in the rest of the country. Class sizes in Seoul high schools tend to be larger than in any other region of the country. One might want to interpret this to mean only that social demand for high school education is greater in Seoul than elsewhere, and that differences in enrollment shares do not imply differences in the quality of education provided.

But enrollment in high school is necessary for graduation from high school, and entrance to college, and in Korea as elsewhere salaries increase directly with level of educational attainment. Studies elsewhere have shown that students' aspiration levels are greatly influenced by the aspirations of their companions. A child growing up in Seoul, therefore, is more likely to want to go on in school, and more likely eventually to obtain a higher income, than children living elsewhere in the country. Seoul, with 12.0 percent of primary school graduates in 1964, had 38.4 percent of all students applying to higher education, and 44.2 percent of all academic high school graduates admitted to higher education in March 1965.

The figures for 1975 show that Seoul's share of new entrants to higher education remained disproportionately high, with 42.5 percent of Korea's academic high school graduates entering college being (apparently) from Seoul. At the same time, however, because of the overall growth of Seoul's population, primary school graduates from Seoul were proportionately 35 percent more in 1975 than in 1965. In other words, while Seoul still provides a relatively greater opportunity for educational advancement than the rest of the country, the differences are not quite as great as ten years ago. The same is also true for Pusan, the only other part of the country whose share of students increases steadily as we go up the academic ladder.

Some of the provinces, particularly Kangwŏn, South Ch'ungch'ŏng, and North Chŏlla, have improved their share of students reaching the higher levels of the educational system over time. Other provinces, however, particularly South Kyŏngsang, Kyŏnggi, and South Chŏlla, have slipped further behind. In those provinces, in other words, children have been at an increasing disadvantage relative to children in other provinces, in terms of their chances of graduating from high school and going on to college.

The implications of Table 43 are made a bit clearer by

distinguishing between academic and vocational high schools and their graduates. In both years, there were almost equal numbers of graduates from the two kinds of institutions but, while more than a third of academic high school graduates were admitted to higher education, less than one-sixth were admitted from vocational high schools, the proportion actually declining between 1965 and 1975. This change is consistent with government policy, which attempts to make vocational high school a terminal program, rather than preparation for college and university training. But the numbers of students in each kind of school have been redistributed in the country between 1965 and 1975. As Table 44 shows, Seoul's share of vocational high school graduates has declined, while that of other provinces has increased. Furthermore, Seoul's share of vocational high school graduates going on to higher education has plummeted, while that of the provinces and Pusan has risen sharply.

The conclusion to be drawn from these figures is that, between 1965 and 1975, educational opportunities have become more than previously a function of residence. Students interested in academic education and attendance at a university should be advised to move to Seoul, as the probability of reaching their goal is higher there than elsewhere. Students interested in a technical career, without higher education, would be advised to move to Pusan, Kyŏnggi province, South Chŏlla province, or North Kyŏngsang province. But if those students want to attend vocational high school and then go on to the university, their best chance is in Pusan or South Chŏlla province.

Not only does Seoul get more than its share of the types of schooling (academic high schools and universities) most likely to yield higher incomes; it also receives more in the form of high-level human resources for education. Table 45 presents the distribution of highly trained teachers at each level in 1965 and 1975. Years of training are determined in part by the level for which a teacher is prepared: the minimal level is high school for elementary teachers, junior college for middle school teachers, and college for high school teachers. Teachers trained

TABLE 44 Provincial Share of Academic and Vocational High School Graduates Entering Higher Education

		Academic High School Grads	Entering Higher Ed.	Vocational High School Grads	Entering Higher Ed.
Seoul	1965	35.5	44.2	20.4	30.3
	1975	34.2	42.5	18.1	16.4
Pusan	1965	9.2	10.4	8.5	9.8
	1975	8.2	9.4	11.3	14.5
Provinces:					
Kyŏnggi province	1965	6.7	4.8	11.5	9.6
	1975	5.0	3.7	13.2	13.0
Kangwŏn province	1965	2.7	1.8	5.5	3.7
	1975	3.5	3.6	5.5	3.1
N. Ch'ungch'ŏng province	1965	3.6	3.0	4.7	4.8
	1975	2.8	2.7	3.7	3.5
S. Ch'ungch'ŏng province	1965	6.1	4.9	8.2	5.5
	1975	8.1	5.6	6.2	5.7
N. Chŏlla province	1965	5.9	4.6	9.2	10.0
	1975	7.7	6.3	5.9	4.0
S. Chŏlla province	1965	8.9	9.0	9.1	9.2
	1975	8.2	8.0	11.8	18.6
N. Kyŏngsang province	1965	14.2	12.4	12.5	10.1
	1975	13.7	12.5	14.1	14.0

(continued)

TABLE 44 (continued)

		Academic High School Grads	Entering Higher Ed.	Vocational High School Grads	Entering Higher Ed.
S. Kyŏngsang province	1965	5.7	4.1	9.4	5.8
	1975	7.2	5.0	8.6	6.1
Cheju Island	1965	1.4	0.9	1.0	1.2
	1975	1.3	0.9	1.5	1.2
National	1965	64,487	29,459	47,289	7,919
Total	1975	137,228	57,007	126,141	11,048

Source: Ministry of Education, *Statistical Yearbook of Education 1965 and 1975.*

TABLE 45 Distribution of Teachers by Level of Formal Education
Regional Share of Teachers Completing at Least N Years

	1965			1975		
	Elementary 15 yrs.	Middle 15 yrs.	Academic High 15 yrs.	Elementary 15 yrs.	Middle 16 yrs.	Academic High 17 yrs.
Seoul	21.2	22.6	27.1	29.6	21.6	58.1
Pusan	6.4	8.1	8.3	4.9	6.5	8.1
Provinces:						
Kyŏnggi province	8.7	9.8	8.1	10.3	10.6	5.8
Kangwŏn province	2.4	3.9	4.3	4.5	4.7	1.6
N. Ch'ungch'ŏng province	4.7	3.4	4.5	6.3	4.4	1.6
S. Ch'ungch'ŏng province	6.3	5.4	6.4	5.4	7.8	3.4
N. Chŏlla province	10.2	8.4	7.0	10.2	6.5	2.2
S. Chŏlla province	11.2	7.2	9.8	8.6	6.5	6.5
N. Kyŏngsang province	19.5	17.6	14.7	10.2	10.7	11.0
S. Kyŏngsang province	8.8	12.4	8.5	9.3	15.5	1.3
Cheju Island	0.6	1.2	1.4	0.8	10.2	0.3
Total	3,986	10,893	11,847	5,826	1.4	1,218
Total all Teachers	79,164	19,067	14,108	108,126	36,689	20,415

Source: Ministry of Education, *Statistical Yearbook of Education, 1965 and 1975.*

above the minimum may not be many, but they are important in forcing a high level of quality instruction. At all levels for both years, Seoul gets more than its share of these highly trained teachers. In 1965, with 12 percent of the elementary school students, it had 21 percent of the highly trained elementary teachers. With 16 percent of the middle school students, it had almost 23 percent of teachers with at least 15 years of formal education. (Data for 1965 are broken down in two-year groupings; almost no teachers had more than 16 years of formal schooling.) Seoul had only slightly more than its share of trained high school teachers in 1965, but by 1975 it had more than half of all those with some graduate training.

If one combines higher quality of teachers with more favorable income circumstances (Seoul's per capita income is higher than the provinces'), then it is not surprising that students beginning school in Seoul have a greater chance than students in other regions of the country of making it into the university.

Sex and Educational Opportunity.
Some progress has been made in reducing disparities between the educational opportunities for boys and girls. Table 46 displays women's share of various statuses at different levels in the system in 1965 and 1975. In all cases, women today have a greater share of education than they did ten years ago. There appears to be a definite move towards parity in most kinds of educational establishments.

Without diminution of these recent achievements, it should be recognized that past differentials in opportunities available to men and women were very large, and that these differentials to some extent survive to the present day. Table 47 shows the female share in total enrollments at the four major levels in the system, beginning in 1939. Under the Japanese, educational opportunities for women were limited. Three times as many boys as girls attended school. Few Koreans went to high school, and the higher proportion of women in high school than in primary school may reflect only the colonial policy of restricting positions of leadership for Korean men.

The U.S. Military Government, as noted earlier, introduced coeducation in Korea and made strong efforts to increase female

TABLE 46 Women's Share of Enrollments in 1965 and 1975

	Percent of Total in	
	1965	1975
Elementary Graduates	43.3	47.8
Entering Middle	37.1	43.0
Graduating Middle	35.0	40.6
Applying to High School	32.9	38.9
Entering Academic High	45.3 ⎫ 35.5	41.7 ⎫ 39.4
Entering Vocational High	19.8 ⎭	36.0 ⎭
Graduating Academic High	41.3 ⎫ 31.6	43.3 ⎫ 38.8
Graduating Vocational High	17.4 ⎭	33.8 ⎭
Applied Higher Education	31.8	34.5
Admitted Junior College, Junior Teachers College	44.6 ⎫ 33.5	58.7 ⎫ 37.2
Admitted College or University	29.3 ⎭	33.3 ⎭
Graduated Junior College, Junior Teachers College	40.3 ⎫ 22.4	58.3 ⎫ 34.2
Graduated College or University	16.9 ⎭	28.9 ⎭

Source: Ministry of Education, *Statistical Yearbook of Education 1965* and *1975*.

TABLE 47 Women's Share of Enrollments as Percent of Total, 1939–1975

	Year							
	1939	1945	1952	1955	1960	1965	1970	1975
Primary	25.1	39.6	36.3	41.9	45.0	47.6	47.9	48.4
Middle			21.8	24.8	24.4	35.6	38.1	42.2
High School	33.0	31.0	16.4	17.9	25.5	33.4	37.1	38.2
University	17.9	14.1	12.3	10.9	17.4	24.5	22.7	26.5

Sources: Jin Eun Kim, "Analysis of the National Planning Process"; Ministry of Education, *Statistical Yearbook of Education 1975*.

enrollments. Those efforts were successful at the compulsory level, but had mixed results at other levels. Women's share of middle school enrollments stayed constant until after 1960, then began to rise with the opening of middle school to all primary graduates. Female enrollments in high school declined proportionately after 1945, as the rapid expansion of opportunities for secondary education attracted many men. Similarly, the expansion of higher education during and after the Korean War attracted more men than women. It is only since the early 1960s, then, that women's share of enrollments has begun to climb steadily, surpassing, in the case of high school and college and university, the levels reached during the Japanese colonial period.

A closer examination of these developments indicates some of the difficulties women face in achieving equality with men in Korean society. For example, the education of daughters may cost parents more than the education of sons. In the early 1960s, it was common for schools to charge higher fees to girls than boys in the same schools.[40] Although women are enrolling in colleges and universities in increasing numbers, women are still found almost exclusively in "feminine" careers such as nursing, teaching, or liberal arts, while men dominate in engineering, science, and other professions whose returns in terms of income and prestige are considerably greater than those of careers followed by women. Women also do not receive equal pay for equal work. Using results from a study of seven banks in Seoul, Chung Han Kim concludes that women are not hired in open competition, while men are. Women must promise to quit their positions if they get married. Female employees who are college graduates receive the same starting salaries as male employees who are high school graduates, and men are given preference in promotions. She concludes, "As has been shown, Korean college women are not fully allowed to participate in the building of Korean economy as Korean men are due to the mere fact that they are women."[41] She then goes on to assert that most women accept this state of affairs as inevitable "under the present circumstances in which Communist invasion of real or imaginative nature constantly threatens the security of the country from within and without."[42]

This pattern of discrimination is not very different from those of most other developing countries (and many developed societies as well), but it does qualify the favorable interpretataion placed on recent enrollment gains for women.

Summary.
We can summarize our findings on access to education in South Korea as follows:

1) Korean education is general at the bottom of the pyramid, comparatively restrictive at the top.

2) Selection is exercised mainly through standardized tests and surprisingly stiff fees.

3) However, the selection process results in little regional discrimination (relative to other countries) and in what is probably a relatively small amount of class discrimination. Education (at least for sons) is a strong and widely shared value, for which Korean families are willing to make substantial sacrifices.

4) Families place a lower value on education for their daughters, who may also be discriminated against in school, although the amount of this discrimination is declining.

5) Overall, our impression is that academic "merit" plays a large part in the system and that, while the school system, as in other countries, serves to transmit social status from members of one generation to their offspring in the next, it has afforded significant opportunities for students from modest backgrounds to rise if they had the requisite ability and determination and if their families were willing to sacrifice for them.[43]

EFFECTS OF EDUCATION ON INCOME

Having discussed access to education, we now come to the second, and harder, question. What difference does it all make?

What effect does education have on the incomes of those who receive it?

In Korea, as in all other countries, people with more education tend to earn higher incomes than people with less education. Figures 3 and 4, above, provided limited evidence that Korea is not an exception to this universal tendency. The great issue in the study of education's economic effects is not whether income is positively associated with educational attainment but what the undoubted statistical association means.

Tests to provide a clear rejection of either the human-capital theory or its opponents have not yet been devised and are probably not possible, since each theory probably reflects some important aspects of reality but is insufficient to stand as a sole explanation of education's multifarious effects.

All empirical research done on South Korea so far has, as far as we know, been in the human-capital theory tradition. This tradition comprises two types of empirical study, each of which has been carried out for the Korean case. The two types are earnings-function studies, which seek to measure the influence of years of schooling and other variables on short-run earnings, and estimates of the rate of return to investments in education.

One of the problems encountered in empirical applications of human-capital theory is how to quantify education in a meaningful way. So far, no satisfactory way has been found: 1) to include all forms of education; and 2) to reflect the quality as well as the duration of education. Early studies included only formal schooling, measured in years of school attendance. More recent work, following Jacob Mincer,[44] has incorporated informal on-the-job training, measured in years of work experience. Studies of the earnings of industrial workers in South Korea by Kang-su Chŏng and Kwang-sŏk Kim[45] and Funkoo Park, reported in the University of Minnesota's *Annual Report* for 1976,[46] follow the newer approach.

These studies, like virtually all similar work, reveal signficiant positive statistical association between earnings, on the one hand, and both years of schooling and years of work experience, on the other. In addition, Park's study reportedly shows some interesting differences between large firms, which reward both schooling and firm-specific experience more highly, and small firms, which appear to regard schooling and outside work experience as substitutes for each other. Both these studies are based on highly restricted segments of the labor force (regular full-time industrial workers) and thus tell nothing about the relationships between education and earnings that prevail in other parts of the economy. Moreover, as studies of statistical association, they tell us that certain education and earnings measures move together to a significant extent, but they do not help us distinguish between the rival theories of why this is so.

Rate-of-return studies have intellectual premises similar to those used for earnings-function studies, with the differences that 1) they attempt to take into account lifetime earnings rather than merely current earnings, and 2) they allow for the costs of education. Rate-of-return calculations for education in Korea have been made by Kwang Suk Kim[47] for USAID, John Chang[48] for the Florida State University educational planning team, and Chang Young Jeong[49] for the Korea Development Institute. These calculations involve complex manipulations of large bodies of data, invoking assumptions that are not always spelled out in the published versions of the research. The final results of the three studies can, however, be summarized, as shown in Table 48.

We believe that all the rates given in this table are *marginal social rates of return.* That is, they are marginal in the sense that they reflect the *additional* income earned by graduates of a particular level of education over those who have completed the preceding, lower level, as well as the costs of obtaining that marginal level of education. They are social in that they reflect the part of educational costs borne by society as a whole through the government, as well as the costs met by the individuals being educated and their families. The John Chang and Chang Young Jeong studies use earnings data from the Occupational Wage Survey, the data source discussed earlier. A

TABLE 48 Estimated Rates of Return
To Investment in Education

| | Kwang Suk Kim (1968) | John Chang (for 1967) | | Chang Young Jeong (for 1971) |
		Adjusted for Unemployment	Unadjusted	
Middle school	12.0	20.0	26.5	8.2
High school	9.0	11.0	13.5	14.6
College	5.0	9.5	9.5	9.3

fundamental difficulty of rate-of-return studies is that they must somehow estimate the future lifetime earnings of persons currently being educated. John Chang and Chang Young Jeong deal with this problem in the usual way, by assuming that the earnings of older people currently employed correctly forecast the future earnings of today's young people, while Kwang Suk Kim attempts an explicit forecast of future earnings. Neither method is very satisfactory, especially when applied to a labor market undergoing massive non-marginal changes.

For what they are worth, the studies (particularly those by Kwang Suk Kim and Chang Young Jeong) indicate rather low rates of return to investment in education, relative both to the 20 percent rate of return on physical capital thought to exist in South Korea in the late 1960s and to rates of return on investment in human capital calculated for other countries.[50] According to the logic of the human-capital approach, these results could be read to indicate over-investment in human capital relative to physical capital (and particularly over-investment in higher education). Kwang Suk Kim did, in fact, draw this conclusion, while John Chang concluded that further educational expansion was needed despite his findings, so as to capture non-pecuniary benefits of education and for two other reasons which appear spurious.[51] In fact, however, low measured rates of return to investment in education do not necessarily indicate that education is overexpanded and should be cut back. As is usual with rate-of-return studies, the results are difficult to interpret—even within the human-capital framework, and (as we have already noted) there is an alternative explanation of them from outside that framework which may have considerable appeal.

Within the human-capital framework, several observations can be made:

1) All three rate-of-return studies apparently assume that the entire variation in income associated with variations in education is causally attributable to education. This is patently wrong because of multi-collinearity: we have seen that socio-economic status is positively associated with income. As far as we know, no research has been done for Korea on the statistical association between education and earnings when socio-economic background is held constant; we shall return to this point. In any case, since only part of the income variation associated with income is independently attributable to education, the rate-of-return studies are biased upward in this respect.

2) They are biased downward, however, by the exclusion of benefits other than productivity gains (allegedly) reflected in higher earnings for the individual educated. The excluded types of benefit are production externalities (that is, increases in productivity which raise the incomes of others), consumption benefits to the individual, and socialization benefits to society as a whole.

3) All the studies are crude in the sense that they measure returns only to the "mainline" forms of schooling, ignoring the several specialized branch forms shown in Figure 1, and lump together all specialized streams of education within the mainline (that is, they take no account of possible differences in returns to arts education, science education, engineering, and so on).

Parenthetically, it would be a useful exercise if a test of the association of education with income, independent of socio-economic background, were conducted. This would provide some evidence on the causal factors at work, since the expected finding that there is such a partial association would suggest that education raises income *either* through productivity increases or through "meritocratic" (as opposed to discriminatory) selection. The contrary finding, that education has little independent effect on income, would suggest that education merely transmits socio-economic status between generations. If this test turned out as expected, we would still be left with the unresolved, and perhaps unresolvable, problem of distinguishing between the productivity-increasing effect and meritocratic selection.

Finally, we offer (without proof) an alternative explanation for the apparently low rates of return to education in South Korea, an explanation based on the selection theory rather than the human-capital theory. It was suggested earlier that earnings-for-education differentials may be small in Korea relative to other low-income countries. The reasons for this phenomenon may relate more to institutional factors which hold down the earnings of elites and near-elites, such as urban white-collar and skilled blue-collar workers, rather than in the operation of competitive labor markets which set the wages of different types of labor (categorized by years of schooling) equal to marginal product. If this is so, then a low measured return to education is inevitable, even though the school system is an important means of selecting individuals to occupy high-status positions.[52] The importance of the school system as a selection device may be even more important in Korea than in most countries (as it was in Japan), despite the relative modesty of the financial rewards.[53] Thus, Korean parents are perfectly rational in seeking all the schooling they can get for their children, if it is assumed that the objective is high-status positions in the economy and society.

Impediments to Equitable Distribution.
To the extent that education is linked with income and social status, inequities in the distribution of access to education

contribute to inequities in the distribution of income and status. Given the virtual destruction of the class structure by the Liberation and the Korean War, and the rapid expansion of education, Korea has been able to distribute access to education with a relatively high degree of equality across regions and social classes, and between the two sexes. But near equality in access really prevails only in the lower levels. The limitation of access to the upper levels makes it more likely that discriminatory criteria will be used in the assignment of entrance into higher education.

Although not extreme (nor even severe in comparison with other countries), there are differences in access to education as a function of rural-urban residence, occupation of parent, province, and sex. These differences have diminished in recent years as education through the 9th grade has become nearly universal. If Korea could continue to expand educational offerings, then it is likely that educational opportunity would be even more equitably shared.

As indicated earlier, access to higher education means higher incomes for those employed. It also means, as Table 17 shows, a greater chance of employment. Persons leaving the educational system are much more likely to be employed within three months after graduation if they have graduated from a university, a vocational high school, or a junior college, than if they have graduated from an academic high school or only a middle school.

The differences in employability of academic and vocational high school graduates merit special attention. These differences have existed for at least ten years, yet academic high schools continue to enroll more students than vocational high schools. Demand for entrance into academic high schools is strong because parents believe that they are a better route to the university (although Table 44 would suggest that is less true today than previously).

But even the superior employability of vocational school graduates varies according to province, as shown in Table 49.

TABLE 49 Employment Rates of Vocational High School Graduates, 1975

	Number of Graduates	Percent Admitted to Next Level	Not Going On, Percent	
			Employed	*Not Employed*
Seoul	22,851	7.9	72.6	12.4
Pusan	14,309	11.2	74.0	15.1
Kyŏnggi province	16,618	8.6	51.5	23.2
Kangwŏn province	6,943	4.9	43.7	25.6
N. Ch'ungch'ŏng province	4,676	8.3	50.9	28.3
S. Ch'ungch'ŏng province	7,801	8.0	41.1	19.5
N. Chŏlla province	7,431	5.9	41.6	35.1
S. Chŏlla province	14,934	13.8	35.8	32.8
N. Kyŏngsang province	17,732	8.7	56.3	23.5
S. Kyŏngsang province	10,903	6.2	51.9	23.3
Cheju Island	1,943	6.9	54.2	7.6

Source: Ministry of Education, *Statistical Yearbook of Education 1975.*

Seoul and Pusan, although they are not the highest with respect to sending students onto the university, have much higher employment rates than the other provinces for their vocational school graduates.

Finally, one must consider the short period of history we are examining. If one dates the present educational structure from 1953, then the educational history of modern Korea extends only slightly more than twenty years. Graduates during that period are only now seeing their own children graduate from the lower levels in the system. Whatever discriminatory tendencies are built into the opportunity structure of the society favoring one class or region over another have not yet had time to be reproduced and reinforced. The equitable distribution of education and income in Korea might be most easily explained on that basis, that a stratification system has not had time yet to rebuild itself. It is reasonable to expect, given the history of other countries, that, as children from parents of one class or one region receive a higher quality education or greater chances for educational advancement and consequently higher incomes and status, educational opportunity and consequently incomes will become less equitably distributed than they are at present.

One policy option open to the government is to spend much more on support of secondary and higher education than it is doing currently (that is, to make attendance at these levels universal as well). But increased public investment in education means decreased public investment in the creation of physical capital. The choice is a hard one. Evidence that rates of return to education are not high relative to returns to physical capital investments and that rates of return *decline* as one goes up the educational ladder hardly encourages the government to expand its contribution to education. Another option is to adopt an incomes policy that keeps the rate of return to higher education low.

Expanded investment in secondary and higher education is especially unlikely if the *political* returns to that investment are not favorable to the present government. The next chapter discusses some of the non-economic functions of education in Korea, and notes the dilemma posed by modernization through education.

FIVE

Education as a Source of Values and Attitudes

Conducive to Modernization

In what ways do Koreans who receive education become different from the rest of their countrymen? Are they more "modern" in their outlook, more rational in their behavior, more radical in their perspective, more "development-oriented" in their values?

To this point we have looked at two kinds of information sometimes used to evaluate the modernizing impact of education. First, we have examined the extent to which the educational system has provided the quantity and quality of inputs one would expect to result in a change in the skills and attitudes of a country's population. We asked whether the form and content of the curriculum might be expected to "modernize." Second, we have provided information on the association existing between levels of education attained and economic states, both those of the individual and those of the nation as a whole. Because "modernization" of a citizenry is supposed to result in economic growth, it seemed reasonable to examine whether growth in education was associated with levels of incomes and national productivity.

Intervening between educational inputs and eventual outcomes are the *outputs* of education, those actual changes in individuals that can be associated with having received education. In this chapter we examine the degree to which educational attainment in Korea is associated with levels and kinds of *attitudes* that might be considered to be conducive to modernization.[1]

We begin by considering what attitudes could, in fact, contribute to the process of social and economic modernization. Then we pass to an examination of the evidence available on the association between level of educational attainment and attitudes. Much of the research that has been done focuses on *political* attitudes; we consider the extent to which education has contributed to the political "modernization" of the Korean citizen, and the impact of this on the political system of the country.

THEORIES OF MODERNIZATION
AND EDUCATION

Although theories of modernization vary in the extent to which they focus on causes of the process, there is general uniformity in the major dimensions of change. Black,[2] a historian, sees modernization as the adaptation of societal institutions to new functions emerging from increased knowledge. Societies are regarded as modern in the degree to which they have highly differentiated social and economic structures. Levy[3] identifies countries as modern in terms of the degree of use of inanimate as opposed to animate sources of power.[4] The process begins in a given country as a result of contact with a more modern society. Both imperialism and curiosity act to induce change in the less modern country, requiring adaptation (and often disintegration) of existing social structures in order to survive and to satisfy the increased appetites generated by contact with a more productive society.

No matter how the process starts, once under way it is irreversible. The adoption of technologies and customs from a more modern society requires increased role differentiation for individuals, and specialization of organizations.[5] Specialization of functions, for individuals and organizations, requires both a broader distribution of skills, particularly those of communication[6] and participation in groups, as well as the development of special talents in small numbers of people and organizations, and opportunities for these talents to emerge.[7] Increased specialization within the system means that persons and organizations become less self-reliant, more interdependent, and therefore require greater efforts toward integration and coordination or control. Integration is achieved through the development of a system of values and norms for behavior that are universally applied.[8] Coordination or control results, with the development of hierarchical systems with multiple layers. The growth of large, specialized organizations, interdependent with each other, makes money and markets increasingly important for purposes of communication. Finally, strong central governments emerge as the only means to hold the system together. Black states that "the concentration of effort required by economic and social transformation is focused primarily at the level of the political organized society, the national state or polity, rather than at the local or the international level."[9] He then goes on to describe graphically the importance of value integration (or homogeneity) as the means of legitimation of the national government:

The political consequences of this concentration of effort at the national level are reflected not only in administrative centralization but also in a significant intensification of nationalism. In the preceding phase, nationalism is concerned with independence and unification and reflects a spirit of freedom from traditional restraints and anticipation of new opportunities. In the period of economic and social transformation nationalism comes to represent a jealous concern of almost psychotic proportions for the security of one's own society and, at the same time, a systematic attack on loyalties of a local or ideological character that might threaten national cohesion.[10]

It goes without saying, of course, that the jealous concern is felt most keenly by those in power, and that the "local" or "ideological" loyalties that threaten national cohesion are always those held by those not in power but seeking to share it.[11]

Changes in the specialization and interdependence of organizations and people require changes in relationships, between social structures and between the individuals who form those structures. Levy lists six critical aspects to be changed. In the cognitive aspect, people and organizations must change from a traditional to a rational way of thinking. Criteria for membership in organizations change from particularistic to universalistic. The substantive definition of problems changes from diffuse (everything related to everything) to specific. Most (but not all) affective relationships change from intimacy to avoidance. People's goal orientations become more individualistic and the stratification system becomes increasingly hierarchical (with money or wealth becoming the main defining characteristic).

The views of modernization described above see education as one of many social institutions that change, and must change, as a result of the process of modernization. Because emphasis is on changes in the entire social system, no single institution is singled out as a major cause of or contributor to the process of modernization.

It is clear from what has been presented, however, that education can play an active, if not causal, role in the process of development of modern institutions and modern men. There are at least five (four suggested by Hannan[12]) ways in which education could have an impact on a national economy and policy. First, education could have direct effects on individuals, on their skills and attitudes, their productive motivation, their appetites as consumers, their docility as citizens. The aggregation of these individual changes could contribute to increased production, improved flow of communication, a more rationally ordered political and economic system, and so on.

Second, the expansion of education, that is the increase in numbers of "educated" people, can permit a reorganization of the social structure. Hannan suggests, for example, that expanding education allows employers to reduce the costs of searching for competent employees. Third, the growth of the educational organization itself can create general conditions for a more effective spread of information. "Educational expansion can be seen as an organizational investment in information processing capacity which has potential effects on economic development."[13] Education also could contribute to "activate" latent "modern" norms and values in individuals with no actual "value added." Finally, education can act as a selective mechanism picking out those individuals with skills and attitudes already present (or capable of being induced) that fit with the development needs of the society. These five contributions of education are not mutually exclusive and could operate together.

EDUCATION AND INDIVIDUAL MODERNITY

The most complete research effort to examine the outputs of education in terms of individual modernization is that of Inkeles.[14] Central to all Inkeles's work is his definition of the "modern man." Modernity in individuals is defined through certain attitudes and behaviors posited to be prerequisites for competent performance in modern society. Although shorter than others available, the following list of ten attributes captures the essence of individual modernity as Inkeles and his co-workers have defined it.

The modern man has a readiness for new experience and an openness to innovation and change. He is disposed to have opinions about a broad range of topics outside his environment. He is aware of the diversity of opinions of others, but does not necessarily accept their opinions. He is oriented to present or future time. He believes in planning as a way of handling his life. This, in turn, implies that he has a sense of efficacy, that is, a belief in his ability to dominate his environment in order to advance his own goals and purposes. Accordingly, he believes in a reasonably lawful world under human control. He is aware of the dignity of others and shows respect for them. He has faith in science and technology. And, finally, he believes in distributive justice, that is, to each according to his contribution.[15]

In presenting this definition, Inkeles took great pains to argue that he was not defining the modern man as contemporary, stating that these attitudes would have defined modernity a thousand years ago and will characterize the "modern" man of the future. The argument also was made that these attitudes do not represent an ideology, that the modern man would be as frequently encountered in a communist as in a capitalist society. Nor is modernity an attribute possessed only by the developed or Western nations, as it would be found in varying degrees in all cultures of the world.

The central hypotheses of the Inkeles research (which make it fundamentally different from McClelland's thesis) are that modern attitudes can be acquired in adulthood and that they are acquired through participation in certain kinds of organizations. The central instrument of the research is the OM (Overall Modernization) scale of attitudes, constructed after considerable analysis of the results of interviews with 6,000 persons in six countries. Scores on the OM scale are taken as indicators of modernity; they are predicted from individual variables such as age, sex, and intelligence, and from experiential variables such as schooling, employment, and exposure to the mass media.

The major findings are these. The most important determinant of modernity is years of schooling. Next most important is experience in factory employment or some non-industrial occupations. Third, exposure to the mass media is associated with higher levels of modernity. Summing up the results with regard to schooling, Inkeles concludes:

Those who had been in school longer were not only better informed and verbally more fluent. They had a different sense of time, and a stronger sense of personal and social efficacy; participated more actively in communal affairs; were more open to new ideas, new experiences, and new people; interacted differently with others, and showed more concern for subordinates and minorities. They valued science more, accepted change more rapidly, and were more prepared to limit the number of children they would have. In short, by virtue of having had more schooling, their personal character was decidedly more modern.[16]

The effects of factory employment were found to be independent of those of schooling and to compensate for a lack of education:

The longer men are in a factory, the smaller becomes the gap in their modernity scores, because the men with little education come, through their factory experience, to catch up with those of higher education. . . . Clearly, men who start out with little or no education also start with a psychosocial handicap in the form of low modernity scores. Yet if these same men succeed in getting into factories, they evidently can, in time, raise their modernity scores to the level of men with far more years of education who have as yet not had the additional benefit of factory experience.[17]

The clear suggestion here is that something about the school and the factory acts to make men more modern in their outlook. Being more "modern" leads to changes in economic behavior. Inkeles and Smith claim:

The modern man is quicker to adopt technical innovation, and more ready to implement birth control measures; he urges his son to go as far as he can in school and, if it pays better, encourages him to accept industrial work rather than to follow the more traditional penchant for office jobs; he informs himself about the goods produced in the more modern sector of the economy, and makes an effort to acquire them; and he permits his wife and daughter to leave the home for more active participation in economic life.[18]

What are the critical attributes of factory and school that make them effective agents of individual modernization? First, it may be important to recognize that some non-industrial forms of employment generate as much modernity as factory employment. Men employed as cabdrivers, newspaper vendors, barbers, and street hawkers, hardly what one would consider "modern sector" jobs, show relatively high levels of modernity according to Inkeles.

Second, the impact of school or factory does not appear to be a function of the degree of modernity of the individual school or factory. Qualities of the school or factory are much less important than the amount of time spent by the person in the institution. Smith and Inkeles argue that *curriculum,* considered by educators to be the core of education, has at best a minor role in generating modernity. Claiming that they know of no curriculum that provides formal instruction in the elements of modern behavior (for example, how to join an organization, how to be open to new experiences, the positive benefits of birth control), they argue that the impact of the school lies in its distinctive nature as a social organization. The modernizing impact of the school comes not so much through formal instruction in academic subjects as through a more general socialization process:

> School starts and stops at fixed times each day. Within the school day there generally is a regular sequence for ordering activities: singing, reading, writing, drawing, all have their scheduled and generally invariant times. Teachers generally work according to a plan, a pattern they are rather rigorously taught at normal school . . . The principle of planning may, of course, also be inculcated more directly through reward and punishment, as when pupils are punished for being late, marked down for not getting their papers in on time, and held after school for infractions of the rules.[19]

The parallel between the socializing structure of the school and that of the factory is obvious and need not be drawn out. What is critical is not so much the *content* of the experience as the degree of organization that obtains, to which the student or worker is subjected. The more organized the set of experiences, the more impact they should have upon the individual.

As Carnoy[20] has pointed out, this makes increased industrialization and longer schooling "a useful development strategy once the structural changes take place that enable mass modernization to proceed." That is, *once* a country is in a position to build its educational and industrial organizations so that they can operate to socialize their members, *then* the spread of these organizations will contribute to the generation of attitudes conducive to adoption of innovations and measures associated with economic development. Carnoy notes that Inkeles does not claim that increased modernity directly generates economic growth, only that it fosters the conditions under which it can take place. The same position was taken by Leibenstein earlier:

> Education in its broadest sense creates not only specific skills but also attitudes about the desirability of certain activities and about the value of education itself. It is quite likely that these attitudes are more important in fostering economic development than are the specific skills created directly by the educational process.[26]

And it could be argued that modern attitudes do not "foster" development so much as they facilitate attainment of the objectives of certain development strategies.

EDUCATION AND POLITICAL ATTITUDES IN KOREA

Inkeles's results, then, make it possible to continue to argue that the expansion of education in Korea from 1945 (or even earlier under the Japanese) could have contributed to the rapid economic modernization of the country. This contribution would be made, however, not so much through the training of scarce "human resources" as through the inculcation in a much larger proportion of the population of attitudes conducive to industrial employment, a new set of consumer behaviors, and political stability.

The results also would suggest that education and industrialization both contributed to individual modernization, *pari passu*. But if one takes this position, then it is difficult to argue that education was a prime contributor to economic growth. One could just as well argue that economic growth through industrialization (for example, under the Japanese) contributed to individual modernization and hence to a higher demand for education. We will return to this problem in the last chapter.

Individual modernization could be a mixed blessing from the national government's perspective. From what has been reviewed earlier, it is clear that Korea's leadership sought to control the value content of education as it expanded, to use education to promote some modern ideas (such as economic productivity) while avoiding others (such as those associated with full citizen participation in Western democracy). Analysing President Park's 1971 book, *To Build a Nation*, Ross Harold Cole concludes:

> Even though members of South Korea's ruling elite were Western-trained they fostered the adoption of only those Western ideals that would contribute to the progress of the country economically. The social, political and cultural aspects of the Korean culture were generally retained. Korea's great economic boom is pointed to as the result of the inculcation of the attitudes of productivity. President Park hopes to keep just *the economic ideas* imported from America in the citizenship education program. He does not want to inculcate what he considers to be the attendant evils of American individualism, materialism and public criticism of government and public officials.[22]

But if Inkeles is right, this hope was doomed to failure, as the very experience of education, especially an education as well-organized and disciplined as that of Korea, would have the effect of modernizing students not only in terms of productive attitudes, but also political attitudes. Inkeles reports that men high on the OM scale are much more active politically, more likely to join organizations, to vote, to contact governmental and political agencies.

As Portes puts it, the secular orientation of modernity is not conductive to support for a developmentalist ideology:

> The success of ideology in promoting support for developmental efforts depends on a general psychological predisposition in the mass of the population. [But] traditional and seemingly apathetic groups are more receptive to development ideologies than those exposed to extensive modernization. Modernity not only encourages the pursuit of individualistic fulfillment but also stresses rationality and distrust of ideological appeals, be they religious or political. "Moderns" may be too sophisticated to believe in developmental miracles.[23]

In a society whose leaders seek to avoid political controversy, where ideological loyalty and national unification are primary values, these "modern" men might well prove to be a source of difficulty for the government. This would be especially true if a government decides to forego the benefits of open democracy in order to insure complete control over political action. We might expect to find, then, that with more education Koreans become more critical of their government and less compliant with its demands.

EDUCATION AND
SOCIAL AND POLITICAL ATTITUDES

Before reviewing evidence to test that hypothesis, we should first determine whether, in Korea, educational attainment is associated with modern attitudes. One set of data is from a 1972 sample survey of Korean men.[24] Because the definitions of "modern" and "modernization" differ slightly from those described earlier, they are presented in some detail. Kim and Kim define modernizing culture in terms of four distinguishable facets of orientation: anomie, Machiavellianism, civic culture, and legal-rational assumptions.

1) *Anomie.* The concept of anomie indicates a condition of normlessness or failure of individuals to agree on and to follow the rules of society. In this study, anomie is measured in terms of a person's confidence or sureness about the social norms and

principles he should follow, and clarity about the pattern of mutual expectations, that is, what he can expect of other people. Anomie connotes a condition in which no strong normative order guides a person's activities or gives him a sense that his life is worthwhile. High anomie would seem contrary to individual modernity.

2) *Machiavellianism.* This is conceived of as a belief that one should suspend honesty, virtue, and trust in the pursuit of power and in getting what he wants. The syndrome is not unknown in social life in historical as well as industrialized countries. Kim and Kim believe that a substantial amount of trust in the probity and goodwill of others is essential for social integration, and therefore that Machiavellianism is bad.[25] To measure the propensity to Machiavellianism, Kim and Kim assessed individual attitudes toward the powerful, views of the proposition that "one should use all possible ways and means to get what he wants," and feelings of generalized distrust in fellow men.

3) *Civic Culture.* This reflects an interest in public affairs and a challenging spirit against injustice expressed through participation in civic action in regard to political and governmental processes. The index of civic culture used here is a measure not of the objective conditions of society but of the individual's willingness to exercise his rights. It clearly is associated with modernity.

4) *Charismatic versus Legal-Rational Orientation.* Rule by charisma or personal whim seems to have been increasingly replaced by legal-rational rules in political and governmental processes. The index is based on an implicit assumption that a prerequisite of political development is a commitment on the part of the population to a rational structure of rules and regulations.

Table 50 presents the specific questions used by Kim and Kim in their research and Table 51 shows the distribution of affirmative responses for each of the four value categories. These responses are tabulated according to age, level of

TABLE 50   Attributes of a Modernizing Culture

Syndromes	Attributes
1) Anomie	a). Since there are not any absolute principles which must be adhered to, in order to live, it is better to live according to the situation. (agree-disagree)
	b). The world is changing so fast that it is often difficult to distinguish what is right and what is wrong. (agree-disagree)
	c). I often wonder why I should continue living. (agree-disagree)
	d). There are so many divided opinions that I often do not know which one to believe. (agree-disagree)
2) Machiavellianism	a). Many people think that, in order for a person to get what he wants, he should use all possible ways and means. (agree-disagree)
	b). Whether you like or dislike a person who is powerful, it is good to become a good friend of him. (agree-disagree)
	c). It is better not to say anything if your words might be damaging to you. (agree-disagree)
	d). A person who easily trusts other people's words will eventually suffer. (agree-disagree)
3) Civic Culture	a). It is unnecessary to obey an unjust law. (agree-disagree)
	b). If the National Assembly plans to make a law which will be either unfavorable or unfair towards you, you must petition to try to prevent it. (agree-disagree)
	c). When you have a difficult problem at a government office, (you will try to meet with others who also feel that they have been mistreated or have been victimized and establish measures to meet the situation; or you will be quiet and do nothing

(continued)

TABLE 50 (continued)

Syndromes	Attributes
	because if you raise a clamor it will be more harmful to you).
	d). A purpose of the court is to prevent citizens from harmful government action. (agree-disagree)
4) Charismatic vs. Legal-Rational Orientation	a). To have a good society, it is more important to have a good leader than to have good laws. (agree-disagree)

education, intergenerational social mobility, and a self-report of standard of living.

Overall the data suggest that Koreans tend to distrust each other, feel normless, feel inefficacious as citizens, and prefer charismatic leadership to a "rule of law." About 72 percent of the people interviewed responded affirmatively to the statements included under Anomie, 74 percent agreed that is is more important to have a good leader than to have good laws, 67 percent *dis*agreed with the statements under the Civic Culture rubric and 85 percent agreed with the Machiavellianism items.

There are, however, some interesting variations in attitudinal scales depending on age, education, social mobility, and standard of living. Consider, first, the relationships between these structural indicators of one's position in society and the syndromes of transitory culture most germane to social integration, Machiavellianism and anomie. The younger generation, born after the Korean War, seem more scrupulous about power than the older group, while the middle-aged fall in the middle. A similar pattern of relationship appears between age and anomie. The older generation reports an acute sense of normlessness, perhaps because they find that their traditional moral ethos is increasingly being undermined by new social habits practiced by other groups. Sixty-seven percent of those below age 30, 71 percent between 30 and 44, and 79 percent above 45 indicated

TABLE 51 Percentage agreement with Attributes of Modernizing Culture
Male Only (N=1088)
1972 Nationwide Interview Survey

	(N)	(N=783) Anomie	(N=801) Charisma	(N=354) Citizenship	(N=927) Machiavellianism
Age	19–29 (332)	67 (72%)	71 (74%)	40 (33%)	82 (85%)
	30–44 (444)	71	74	30	85
	45–65 (312)	79	76	27	89
Education	None or Little (361)	82	78	26	82
	Middle or High (470)	74	72	32	85
	College (257)	54	71	42	89
Mobility	Downward (150)	65	65	40	80
	No Change (888)	73	75	31	86
	Upward (50)	74	76	46	82
Standard of Living	Low (426)	65	76	32	87
	Middle (631)	73	73	33	84
	High (31)	74	58	29	87

that there are no absolute principles governing social relations; they are confused about what is right and what is wrong, and fatalistic in their conception of personal life.

Education is related to Machiavellianism in a positive linear way, while it is inversely correlated with anomie. The more educated one is, the more one agrees that is it all right to seek power by any means that work. On the other hand, as one advances up the educational ladder, there is an increased sense of personal efficacy; only 54 percent of the college-educated group report feelings of anomie, compared to 82 percent of those with little or no education.

Intergenerational social mobility is related to the two major syndromes of social integration. A great majority of those polled, 82 percent, belong to the category in which the occupational status between themselves and their fathers has not changed substantially. Only a tiny fraction of the sample (5 percent) moved up higher on the ladder of occupational prestige from the position occupied by their parents. Those who didn't advance any higher than their fathers feel least anomic. Differences as a result of social mobility are not large.

Contrary to what some modernization theorists might predict, the sense of normlessness increases as the standard of living improves, while the poor, in their approach toward power and social life, tend to be as Machiavellian in their attitudes as the rich.

These findings suggest that education definitely increases one's sense of personal efficacy and enhances enterprising social behavior. The Kim and Kim data indicate a generally low level of civic culture and high expectation for charismatic authority. This tendency might be related to a condition in which social relations among men appear to be regulated neither by trust nor by normative principles but presumably by political power alone.

On top of the civic scale stand the young, college-educated, and upwardly mobile, while the old, the uneducated, and the poor fall at the bottom. A small number of people in the upwardly mobile category seem ready to challenge unfavorable legal measures in politics in a more assertive manner based on informed opinion about legal institutions. But more than half the people in the upwardly mobile group took positions in favor of passive withdrawal from active civic participation.

In summary, the results of this research suggest that Korean education *does* have a significant impact on attitudes toward social and political life. There is, for example, a clear difference between what college graduates feel and the rest of the population feel. Those with more education demonstrate a higher regard for civic action, feel less confused about the ways in which social interactions should be regulated, and are more favorably inclined toward the use of legal (as opposed to charismatic) authority to build the new social order. They are also, however, most inclined to state that power should be taken by whatever means possible. We should expect to find, therefore, that with more education people are more critical of authoritarianism and centralization in the present government, and more likely to engage in opposition to that government.

EDUCATION AND
ATTITUDES TOWARD THE GOVERNMENT

In general, education in Korea, as elsewhere, increases politicization. It heightens public awareness, civic sensitivity, and a sense of social efficacy. Young-ho Lee,[26] for example, found that the more the Koreans are educated, the more they tend to be politically oriented. They also are more concerned about national issues.

Education does not necessarily lead to support for democracy. While Korean students in the late 1960s seemed to support democracy as an ideal political system, they were split almost down the middle on its suitability to Korea. Various surveys tend to support the view that college students were sharply divided on the issue. T'ae-gil Kim[27] asked 1,604 students across the nation in 1964 whether they would "starve under democracy" if they had to "for the sake of democracy even if dictatorship might improve the standard of living"; 46 percent of those polled said they would, while 43 percent said they would not. Commitment to democracy varied little with the class background of these students. Four years later, Sŏng-jik Hong[28] asked similar questions of 1,895 college students spread over 12 universities, with similar results. Thirty percent of the group expressed the view that Western democracy is suitable to Korea because it helps to foster individual liberty and national modernization, but 38 percent disagreed by reason of the cultural and social uniqueness of Korea. Almost one-third of Hong's group revealed an ambivalent attitude toward the issue, saying that democracy is suitable in some areas but not in other areas. A 1970 survey of students' opinions on democracy[29] reported that 40 percent of the 135 students interviewed felt that democracy is unsuitable to Korea while the rest disagreed with the notion. A 40–60 split also held for the proposition "Political freedom is less important than material well-being."

At the same time, increased education leads to less trust in the *government*. This is true for workers as well as for students. Sae-gu Chung[30] found that trust in the government starts high in the 5th grade and declines steadily. The loss of trust is greatest in terms of belief in the morality of government, less with respect to whether the government operates for the benefit of the people. Chi-Young Ham[31] also reports that trust in government declines with education. He asked 1,878 students in primary, middle, and high schools, 412 of their parents, and 247 teachers to tell him who should bear the heaviest responsibility for the failure of democracy in Korea, the people or the politicians. Almost five times as many of the primary school students assigned responsibility for the failure of democracy to the people as blamed the politicians. The proportion declined steadily in the upper grades, and was lowest among parents and teachers, who distributed the blame equally.

Se-jin Kim interviewed 9,171 workers in 52 industrial plants to determine their sense of political efficacy. He describes the typical worker in these large modern plants as having "eleventh grade education (1st year high school), about 26 years of age, monthly income of about seventeen thousand wǒn ($42.50), some degree of technical skill, and considerable rural orientation."[32] Arranging workers by their level of education, from primary to college, Kim reports a declining belief among the workers as to their ability to influence political decision-making, and less trust in elections.

From primary school to the college level, national concerns are widespread, but support for governmental policies varies inversely with the number of years of formal education. Pollsters in 1973 asked 1,284 youngsters questions about anti-communism and the government's modernization policies, among other topics.[33] In most of these queries, the younger members of the sample showed affirmative attitudes while the more advanced students, especially college youth, indicated strong dissent on grounds of patriotism.[34]

STUDENT CRITICISM OF THE GOVERNMENT

There are at least two possible explanations of the negative association between level of education and support of the present government. One type of explanation turns on the expectations that students have about the benefits education will bring them. The second turns on the roles vis-à-vis political participation that are assigned to students, university students in particular, in Korean society.

EDUCATION AND EMPLOYMENT

Around the world, "modern" education leads to expectations on the part of graduates that they will be offered or find employment befitting the new status they have acquired. "Educated unemployment," the newest nightmare facing the educational policy-maker, is often ascribed to the aspirations induced by education itself. These aspirations vary in terms of the status and economic rewards associated with the particular level and type of education completed, and the fit between the job offered and the type of education or training received in school. If it were always the case, as the most simplistic version of the education-as-an-engine-of-development theory has it, that the availability of educated human resources results in increased and more modern economic activity, then graduates' expectations would always be met. We would find that graduates do, in fact, get the kind of employment they expect, both because educational institutions socialize them properly and because the economy has expanded to take advantage of the skills offered by the new graduates.

But that happy outcome depends on a direct response of education to occupational opportunities (or the needs of the economy), rather than to other pressures. If education is, in fact, controlled by "social demand" forces, it is possible for the system to produce graduates much more rapidly than they can be absorbed into the economy in positions consistent with graduates' expectations. As we have seen in previous chapters, the educational system of Korea historically has grown more rapidly than the economy. Numbers of graduates, especially at the secondary and higher education levels in the early 1960s, have increased more rapidly than the capacity of the labor force to absorb them at conventional or expected levels of occupational status. One result, a short-term phenomenon, is unemployment, as graduates do not find jobs that meet their expectations. A longer-term consequence is feelings of frustration, as graduates are forced to take jobs of lower status and economic reward than expected, often with tasks and settings different from those for which training was received.

Table 52 suggests the extent to which graduates of Seoul National University were able to find jobs compatible with their training during the period 1958–1969. As can be seen, liberal arts graduates increasingly over the period felt that their training was not compatible with their current occupation. While 60 percent of university graduates in 1958 found occupations that were highly compatible with their majors, only 15

TABLE 52 Occupational Compatibility with College Majors: Graduates from the College of Arts and Sciences, Seoul National University, 1958–1969

Question: To what extent is your current occupation compatible with your college major?

	Liberal Arts & Social Sciences (including 85 females)			Natural, Physical and Applied Sciences (including 104 females)		
Year	Highly Compatible	Somewhat Compatible	Little or No Relevance (N)	Highly Compatible	Somewhat Compatible	Little or No Relevance (N)
1958	60	20	20 (70)	83	6	11 (96)
1959	53	23	22 (61)	85	7	8 (85)
1960	47	17	36 (151)	77	9	14 (89)
1961	43	20	37 (163)	84	2	14 (108)
1962	43	19	38 (121)	73	10	17 (95)
1963	44	23	33 (206)	70	9	21 (116)
1964	44	25	31 (221)	75	9	16 (141)
1965	39	24	37 (239)	73	6	21 (146)
1966	41	17	42 (168)	70	14	16 (111)
1967	46	27	27 (91)	57	18	25 (73)
1968	36	19	45 (120)	68	9	23 (81)
1969	15	10	75 (54)	70	5	25 (66)
Total (N)	(720)	(359)	(586) (1,665)	(898)	(101)	(208) (1,207)
% average	43%	22%	35% 100%	74%	8%	18% 100%

Source: Sungkwun Im and Kwanyong Rhee, "A Preliminary Study on the Occupational State of Graduates," *Seoul National University Research Review* 8.1: 31–42 (June 1971).

percent were able to do so in 1969. A similar, but less marked, trend is found for graduates in the natural, physical, and applied sciences. In those areas, while 83 percent of 1958 graduates found compatible employment, only 70 percent were able to do so in 1969. Seoul National University is the most prestigious university in Korea, and it could be assumed that its graduates would have first choice of job openings in the labor market. It would follow, then, that graduates of other universities experienced even greater problems in finding employment compatible with their university education.

More detailed information, based not on self-report but on the actual fit between education and employment, is presented in Table 53, which compares the occupations of graduates of the SNU College of Agriculture between 1955 and 1969. Few if any graduates now go into teaching, which might be a reflection of the expansion of teacher-training institutes at the secondary level. Government employment in agriculture-related jobs peaked in the early 1960s but declined to an overall low in 1969. Only study abroad and employment in the police or military have increased during the 15-year period, suggesting that occupational opportunities, for these graduates at least, are few in proportion to the supply of graduates.

THE SOCIAL MEANING OF EDUCATION

Unemployed graduates could well have developed antagonisms towards the government for failure to create the conditions under which they would obtain the employment "deserved." But it is likely that education has a much more important significance than job preparation in Korean society, and that the economists' explanation of disaffection on the part of the educated is only partial.

Both Korean students and adults in general tend to place more emphasis on "moralistic" aspects of education than they do on education as professional training. For example, Hichul Henry Whang[35] asked members of Provincial Boards of Education, teachers, and parents (selected to represent Seoul and a rural

TABLE 53 Occupational Fields of Graduates from College of Agriculture,
Seoul National University, 1955–1969

(row percentages)

	Farming	Teacher	Government Official in Agricultural Areas	Government Official in Non-Agricultural Areas	Self-Employed	Company Clerk	Study Abroad	Police, Soldier, Military Service	Others	Total (N)
1955	7	32	23	3	7	11	3	13	1	100% (187)
1956	8	35	21	4	11	14	2	5	0	100% (254)
1957	7	23	28	6	11	17	2	2	4	100% (258)
1958	6	22	39	4	13	8	4	2	2	100% (228)
1960	5	22	43	9	7	8	5	1	0	100% (252)
1961	9	18	35	8	8	10	8	2	2	100% (220)
1962	6	5	49	5	12	13	7	2	1	100% (200)
1963	5	8	40	8	12	16	8	1	2	100% (301)
1964	8	9	38	6	6	19	9	3	2	100% (348)
1965	7	4	26	6	6	19	9	21	2	100% (307)
1966	5	2	24	11	6	19	10	18	5	100% (211)
1967	8	1	33	3	6	12	7	24	6	100% (157)
1968	3	1	18	5	3	10	8	51	1	100% (154)
1969	4	2	13	3	4	12	15	47	0	100% (165)
Total (N)	(202)	(427)	(1015)	(202)	(273)	(459)	(215)	(367)	(82)	(3,242)

Source: Sung Kwun Im and Kwanyong Rhee.

area) to indicate their priorities among a set of 16 goal statements for primary and secondary education, such as "Understanding the role of various family members," or "Loyalty to
Korea and the Korean way of life." The 16 statements can be
classified into four categories of goals or functions: Intellecutal,
Social, Personal, and Productive. Each of the three groups in the
study gave highest priority to Intellectual goals, and lowest to
Production goals. The major tasks for primary education were
assigned to the areas of Communication of Knowledge and Moral
Integrity. The highest priority tasks for secondary education
were Cooperation in Day-to-Day Relations, Moral Integrity, and
the Creation of Knowledge. Differences among the three groups
of judges were slight. Lowest priority at both the primary and
secondary levels was given to Vocational Training and Selection,
and to Consumer Skills. These data suggest that, if parents and
local educators believe education has some contribution to make
to economic development, it is not to be made through training
in specific skills or knowledge about economic processes or
national needs.

University students tend to conceive of the purpose of higher
education primarily in terms of cultivating one's "virtue." The
pursuit of knowledge is secondary to this primary orientation.
Students are concerned primarily about social values, or the
perceived lack of them. Since 1960, researchers have been asking
university freshmen almost every year to indicate what they
consider the most valuable pursuit one could commit oneself to,
not only in college but throughout one's life. The questions
asked range from Health to Social Values, each broken down
into several more specific questions. Table 54 summarizes the
results of these surveys from 1960 to 1972. In the 1960s,
students were largely concerned about individual matters such
as Friendship and Personality (read "Virtue"). Academism came
next. But in the 1970s, students born and reared after the
Korean War have begun to identify social mores as the most
troubling concern. A large majority of the respondents now

TABLE 54 Changing Value Concerns of Korean College
Students, 1960–1972
(rank order based on percentage scale)

	(1) 1960	(2) 1966	(3)[a] 1967	(4) 1968	(5) 1968	(6) 1969	(7)[a] 1971	(8) 1972
Health	5	5	7	6	8	7	8	7
Personality	2	2	3	4	4	2	4	4
Familism	8	8	6	8	6	8	6	8
Academism	4	4	2	2	2	3	2	2
Friendship	1	1	1	1	1	1	3	3
Love	7	7	8	7	7	6	7	6
Employment	6	6	5	5	3	5	5	5
Social Values	3	3	4	3	5	4	1	1
(N)	210	1,207	2,876	1,237	1,089	2,280	2,849	1,366

Sources: (1), (2), (4): Kwanyong Rhee, "A Study on Mooney Problem Check List,"
Research Review, Seoul National University 7:2 (June 1970),
p. 29.
(3): Central Education Research Institute, A Comprehensive Study on the
Contents of Higher Education (Seoul, 1967), p. 57.
(5): Kyungbuk University, Research Review, 1968, p. 19.
(6): Ehwa University, Student Guidance Center, Research Review, 1969,
p. 6.
(7): Sukmyong University, Student Guidance Center, Problems of Korean
College Students and Some Approaches in Guidance and Counseling,
1971, p. 10.
(8): Sukmyong University, Student Guidance Center, Research Review,
1973, p. 9.

Note: [a]Nationwide samples. Other studies were based on responses from respective
college population.

consistently expresses concern about "the decay of moral
ethos," "lack of unifying cultural movement," and "anomie."
Next most important in their minds is the pursuit of
knowledge. Such issues as Love, Employment, Health, and
Family all ranked generally low throughout the period. These
findings suggest that the meaning of higher education as
interpreted by Korean students is largely traditional (but not
necessarily antithetical to development) in the sense of its stress
on the individual's moralistic cultivation, pursuit of knowledge,
and social harmony.

Another survey conducted in 1964[36] is basically compatible with the annual freshman survey in its major conclusion. Asked "Which one of the following values will you choose to pursue in life?" about one-third of the 1,660 students first chose Virtue. For the entire sample, cross-cutting sex, class, and regional backgrounds, Virtue stood out as the most important personal goal in life. Knowledge came second, Wealth third and National Service fourth for the male group. (See a condensed summary in Table 55.) After Health and Longevity, Love and Friendship seemed important to most of these groups. Personal Fame and Power were at the bottom of the scale. One gets a strong impression from these studies that the ideal image of society and the role of education in it held by contemporary students is almost identical to that advocated by their Confucian scholarly ancestors several hundred years ago. "The moral codes of Korean students," Rettig and his associates[37] found, "are more severe than those of the American students, in spite of the fact that the majority of Korean students profess no religious group membership." In 1959 and again in 1962, some 500 students of Seoul National University and an equal number of American students at Ohio State University were asked to judge 50 moral issues. The heirarchy of moral judgments did not differ much in the two studies, but Korean students increased sharply in economic morality between 1959 and 1962.[38]

Additional evidence strongly supports the view that the manner in which Korean students judge moral issues, ranging from premarital sex to human rights, has become rigidified over the years. Korean researchers found in 1960, for example, that the college youth who had just overthrown the Rhee regime were as rigid in their mental framework as the Tories in England. In this survey, as in a study by H. J. Eysenck,[39] moral attitudes were measured in terms of positive or negative responses to 60 questions on a rigidity-flexibility (or toughmindedness versus tendermindedness) scale, the average percentage difference taken as the position of the group on the dimension. The moral judgment of Korean youth, measured in this way, seems

TABLE 55 Students' Values
Which one of the following values will you choose to pursue in life?
(rank order based on percentage scale)

	Male	Female	Family Class Background			Regional Background		
			High	Middle	Low	Seoul	Town	Rural
Health and Longevity	5	8	6	6	3	7	5	3
Knowledge	2	4	3	3	2	3	3	2
Virtue	1	1	1	1	1	1	1	1
Wealth	3	7	5	4	6	4	6	6
Friendship	7	3	4	5	5	6	4	5
Love	6	2	2	2	4	2	2	4
Fame	12	12	12	12	12	12	12	12
Power	9	11	10	11	11	11	10	11
National Contribution	4	9	8	8	7	9	8	7
Creative Work	8	5	7	7	8	5	7	8
Escape from Reality	11	10	11	10	10	10	11	10
Religious Life	10	6	9	9	9	8	9	9
(N)	(915)	(745)	(554)	(823)	(205)	(514)	(482)	(586)

Source: Condensed from T'ae-gil Kim, pp. 245–268.

to have become more and more rigid between 1960 and 1968 (see Table 56).

Seen in the light of these findings, Korean student criticism of the government appears to be largely an effort to improve the system in keeping with underlying cultural and ideological values. Student dissent is *not* unorthodox in the sense of questioning the basic ideological values, but rather conservative and orthodox. It does not seem likely that complaints stem principally from unsatisfied job ambitions.

TABLE 56 Ideological Dimensions of Korean Students Compared with Original Eysenck Results

| | *Dimensions* | |
Korean Students	*Conservative-Radical*	*Rigidity-Flexibility*
1960 (N=281)	5.7	14.1
1966 (N=233)	5.5	11.6
1968 (N=5,883)	5.5	11.7
1957 Eysenck Study:		
Fascists (N=250)	7.0	8.4
Conservative (N=250)	5.3	14.2
Socialist (N=250)	10.3	14.2
Liberal (N=250)	7.0	17.3

Sources: Eysenck; Ch'ang-yŏng Chŏng and Myŏng-hwi Kim, "Hyŏngmyŏng ŭi simnihak," *Han'guk ilbo,* September 19, 1960; Michyun Choi, "Social Attitudes of Yonsei and Korea University Students," unpublished MA thesis, Korea University, 1971; Yong-sin Chŏn, "Han'guk taehaksaeng ŭi chŏngch'i-jŏk t'aedo," *Koryŏ Taehakkyo nonmunjip* 15:33–51 (1969).

Note: Eysenck's scales are based on responses to a series of questions. In the Conservative-Radical dimension, low=conservative attitudes. In the Rigidity-Flexibility dimension, low=rigid attitudes.

THE SOCIAL ROLE OF THE UNIVERSITY STUDENT

To understand this more clearly one has to look at how Korean society traditionally has defined the role of the university student. Students were the vanguard against the Japanese imperialists in 1919. Student-led riots provoked the overthrow of Syngman Rhee. Activism in politics is expected of students in time of crisis. The reasoning that it is their right and duty to "rise up" seems firmly institutionalized in Korean culture. In numerous statements prepared by students themselves on various occasions, including the dramatic uprising against the Rhee Administration in 1960, the message is clear. Korean students, as the guardians of national consciousness, want to be an integral part of national development. Available evidence indicates that they have a definite conception of their political role and firm ideas about their action.

A clear majority (68 to 80 percent) of the 2,923 student respondents to the 1970 survey believed that university students have the responsibility to participate in social and political issues.[40] They stated that they definitely are the elite of the society, that the political and social views of the educated should be reflected more closely in politics than should those of the less educated. Students saw their own views on politics and social issues as legitimate and valid, and argued that conscientious participation in the political movement to bring about social justice is more important than the study of academic subjects.

For various reasons, student dissent constantly has run up against militant suppression by the government. There has been a cycle of dissent-revolt-suppression-dissent almost continuously since 1945. Being unable to develop a radical ideology of nationalism and confined within the contours of a conservative, anti-Communist political tradition, the student movement has become a major social force against the existing regime largely on *moral* grounds. Sustained by the legacy of Confucian tradition and reinforced by formal socialization, the ideas of moralistic elitism vitalize political activism. Political participation in various forms of protest, including street demonstrations and passive resistance, seems to stem from a belief that studenthood is a moral embodiment of national consciousness, and that existing leadership and institutions are illegitimate as a result of their failure to live up to the principles of democratic nationalism. When students were asked to rate the performance of major political institutions, including the presidency, National Assembly, political party system, and electoral system, along a trust-distrust and worst-best scale, the system failed miserably in all categories. Three-quarters of those polled said that the intellectuals remain silent before injustices and corruption out of fear for their security. A resounding 72 percent agreed with the statement "For the sake of national development, the old generation must be replaced by a new generation."[41]

The more naive the patriotism—characteristic of those students who came to cities from provincial areas with ambitious dreams —the higher the sense of national humiliation runs in the bloodstream of the youth. It is not surprising, therefore, to discover the source of student activism in education-related urbanization. Protest movements invariably are led by successful candidates in major universities of Seoul who have come from provincial areas. Similarly, activism is usually strong in universities in which the proportion of migrant students is high.

The basis of support for the student movement also is not in urban areas but in the provinces. The idea that students "should participate in political and social activities" seems prevalent among the rural population. It is most likely that the activists are implicitly inspired by the moral support rendered to the successful students of their own community. As we see in Table 57, the degree of support for the student movement is highest among farmers (supposedly the least modernized group in society). While only a small percentage of military personnel, businessmen, and professors indicate active support, more than one-third of the farmers in the poll sample said they actively endorse student activism.

EDUCATION AND ITS
RELATIONSHIP TO "DEVELOPMENT"

In general, the studies that have been reviewed in this chapter support the assertion that education in Korea has some

TABLE 57 Social Support of Students' Political and Social
Activities by Social Groups, 1965
(row percentages)

Question: To what degree do you think college students should participate
in political and social activities?

	Active	Intermediate	Passive	Others	Total (N)
Army Cadets, Freshmen	13	47	37	3	100% (174)
Army Cadets, Seniors	6	37	56	1	100% (161)
Military Officers	10	37	46	7	100% (194)
Farmers	35	28	20	17	100% (352)
Businessmen	11	40	46	3	100% (261)
Professors	15	51	28	6	100% (392)

Source: Condensed from Sung Chick Hong, *The Intellectual and Modernization*
(Seoul, 1967).

modernizing effects on individuals. Persons with higher levels of
education appear to have more confidence in their ability to
affect their social and political environment, and to believe that
society is best when ruled by laws instead of by charismatic
individuals. Those persons who have gone further in the educational system are more likely to express concern about national
issues, to be concerned with justice, and to have a future
orientation. All of these relationships are consistent with what
Inkeles suggests are the modernizing outcomes of education, and
the changes induced are consistent with those that theorists say
are necessary for a country to modernize.

On the other hand, the research presented also suggests that
some of the modernizing influences that education has on
individuals are inconsistent with social trends and specific
government policies and actions and therefore may not contribute to economic development. To the extent that close
government control is necessary for, or a major factor in, the
organization and modernization of the Korean economy,
educational outputs that lead to challenges of the government's
authority and legitimacy do not contribute to societal modernization. Study after study shows that with increased education

Koreans have less confidence in their government and attribute less legitimacy to it. Student dissent, often in the form of violent behavior, is one manifestation of this phenomenon. It is scholars and intellectuals who are jailed by the Park Government, accused of subversion, rather than members of the working class or persons with lower levels of education.[42] If one is willing to accept that dissent against the government is at least a potential threat to government-controlled development plans, then education can be said to have some counterproductive aspects.

Some persons, viewing these findings, might wish to conclude that the problem is simply one of imbalance between levels of development in various sectors of the Korean society. For example, if it could be argued that the economy has modernized more rapidly than education (or vice-versa), then perhaps civil dissent and violence can be traced to these unequal rates of growth. Increased government effort to modernize education (or the economy) would, if this perspective were correct, result in a reduction of tensions (and increased development).

A study by Sofranko and Bealer[43] suggests that unequal rates of modernization across different sectors of a society are not related to levels of violence. They found no relationship between "imbalance scores" for political, economic, educational, social welfare, and communication modernization, and the frequency of civil disturbances in 75 countries. In other words, a more balanced pattern of development across sectors does not guarantee less resistance to government policies.

A more likely explanation is that there are different types and strategies of development, and that what is functional for a given development strategy may be dysfunctional for another. The set of values espoused in the visions of modernization championed by Black, Levy, Inkeles and others are drawn from the political and social history of the United States and Western Europe. These countries followed a particular path toward development in which a given type of social structure and political process was functional. The "modernizing" influence

216

of education, with its tendency to stimulate individual creativity and independence of action, might well be functional in a capitalist economy in which social stratification and class differences in access to power are justified in terms of "merit" or "intelligence." Inkeles notes that modernity is much like a kind of *social* intelligence. The question is whether this "intelligence" is functional in all situations, or whether there may be some kinds of development patterns in which this particular combination of intelligence contributes neither to individual welfare nor to the welfare of the total society. (In such a case, of course, the issue should become whether that pattern of development is worth the social costs entailed.)

SIX

Education and the Development of Korea

Analysis and interpretation of the relationship between education and development is a troubled, unsettled area of intellectual inquiry. Manpower requirements analysis, international comparisons, even the cost/benefit approach have all had their days. Each has illuminated a part of the "true" picture, but obscured other parts. In desperation, perhaps, skeptics have turned to "sociological" theories that stress the "screening" or "acculturation" functions of education. One effect has been to reduce sharply the number of writers who still use terms such as "human capital" and "human resources as the wealth of nations." Most specialists in the field are unsure about what these terms mean and what relationship they bear to education. But the new approaches also afford only partial explanations.

In this final chapter we summarize the arguments and evidence to support various views of how education may have contributed to the development of Korea. We ask two major questions: How much and in what ways has education contributed to Korea's rapid economic growth since 1945? What can the Korean experience tell us about the potential contribution of education to the development of the poor countries? We begin by once again calling attention to the remarkable accomplishments of Korea.

THE GROWTH OF EDUCATION AND ECONOMY IN KOREA

The information contained in Chapter 1 of this study documents the rapid expansion of education in Korea during the past thirty years. Chapter 3 summarizes the statistical information with respect to growth of the economy. At the close of World War II, Korea was a poor and backward nation, just emerging from a history of colonial repression. But, despite limited resources, in a relatively short period of time it had built an educational system that outstripped—in terms of provision of educational access to children—those found in countries with much larger stocks of resources and higher levels of national income. By 1965, for example, Korea had an educational system equivalent to that found in countries with an average GNP of $380, although its own per capita income at that time was only $107. Its economic growth had been so rapid that in the space of just a few years the country had moved from the ranks of the very poor up into the middle range of countries in terms of income level, industrialization, and urbanization.

If the Koreans had managed this remarkable record in one single cycle, perhaps we would be less impressed with their accomplishments. But the country has overcome not just the results of a colonial legacy, but also the results of a bloody and destructive war in which most of the stock of human and physical resources was lost. Growth of education and expansion of the economy have been possible *despite* the heavy burden of military expenditure associated with the Cold War aftermath of the 1950s conflict.

Growth in education came first, and was followed by the economic boom. For some that is prima facie evidence that education is an important contributor to economic development. But facts do not explain themselves. Although the sequence of (A) educational expansion, (B) accelerated economic growth is logically consistent with the hypothesis that A caused B, it in no way contradicts the alternative that B was caused by some unknown C. Accordingly, we ask explicitly what, if any, causal link there is between the prior event and the subsequent one.

One of the requirements for proof of causality is that the B *always* follows A. Educational expansion of the kind experienced has occurred in a number of low-income countries whose governments sought (or were pressured by their constituents to seek) development of one of the more popular and easily attained modern institutions, the formal school system. If in each of these cases, or most of them, the expansion of education had been followed by accelerated economic growth, then there would at least be reason to suspect the existence of a straight-forward causal relationship.

The facts, however, are otherwise. A far more common result of rapid enrollment expansion, observable in numerous countries, is simply an educational system that is increasingly incongruent with the economic and social structures, marked by high levels of unemployment among the educated, and widening income differentials.[1] Many individuals and countries have paid a heavy price in frustration and instability for high rates of educational expansion. Although there will always be those who argue that development of education and other social programs will in time lead to accelerated economic growth, a systematic test of the hypothesis by the United Nations Research Institute for Social Development[2] produced highly ambiguous findings.

If asked to comment on research findings such as these, education specialists would undoubtedly argue that the analysis is couched in unwarrantedly crude terms. Hypothesis tests based solely on enrollment statistics imply that the content and *quality* of education are unimportant, that only the *size* of the system matters for economic and social development. If educational enrollment was followed by accelerated economic growth in Korea but not elsewhere, it could be said that there is something about the nature or quality of Korean education that made it especially conducive to economic growth. Can one perhaps hope to find in Korean education some unique quality which could be transferred to educational systems in other low-income countries, thus improving their contributions to development?

In Chapters 1 and 2 we reviewed some of the unique features of education in Korea. Some of its attributes should, in terms of conventional wisdom, contribute to *low* educational quality. For example, class sizes in Korean schools are very large; on the average, teachers face about twice as many students as developed-country educational specialists claim is desirable. Classes are large not only in primary schools but also in secondary and technical/vocational schools. Second, although many educators favor automatic promotion as a device for reducing inequalities introduced by "streaming" and "screening" in education, it runs counter to recommendations for ability grouping and special training of the more talented students. Automatic promotion is complete in Korea at all levels of the system. Third, educational specialists argue that the most effective education is one that teaches students *how*, not *what*, to think. Emphasis on rote memorization, learning of facts rather than principles, encyclopedic curricula—all these are seen as counterproductive and are often cited as typical of education in backward areas. Yet these features also characterize education in Korea.

There have been four major influences on the nature and content of Korean education:

1) Confucian traditions
2) political pressures for national survival, anti-communism
3) democratization, Deweyism
4) desire for modernization, interpreted to mean increased familiarity with and competence in science and technology.

There has been much conflict between the proponents of these four perspectives. In the early years of independence, advocates of democratization dueled with traditionalists. Although one prominent Korean educator decried the influence of Deweyism to us, it would seem that today the democratizers have lost out, and that the character of Korean schools owes more to historical factors pre-dating the U.S. Military Government than to the post-war period during which American advisors and some American-trained Koreans tried to implant a different educational philosophy.

On the other hand, there are other features of Korean education that would be looked on positively by most education specialists. Most striking is the extent of private spending on schooling. Strong "social demand" for education is a universal feature of low-income societies (and, for that matter, of high-income societies) in the world today. In nearly every developing country there is steady growth in the demand for school places, putting tremendous pressure on governments to expand enrollment capacity, first at the primary level and then at progressively higher levels as ever-larger cohorts of the schooled move up into the proper age ranges. This demand is present in Korea, too, but what distinguishes Korea from most other countries is the pattern of educational finance. In all countries education offers an opportunity to earn a higher income and attain a higher social status. In most countries this is a highly attractive opportunity because it is available at little cost to the students and their families (although even this cost is sufficient to weigh heavily on the poorest families); most of the cost is borne by the public. Not so in Korea. We have seen that Korean families have had to carry most of the financial load, paying fees even in public schools and relying heavily on private schooling when the government was slow to expand the capacity of the public schools. It is the willingness of large numbers of Korean families to pay substantial sums, large especially relative to their modest incomes, that is perhaps the most impressive feature of the case we have been studying.

We can ask ourselves *why* social demand has been so strong in the Korean case. Part of the answer is no doubt cultural—that is, the importance accorded to study and the role of the scholar in Confucian tradition. Perhaps even more important, however, is a factor discussed briefly at the end of Chapter 4. Korean society is unusually homogeneous in terms of language, religion, and culture; moreover, its traditional system of social class was all but destroyed in the upheavals created by foreign military occupation, war, and national partition. These facts may well have weakened many of the influences that strongly condition social mobility in other countries, leaving education as a uniquely important means of individual advancement. This would explain the observed fierce competition for places in the higher levels of a school system, which may do little to make people more productive but has practically everything to say about whether they will be successful in gaining access to high-income jobs and enviable social positions.

Associated with this importance of education is the privileged social position of the teacher, a cultural heritage from the Chinese, reinforced under the Japanese. In Korea the teacher's social status is so great that it has been possible to attract large numbers of educated *men* to teach in primary grades. In relatively few other countries does one find a majority of teachers both male and highly educated.

This attribute goes hand-in-hand with the ability of Korean teachers to command absolute respect from their students. While teachers in many other parts of the world may spend much of their class hours on problems of discipline rather than instruction, the Korean teacher can expect that students will discipline themselves.

This last feature of Korean education must provoke mixed feelings in American educators. Bowing to the teacher, uniforms, mass calisthenics, reciting in unison are educational practices long ago rejected in favor of policies of student freedom to develop capacities to the fullest, and consequent restriction of teacher control over student behavior. Behavioral conformity is, for Americans, anti-modern.

In summary, although it is clear that Korean schools have

some unique features, it is not certain in what ways those features might contribute to the modernization of the society. In the sections that follow we review three theoretical frameworks that may be helpful in organizing our data.

EDUCATION AND
HUMAN RESOURCE DEVELOPMENT

The oldest argument for a causal link between education and development states that schooling is critical for the development in individuals of those skills and attitudes required for economic growth and political stability. In Chapter 3 we reviewed some of the assumptions underlying this theory—that education makes people more entrepreneurial, more productive, more efficient, more mobile. This happens, the assertion is made, through a process in which individuals are transformed through education.

The specific contributions of education—its "value added"— are assumed to be recognized by the market, and therefore one can look to the economic value of education as evidence for its contribution to development. This value is recognized in various ways. First, the more highly educated people are paid more than those with less education. People want education because they know it contributes to individual advancement.

These relationships hold in Korea as much as in other countries. Those with higher levels of education do (in most cases) receive higher salaries than those with lower levels of education. (Teachers are one striking exception.) The rate of return to education is positive, and often significantly high. There is a high social demand for education.

What is less certain, however, is that these findings confirm the assumptions with which they are associated. If education is rewarded because the skills taught meet the needs of the economy, there should be little educated unemployment, and a good fit between manpower requirements and the output of schools. If there is a value-added process in education, it should be possible to associate differences in educational quality that people experience with differences in the economic rewards they receive. The more education one has, the more the rate of return to education might be expected to increase, since the skills imparted would be even more rare.

With respect to the development of the Korean economy over time, the theory would lead us to expect that education had moved sharply from a traditional to a modern emphasis, from an academic, humanistic approach to one emphasizing vocational preparation and skill training. Because non-formal education is often asserted to be less tradition-bound, it would be expected to have played an important role in the development of the labor force. Over time the equality of education should have improved: improvements in quality would be reflected in increased unit costs, or smaller class sizes and higher teacher salaries.

The evidence we have presented at best only partially confirms these hypotheses. Education expanded much more rapidly than could the economy prior to 1960, to such an extent that educated unemployment was regarded as a serious problem. For a number of years the number of graduates, especially in certain technical fields, exceeded the manpower requirements of the economy. Some analysts[3] feel that the situation has never been fully rectified, that there is *too much* investment in human capital.

One response to this situation has been to suggest that it was the *pool of available talent* that made possible the economic takeoff of Korea. This pool might be a necessary condition, but it is not sufficient. If it were, one would expect high rates of economic growth in countries (such as India and the Philippines) that are approaching their second or third decade of educated unemployment. This is, of course, not the case.

We now have available research from a number of countries that fails to demonstrate a powerful relationship between differences in conventional measures of educational quality received by students and either the amount of learning they have acquired or rewards handed out by society. That is, it seems to make little difference whether a student has a well-trained teacher or not, is in a large or small classroom, has access to textbooks or a modern curriculum; how long one is in school is important, but apparently not what happens to him there.[4] There are serious methodological problems with the research that has produced these findings. As teachers ourselves, we are unwilling to believe that it does not make a difference (in terms of learning) when we prepare our classes and apply the benefits of years of training. But the economy, the labor market, apparently is not particularly sensitive to the differences in graduates from one or another kind of experience.

We have no research results of this kind for Korea. But if they were similar to those from all other countries in which studies have been done, they would read as follows. Graduates from Seoul National University command higher salaries than those from a provincial university, irrespective of their grades or position in the class. A graduate from a university commands a higher salary than one from high school, no matter what his level of intelligence or knowledge. More important, when one introduces social class measures into the predictive equation, school differences (of the order Seoul National versus a provincial university) become small, and social class (education and income levels of parents) account for most of the variance in earnings of graduates.

These comments should not be interpreted as disparagement of the Korean educational system. It has many praiseworthy features. Even though the rote learning tradition and heavy reliance on national examinations seem unlikely to foster creativity and productivity, the system is relatively open to students from varying social backgrounds (much more so than in other developing countries), and there is no doubt that Korean students are bright. We believe that students learn in schools all around the world, and that much is learned in Korean schools. The argument, however, is over whether *differences* in the amount and kind of that learning can be associated with differences in incomes, or whether in fact economic roles and rewards are *not* assigned principally (if at all) on the basis of value added through education.

In Korea, as elsewhere, there is a positive rate of return to education. As we have pointed out in Chapter 4, the rates of return in Korea are lower than rates of return to physical capital, a finding unlike other countries. Second, the rate of return to higher education is lower than that of return to secondary education. (Hence the assertion that there is too much education). Finally, it is possible for individuals to have high rates of return to their investment in education without any equivalent increase in gross national product, as can be seen in a number of countries with very low growth rates and high returns to education. What most influences the rate of return are income differentials between persons with different levels of educational attainment. We have argued that it is likely these differentials are more a function of structural factors in the economy and polity—specifically access to power by those with more education—than they are a result of differences in contribution to national productivity. In Korea those differentials are less than in other countries or, in other words, there is a more equitable distribution of income in Korea than in most countries.

If the development of education in Korea *after* 1945 was a contributor to modernization and growth, then one would expect to find significant changes in the system from that time forward. These changes would, one could expect, move from a traditional to a modern emphasis. There were changes. Some were lasting, others were not. The system expanded and new curricula were tried out. Most of the more "modern" innovations seem to have been abandoned (coeducation is an exception). The evidence presented in Chapters 1 and 2 suggests that, although objectives were set for the introduction of a vocational/technical emphasis in schools, in fact not much progress was made toward that goal until well after the economic takeoff had occurred. Although there was emphasis on individualism and productivity in the curriculum in the 1950s, that was replaced in the 1960s by more emphasis on collectivity and conformity. There were and apparently still are sharp disparities between objectives held by the national executive and those held by administrators and teachers (and parents) at the local level, where the work of education takes place. What distinguishes the curriculum of Korean schools from that of countries whose attempts at development have failed is not its emphasis on science and technology. The major difference seems to be that Korean education places a heavy stress on moral education and discipline. It is hard to fit this characteristic into the human resources development explanation of education's contribution.

Although the educational history of Korea since 1945 is dominated by schools, non-formal education has not been totally ignored. Between 1945 and 1950 literacy and civic education (citizenship formation) were the primary objectives, well financed and apparently highly successful. It is possible that, had the war not intervened, the takeoff would have followed in the early 1950s; but the hard evidence is that, with increasing education of the population and the frustrations arising from the war, in the post-war period the economic and political systems got worse, not better.

Korea made a significant investment during the 1960s in family planning education, with its famous Mothers' Clubs reaching large proportions of the fertile female age-group. The effects of that campaign, in terms of reduced birth rates and the declining growth rate of the population, began to appear *after* the economic takeoff had occurred. Finally, the New Community Movement (Saemaul Undong) is a significant contribution to the use of non-formal education in an integrated campaign for total community development. As we noted earlier, some elements of the movement were taken from the Japanese experience in Korea in the 1930s. The movement did not begin to assume any significant size until after 1970. On the basis of the information we have gathered, Korea seems to have invested relatively small amounts in skill training for workers, through out-of-plant training programs, apprenticeship schemes, or on-the-job training. Training there must have been, as hundreds of thousands of workers left rural areas to enter industry. But that training was not, according to the information we have, either well organized or systematically evaluated.[5]

The absence (during the 1960s) of a large skill-training program is not surprising, however, given the path toward industrial development that Korea chose. Unlike other countries in which worker training has been an important part of the development plan, Korea avoided large-scale heavy industrial production in favor of labor-intensive, low-technology enterprises of fairly modest scale. The skills required of workers were easily learned, especially given basic literacy and the manual dexterity which might be associated with people fresh from rural areas, accustomed to working with their hands.

Ironically, perhaps the most important type of out-of-school education in the Korean experience has been one that directly supports students' performance in the formal school system. We refer to the extensive use of after-hours tutoring in academic subjects noted above.

As we have pointed out, it strains credulity to suggest that the formalistic education imparted by Korean schools, from the 1st grade through the university, was directly functional for the kind of industrial employment associated with the Korean miracle. Korean schools teach a good deal, but not what workers need to know in agricultural and low-technology industrial employment. We expect that what Korean students learn in school, even those graduating from the middle school, far exceeds what they need to know for gainful employment.

Finally, we have presented evidence to show that Korean education, though no doubt high in quality, has not *improved* according to conventional indicators of educational quality. Class sizes have remained the same or increased; unit costs have not grown proportionate to the national income. At the higher levels, the government now invests proportionately less than it did ten years ago. Private investment in education is a shrinking portion of real income.

Although the national government has exercised tight control over both public and private education, this control does not seem to have been intended to insure high quality. Plans have not been followed, in some cases were not financed. There is no systematic evaluation of the outputs of education. Private education has grown, proportionately, more than public education. Any contribution of education to modernization in Korea cannot be claimed as a result of careful analysis and planning.

EDUCATION AND
INDIVIDUAL MODERNIZATION

One way to hold onto the human-resources-development-leads-to-national-development theory is to argue that it isn't really skills that are so important, but rather attitudes and values that dispose individuals to modernization. There are at least two variants of this approach. One would argue that modern attitudes and values lead *individuals* to act as entrepreneurs, to act to increase their personal productivity, and that it is the aggregate effects of these modernized individuals that result in economic growth. Another version would argue that development occurs through planned and organized efforts for which compliance and conformity by individual citizens are important: modernity is defined in terms of identification with a nation-state and active participation as a consumer as well as producer in the national economy. There are also positions which combine these two emphases.

In both cases, education is seen as a critical factor for the development of modernity in individuals. In the simplest approach, the presumption is that this transformation of persons is a function of the content of the educational process, that is, of the school curriculum. We have presented evidence that suggests both that the content of Korean education should not, on face value, be modernizing, and that changes in curricula over time seem to be moving away from what we could consider "modern" values, or at least those consistent with individual entrepreneurship. Especially at the higher levels of education, curriculum and examination content would seem to discourage creativity and innovation.

On the other hand, in Chapter 5 we presented data which show that educated persons tend to be more "modern" in their perspective than those with lower levels of education. The explanation offered to account for this paradox is that what transforms individuals, at least in terms of these attitudes and values, is not so much the content of the educational process as it is the structure of the schooling process. In schools, students learn rules, the importance of time, the use of non-personal evaluation, the importance of quantity, and a variety of other social facts which constitute the syndrome of "modernity." These attitudes are not taught so much as built into the experiences of schooling.

In studies conducted in other countries, persons with more years of education tended to have those attitudes that most people would agree were consistent with life in a "modern" society, especially one in which strong emphasis was placed on acquisition of material goods and social participation. What data are available for Korea are consistent with the findings from other countries. The data for Korea also indicate, however, that persons with higher levels of education are increasingly critical of government policies; university students particularly react against the attempt to associate development with a verticalist society in which collective conformity replaces individual freedom as a value.

There are several major criticisms of this individual-modernization theory.[6] First, only the existence of structural effects of schools on attitudes has been postulated; there is little research that identifies specific structural features and associates them with attitudinal change. On the other hand, there is an abundance of research that presents negative findings—that is, fails to demonstrate relationships between differences in the extent or intensity of the various kinds of structural aspects of educational institutions and differences in the attitudes and values of students in those institutions. (For example, the differences in values between a graduate of a primary school and a graduate of a secondary school are greater than the differences between graduates from two very different secondary schools.)

Second, most research on values and attitudes in children suggests that such values and attitudes are unstable over time. While some fundamental personality differences may be maintained, in general little of the attitudinal position of an adult can be predicted from knowledge of his attitudes on graduating from the 6th, 9th or 12th grade.[7] Third, there is little evidence to link specific attitudes and values before employment with occupational performance; witness the unceasing efforts of personnel directors to find the test that will identify the good and faithful employee. Although Inkeles and his associates, as described in Chapter 5, were able to associate adult behavioral characteristics with contemporary attitudes, we have little evidence that these attitudes have effects over time.

A final criticism of the individual socialization-into-modernity theory argues that it is possible, and just as plausible, that the association between values and education is a function of selection, not of transformation or value added. That is, the critique argues, those with higher levels of education hold more modern values because those with less modern values were selected out previously. Given the nature of the content of examinations in Korea—heavily based on memorization, often of traditional material—and the ubiquity of automatic promotion, it does not seem reasonable to assign blame or credit to the schools for the modernity of their graduates. An alternative is that there is a process of self-selection. Success on the examinations depends on long hours *out of school* preparing for them. This is associated somewhat with social class (as tutors are expensive) and certainly with parental ambitions for their children. The hypothesis is interesting, but we have no data to test it.

THE INSTITUTIONAL EFFECTS
OF EDUCATION ON MODERNIZATION

Each of the perspectives we have reviewed has assumed that education contributes (or not) to the development of a society through its effects on individuals (or their life chances). The human-resources development approach and its cousin, education-leads-to-individual-modernity, both propose a sequence in which education produces changes in individuals, and then these individuals one by one or in the aggregate produce a new society. The evidence to support the theory comes from data based on individual incomes, individual attitudes, and values.

The critics of these approaches, subsumed under the status-conflict or selection models, use the same kind of data. The associations between individual income and education are explained in terms of individual positions in the social structure. Education selects the most talented, or motivated, or conforming individual to positions of power and prestige.

But economic and political development is a collective phenomenon. It depends on individuals, of course, but only as they are able to act together to reach common objectives, only as they interact and as a result of their collaboration (or conflict) produce results that cannot be described adequately in terms of the individual contributions. And the performance of an economy or a society does not depend on the status or ability or motives of individuals at any one time so much as it does on the day-to-day pursuit of objectives following rules and patterns of behavior that apply to *categories* of persons in which the attributes of individual membership are relatively unimportant.

Just as there is a wide variety in the ways in which an enterprise can organize itself to pursue an economic objective, so too there is considerable latitude in the mix of individual skills and attitudes necessary for an organization to function well.

Because education has been conceived principally in terms of its effects on individuals there has been a tendency to assume that its contributions end with graduation. The hottest fad in international education today is the "continuing education" movement, an attempt to counter the notion that everything important can be learned in childhood, but also a confirmation of the notion that schooling affects only those who go to school, that schooling is the only (or best) source of learning.

Little or no attention has been paid to the effects that education may have on society directly, rather than aggregated effects on individuals. There has been little research or theorizing about the importance of education as an *institution* in society, with a social significance that transcends individual members and individual transformations. Meyer points out that

> education is a highly developed institution. It has a network of rules creating public classifications of persons and knowledge . . . It is . . . a central element in the table of organization of society, constructing competencies and helping create professions . . . educational systems . . . rationalize in modern terms and remove from sacred and primordial explanations the nature and organization of personnel and knowledge in modern society . . . Such an institution clearly has an impact on society over and above the immediate socializing experiences it offers the young.[8]

Education not only socializes young people, selects among its students, and gives credentials to graduates so that they are entitled to certain rewards and privileges in society; it also legitimizes a social structure in which certain kinds of knowledge are defined as valuable, and in which only certain persons are defined as capable of managing that knowledge. This legitimization has effects on both students and graduates. Students tend to adopt values and attitudes considered appropriate to their present status as student in a given type of school, and the position that will be theirs upon graduation. As we saw in Chapter 5, university students in Korea (at least in some elite institutions) assume certain responsibilities in society *because* they are university students. They are not so much transformed by the educational process as they are "chartered" by it.[9] Later, as graduates, they will assume other attributes fitting for a graduate of their institution.

Education is in "modern" societies a principal criterion for the assignment of persons to social and economic roles. Government officials must be university graduates. Only engineers (that is, those who have a degree in engineering) are allowed to direct certain kinds of industrial and construction projects. Only lawyers can practice in courts—a lawyer is a person certified on the basis of his education.[10]

Persons in positions assigned to those with certain levels or kinds of education take on the attitudes and values that go with those positions. High school graduates are expected to think and act in ways that are different from those of primary school graduates. The university graduate in turn has a different set of role expectations. Because these expectations are widely shared in a modernized society, a person with a "degree" finds that others are willing to accord him certain privileges with no need to demonstrate his abilities. At the same time, these expectations push the degree-holder into a certain pattern of behavior.

Those who have not gone to school also have a role definition —the person who is "intelligent" although he has not gone to school is so rare that his appearance merits public comment. Even though there is ample evidence that there is tremendous overlap in terms of intellectual ability between those who have finished university and those who have not, people automatically assign to the graduate respect denied to the dropout. We have noted that in Korea those students who fail examinations accept their lower incomes and status with no questioning of the system. With those lower incomes and status are also accepted certain definitions of self-worth. The acceptance of lower levels of income is critical in a strategy of economic development that calls for low levels of consumption and high levels of productivity.

Meyer proposes that the legitimation effects of education can be divided into four categories on the basis of two cross-cutting dichotomies. The first dichotomy deals with the audience of the educational program, elites or masses. The second dichotomy distinguishes between education as a theory of knowledge (that is, an ideology stating what it is important to know) and education as a theory of personnel (that is, stating what kinds of positions in society are important). The first major category of effects he calls "The Authority of Specialized Competence . . ."

> . . . the creation of academic economics means that new types of knowledge must be taken into account by responsible actors. The creation of psychiatry means that former mysteries must now be dealt with in the social organization. The creation of academic programs in business management brings arenas of decision making from personal judgment of luck to the jurisdiction of rationalized knowledge. Social problems call for human-relations professionals (occasionally even sociologists). Safety or environmental problems call for industrial or environmental engineering.[11]

One can appreciate that the legitimation effects of education are likely to be stronger in a country with a 2,000-year tradition of respect for the educated man.

By the end of the period of Japanese colonial rule, about half the primary school age population of Korea was involved in the educational system. The only route to participation in the Japanese colony was through education. Teacher training and military training were the principal routes for a number of Koreans who later became leaders in the Republic of Korea (including President Park, who attended normal school in Japan and a Japanese military school in Manchuria).

Occupation by the Americans re-emphasized the importance of education as a means to identify those areas of knowledge of

importance, and therefore the persons who wield special com-
petency. In addition to a rapid expansion of primary education,
the Americans invested heavily in expansion of higher education
in Korea, and through scholarships for Koreans to study abroad.
Public Administration, Medicine, Agriculture, and Engineering,
programs that previously had received less attention, were now
the best financed, and became the most promising route to a
prestigious job in the government.[12] Public-sector employment
in Korea was always more sought after than private-sector
employment, given the Confucian legacy and the impositions of
the Japanese Colonial Government. When the Republic of
Korea created new educational programs and categories, it was to
be expected that graduates of those programs (especially those
from the prestige universities) would soon occupy critical
positions in the government. Management of the nation's affairs
thus passed from the hands of those trained in traditional
bureaucracy and public administration to a new generation of
technocrats. In addition to the new roles created by the
universities, specialized competence also came from an expansion of the military with a heavy emphasis on formal training in
modern management concepts and techniques. It was this new
category of competent leaders that was to take power in 1961.[13]

These new leaders were certified by the educational system as
possessing elite status because they were trained in the best
schools and in the "new knowledge." Elite definition and
certification is the second major class of legitimation functions
of education identified by Meyer. He writes:

> Education . . . not only creates "economic knowledge" which must
> be taken into account by rational actors. It is also a structure helping
> to create the role of economist, to justify economists' authority
> claims in society, and to define precisely who is an economist.
> Education thus creates, not only psychiatry, but psychiatrists; not
> only modern management ideology, but M.B.A.'s.[14]

The preparation of students in "modern" knowledge and status
imparted only by the school demands the employment of

these persons in important positions, and justifies assigning them salaries equivalent to or higher than those received by persons with more traditional training. Even if no learning took place in the middle and high schools and universities of Korea, one could argue that the expansion of these kinds of institutions, and the repeated insistence of public figures on their importance for society, would result in employment of their graduates.

The effect would also be to persuade parents that their "educated" sons (and in a few instances, daughters) could accept employment in an industrial occupation, could take positions previously occupied by persons with low levels of education, could encourage entrepreneurial activity even if *traditional* Confucian values frowned on that kind of activity. Education—meaning in this case the possession of a certificate— would replace scholarship as the defining characteristic of a respectable person, and in time would replace occupation as the source of prestige. Because in Korea respect was based not only on the material wealth of an individual but his standing (as demonstrated by successful performance on examinations), it was possible for the expansion of a new source of respect (the university degree) to occur without serious distortions to a reasonably equitable distribution of national income. That is, we would argue that the expansion of education in Korea did not lead to widening income gaps as educational expansion has in the great majority of developing countries, not because educated persons in Korea were less productive than those in other countries, but because the social value of education was not in the salary it could command, but the social position.

The net effect of this was to make it possible to do in Korea what other countries have often failed to accomplish, to persuade well-trained (through education) persons to occupy positions requiring education and training, but in themselves lacking social status. The critical variable was not education, but a culture (and set of political and economic decisions consistent with the values of that culture) that tended to reduce the relationship among education, occupation, and social status.

The third category of legitimation functions is called by Meyer the "Universality of Collective Reality." As elsewhere in the world, education serves to create a nation-state by providing a common language, a common set of heroes and myths, the basis for a common civic order, and common perspective on reality. Given the homogeneity of the Korean population, the high level of education already present in the society, the existence of and allegiance to local and national political structures, it is doubtful that this particular function of education was important in Korea. As we have described earlier, considerable attention was given, however, to defining a set of values that would legitimate the current regime. Both during the period of Syngman Rhee and under the present government, education has been designed to reinforce the authority of the government. As will be recalled, Black defines excessive nationalism as a natural stage in the modernization of a nation. Ross Harold Cole writes:

> The fervor with which anti-communist education was stressed as the Park government solidified power had other implications. The original position of the military junta . . . was to destroy the communists and reunify the fatherland. That stance was particularly beneficial to the government at a time when the junta leader-turned-president was striving to unify the people of South Korea . . . Exploiting the presence of the hungry aggressors to the North who were lurking in wait to crush South Korea, added emotional tenor and near religious fanaticism to the sense of urgency and utter necessity of preparing and building Korea immediately . . . Anti-communism became the basic rationale for economic development.[15]

Through direct socialization of students in schools (where even today anti-Communist posters are common), the organization of university students into para-military units with the mandate to seek out subversives, the repeated pronouncement and analysis of the National Charter of Education, the use of school students in demonstrations in favor of the government, and other activities, the educational institution reinforces a national culture in which the President is defined as a benign authority pursuing the interests of all Koreans. Until 1975, this policy had not been successful, but in the past two years the government has made additional efforts to command university student support.

Education not only specifies what knowledge and values are important for participation in the nation-state; it also certifies that individuals are competent as citizens and therefore entitled to the rights and responsible for the duties of citizenship. This is the fourth legitimation function. With the expansion of education comes the expansion of citizen participation in the political process. This has occurred in Korea as in other countries, although as we have noted in recent years the government has tended to thwart movements for increased participation. The movement away from an open parliamentary democracy to a more paternalistic and corporate form of government has necessarily required a reduction in the rights of citizens to free expression and redress of grievances, or so the government sees it.

We would predict that, with continued expansion of education, the Korean government must also continue to be repressive, or permit a fundamental change in political structure.

What we have learned in this analysis of the educational system of the Republic of Korea can be summarized as follows. Both the expansion of education and the growth of the economy of Korea are unique events in the history of development. There is a relationship between the two phenomena, but it is not a simple cause-and-effect or facilitation linkage. The evidence is not consistent with a conclusion that education generated growth, through some transformation of individuals from traditional to modern men or through the formation of "human capital." It does seem likely that changes occurring in other sectors of the Korean society occurred also in education, and that consistency was helpful in the development process.

Education in Korea does not appear to have expanded as a response to technological improvements in the economy requiring higher levels of ability among workers. Nor is there evidence that increases in the number of educated people anticipated (in some causal way) the economic boom of the 1960s. The latter statement does not deny, of course, the possibility that the availability of large numbers of literate and modestly educated workers facilitated the organization of the economy under the Park Military Government in the early 1960s. What is clear is the role assigned to education in the socialization of the population (that is, students and adults) into the basic attitudes of compliance with a strong central government. Although the government promotes education as contributing to economic development, major trends have not been toward skill acquisition and developmental values (as Westerners may see them) so much as toward identification of students with the future of Korea as a corporate state. The expansion of education obeyed, therefore, not only social demand for increased educational opportunity (because educational attainment is a key determinant of occupation) but also the desire to legitimize the new economic and political system. We believe that education did play a critical role in the modernization of Korea; it did this primarily by assisting a strong government with "modernizing" policies to impose its will upon the nation.

Notes

Preface

1. For convenience, we shall sometimes refer to the Republic of Korea simply as Korea, although that term correctly applies to the entire Korean peninsula, that is, North and South Korea combined.

2. By comparison, Taiwan, protected by the Seventh Fleet, spent only U.S. $15 per capita on military expenditures and $9 on education. Figures are from United Nations sources.

3. UNESCO, *Republic of Korea: Educational Services in a Rapidly Growing Economy*, 2 vols. (Paris, 1974), p. 11.

ONE   The Development of Education Since 1945

1. Preschool education is of little significance in Korea. About 2% of the age group is enrolled, and this proportion has remained constant since 1966, when private elementary schools eliminated their entrance examination. Almost all are privately operated. See Un-Hwa Yi, "Pre-school Education in Korea," *Korea Journal* 12:12:28–31 (December 1972).

2. Hyung-jin Yoo. "New Entrance Examination for High Schools in Korea, 1973," paper presented at the World Congress of Comparative Education Societies, Geneva, June 28, 1974.

3. Manzoor Ahmed, "Republic of Korea: A Multipurpose Farmer Education Program," in M. Ahmed and P. H. Coombs, eds., *Education for Rural Development* (New York, 1975).

4. UNESCO, *Progress of Education in the Asian Region: Statistical Supplement* (Bankok, 1972).

5. Byung Sook Choe, "The Impact of the Government Policy on the Development of Education in the First Republic of Korea, 1948–1960," unpublished PhD dissertation, University of Pittsburgh, 1971.

6. Ibid.

7. Elizabeth Cecil Wilson, "The Problem of Value in Technical Assistance in Education: The Case of Korea, 1945–1955," unpublished PhD dissertation, University of Maryland, 1959.

8. Byung Sook Choe.

9. Myung Han Kim, "The Educational Policy-Making Process in the Republic of Korea: A Systems Analysis," unpublished PhD dissertation, North Texas State University, 1974, p. 67.

10. Parent-Teacher Associations were reorganized in 1970 as the Yuksŏnghoe, with essentially the same objectives as previously held: to collect voluntary membership fees to aid the school; to promote cooperations between parents and school authorities.

11. Richard Werth, "Educational Developments under the South Korea Interim Government (SKIG)," *School and Society* 69.1793:305–309 (April 1949).

12. Byung Hun Nam, "Educational Reorganization in South Korea under the United States Army Military Government, 1945–1948," unpublished PhD dissertation, University of Pittsburgh, 1962.

13. Jin Eun Kim, "An Analysis of the National Planning Process for Educational Development in the Republic of Korea, 1945–70," unpublished PhD dissertation, University of Pittsburgh, 1973, pp. 141–142.

14. Ibid.

15. Ibid., p. 107.

16. Hyun-ki Paik, "The Present Status of Education," *Korea Journal* 3.4:4–15 (April 1963).

17. Kak Kim, "Education Undergoes Drastic Revisions," *Korea Journal* 1.4:19–20 (December 1961), p. 19.

18. Ibid.

19. Cornelius Osgood, *The Koreans and Their Culture* (New York, 1951).

20. Ross Harold Cole, "The Koreanization of Elementary Citizenship Education in South Korea, 1948–1974," unpublished PhD dissertation, Arizona State University, 1975, p. 200.

21. Ibid., p. 402.

22. Hyŏn-gi Paek, "Han'guk kyoyuk kyehoek ŭi pyŏnch'ŏn," *Chungang kyoyuk Yŏn'guso sobo*, 9.4:37 (December 1968).

23. Mun'gyobu, *Hyŏngmyŏng chŏngbu mun'gyo sich'aek* (Seoul, 1961).

24. Central Education Research Institute, "A Study of Education Administration in Korea," Research Bulletin No. 45, Seoul, 1967, pp. 33–34.

25. Jin Eun Kim, "Analysis of the National Planning Process."

26. Chong Ch'ol Kim, "Long-Range Educational Planning in Korea," *Korea Journal* 11.10:5–11, 15 (October 1971), p. 15.

27. Hyun-ki Paik, *A Content Analysis of Elementary School Textbooks and a Related Study for Improvement of Textbook Administration* (Seoul, 1969), p. 64.

28. For an example of curriculum research, see Yungho Kim et al., *Toward a New Instructional System* (Korean Educational Development Institute, 1973).

29. Nor were changes in curriculum concepts always carried out faithfully in the textbooks that form the basis of teaching in Korean schools. For example, the 1953 curricular reform stressed:

1) content from matters close to student life;

2) priority to technical knowledge for practical life;

3) content reduced in favor of flexibility;

4) students encouraged to take active attitude toward study;

5) curriculum for actual life rather than study;

6) importance of vertical and parallel relationships among subjects stressed.

"However, the contents of the textbooks compiled in accordance with the compilation policy based on the curriculum did not actually comply with the suggested reforms. Indeed, the next textbooks stressed 'education by textbook' even more than previously." Hyun-ki Paik, *A Content Analysis,* pp. 61–62.

30. See Ross Harold Cole.

31. Hyun-ki Paik, *A Content Analysis,* p. 41.

32. Ross Harold Cole, p. 285.

33. Ibid., p. 321.

34. Ibid., pp. 322–323.

35. See Hung Yung Kim, "A Comparative Analysis of Developmental Values Found in the Children's Stories from the Old and the New Language Arts Textbooks in the Republic of Korea," unpublished PhD dissertation, Ball State University, 1974.

36. Based on David C. McClelland, *Motivating Economic Achievement* (New York 1971).

37. The Ministry of Education reported that 23% of the 43,000 classrooms available in 1950 were burned out or destroyed and another 25% half-burned or half-destroyed. See Ministry of Education, *Education Monthly* 41:106–107 (September 1958). Chapter 2 describes the post-war effort to rebuild the school system.

38. For a review of studies on early leaving, see Russell Beirn, David C. Kinsey, and Noel F. McGinn "Antecedents and Consequences of Early School Leaving," *Bulletin of the International Bureau of Education* 46.182 (first quarter, 1972).

39. Myung Han Kim, "The Educational Policy-Making Process."

TWO   *An Evaluation of the Uniqueness of Education Growth in Korea*

1. Reviewing data for 1955-1965, Zygmont Gotkowski suggests that most development took place in the already advanced countries. "The Evolution of Developmental Gaps Between Rich and Poor Countries, 1955-65: A Methodological Pilot Study," *International Social Science Journal* 27.1:38-52 (1975).

2. For a more sanguine perspective, see Joseph P. Farrell, "National Planning Systems in Latin America: Their Environment and Their Impact," *Educational Planning* 1.1:20-33 (May 1974).

3. Frederick H. Harbison and Charles S. Myers, *Education, Manpower and Economic Growth* (New York, 1964).

4. David C. Cole and Princeton N. Lyman, *Korean Development: The Interplay of Politics and Economics* (Cambridge, Mass., 1971), p. 296.

5. Frederick H. Harbison, Joan Maruhnic, and Jane R. Resnick, *Quantitative Analyses of Modernization and Development* (Princeton, 1970).

6. To the extent that growth in education preceded growth of the GNP (and now lags behind), Korea should look even less distinctive in 1975. That is, given a rapid rate of growth of GNP between 1960 and 1975, Korea would move to a category of more advanced economies *expected* to have more developed educational systems.

7. "While Koreans of the 17th century . . . had no difficulty in addressing each other without offending anyone's status consciousness, the people of contemporary (post-1945) Korea could find no commonly established term by which to address each other outside of their own organized occupational groups." In a society where the ruling class standard had been destroyed without being replaced by a new form of status distinction, educational and political positions became the most important criteria of vertical social stratification. Quee-Young Kim, "Social Structure and Student Revolt: A Quantitative Analysis of the Korean Case," unpublished PhD dissertation, Harvard University, 1975, p. 1.

8. Manuel Zymelman, "Patterns of Educational Expenditures," World Bank Staff Working Paper No. 246, November 1976.

9. Byung Hun Nam, "Education Reorganization."

10. Tai-si Chung, "Korean Education: Yesterday and Tomorrow," *Koreana Quarterly* 12.3:66-76 (autumn 1970).

11. "Educational Reorganization," p. 96.

12. Immediately after the Korean War, aid went to reconstruction of classrooms and schools destroyed during the conflict rather than to creation of new capacity.

13. The burden of fees was heavy for some families. "In the autumn of 1954 there were newspaper accounts of a few fathers who committed suicide because they were unable to raise the fees necessary to send their sons to middle or high schools." Elaine Milam Barnes, "The School of Taegu, Kyongsang Pukto [North Kyŏngsang] Province, Korea, in 1954-1955: An Investigation into the Interaction between Culture and Education," unpublished PhD dissertation, University of Maryland, 1960, p. 63.

14. Sidney R. Grant, "General Characteristics of the Formal Education System at the Primary and Secondary Levels in South Korea with Special Reference to the Feasibility for Innovation," Appendix A in Morgan and Chadwick, eds., *Systems Analysis for Educational Change* (Tallahassee, 1971), pp. 153-186.

15. Robert Morgan and Clifton B. Chadwick, eds., *Systems Analysis for Educational Change: The Republic of Korea* (Tallahassee, 1971).

16. Published in Seoul, 1974.

17. Yunshik Chang, "Education in Korea, 1945-1970: A Comparison of North and South Korea," Workshop on Korean Modernization: North and South, University of Puerto Rico, 1976.

18. Yong Hwan Chung, "A Study of Some Aspects of Educational Administration with Implications for the Korean Public School System," unpublished PhD dissertation, University of Oklahoma, 1965.

19. Ibid.

20. See Beirn et al.; and Ernesto Schiefelbein, "Repeating: An Overlooked Problem of Latin American Education," *Comparative Education Review* 19:468-487 (1977).

21. Shin-Bok Kim, "A Systematic Sub-Optimization Model for Educational Planning: with Application to Korea," unpublished PhD dissertation, University of Pittsburgh, 1973.

22. Ministry of Education, *Education in Korea 1973*.

23. See Hung-jin Yoo, "New Entrance Examination."

24. Uk Hwan Kim, "An Examination of the Interplay of Culture and Education in Korea: A Comparative Study," unpublished PhD dissertation, Claremont Graduate School, 1972, p. 226.

25. ". . . one might conclude from looking at the Korean exam system that Korean education was highly competitive, but in the personal situation of the classroom no one seems to fail. So at access points that are impersonal, the system can be ruthless; in the personal face-to-face realm, respect for person seems to take precedence over objective 'merit'." Grant, p. 185.

26. "The role of the student is one of silent obedience and unquestioning acceptance of the material presented to him. He is required to memorize the contents of the texts for the purpose of passing examinations rather than developing intellectual capacity." Uk Hwan Kim, p. 219.

27. Wilson, pp. 202, 216.

28. "The Impact of American Culture on Korea Through Educational Exchanges," *Koreana Quarterly* 9.4:74-87 (winter 1967).

29. Jin Eun Kim, p. 21.

30. Sun Pyo Choi cites one source to the effect that, in 1943, some 57% of the Korean age group were enrolled in primary school, almost 9% in middle and secondary school, and 9.5% in college and university. He discounts the development value of this education, however, arguing that it only served to socialize people into obedience, through a heavy emphasis on moral education. Sun Pyo Choi, "The Problem of Reconstructing Korean Education in Historical Perspective," unpublished PhD dissertation, University of Illinois, 1960.

31. See, for example, Sung-hwa Lee, "The Social and Political Factors Affecting Korean Education, 1885-1950," unpublished PhD dissertation, University of Pittsburgh, 1958; and Hung Koo Pak, "Social Changes in the Educational and Religious Institutions of Korean Society under Japanese and American Occupations," unpublished PhD dissertation, Utah State University, 1964.

32. Many were located in Japan. President Park was trained in one such institution.

33. Korean Society for the Study of Education, *The Saemaul Education in the Republic of Korea,* (Seoul, 1974), p. 57.

34. Han Young Rim, "Japanese Totalitarian Education in Korea, 1910-1945," *Koreana Quarterly* 1.2:85-92 (1960), p. 91.

35. Sun Pyo Choi.

36. Frank L. Eversull, "Some Observations on Higher Education in Korea," *School and Society* 65.1674:51-53 (January 1947), p. 52.

37. See Herbert Passin, *Society and Education in Japan* (New York, 1965) and Nathan Glazer, "Social and Cultural Factors in Japanese Economic Growth," in Hugh Patrick and Henry Rosovsky, eds., *Asia's New Giant: How the Japanese Economy Works,* (Washington, The Brookings Institution, 1976).

38. Wilson, pp. 76-77.

39. Herbert Wesley Dodge, "A History of U.S. Assistance to Korean Education, 1953-1966" unpublished PhD dissertation, George Washington University, 1971, quoting a 1954 UNESCO report.

40. Hyung Koo Pak, p. 64.

41. Donald K. Adams, "Education in Korea 1945-1955," unpublished PhD dissertation, University of Connecticut, 1956.

42. Sung-hwa Lee, "The Social and Political Factors Affecting Korean Education."

43. Won-Sul Lee, "The Impact of United States Occupation Policy

on the Socio-political Structure of South Korea, 1945–1948," unpublished PhD dissertation, Western Reserve University, 1961.

44. Byung Hun Nam, "Educational Reorganization."

45. Hyung Koo Pak, "Social Changes."

46. Harold H. Koh, "The Early History of U.S. Economic Assistance to the Republic of Korea, 1945–1955 (mimeographed, Cambridge, Harvard Institute for International Development, September 1975).

47. Sung-hwa Lee, "Social and Political Factors." It is difficult to evaluate statistics on literacy in Korea. The Korean alphabet, Han'gŭl, has only 24 characters, and reading can be learned in a relatively short period of time. Literacy figures are reported on the basis of knowing Han'gŭl. But without knowledge of about 1,000 additional Chinese characters, it is impossible to read most books and newspapers.

"There are several factors which contributed to this rapid decrease in illiteracy and the first is the national campaign for literacy conducted by the Ministry of Education, which achieved great results, namely, during 75 days in March through May, 1954, 84,000 literacy classes were organized at which 1,970,000 persons learned the Korean alphabet . . . The second condition . . . is the fact that Korean letters are easy to teach and learn . . . it takes 14 to 28 hours for a normal adult to learn to read and write simple sentences and, upon reaching this state of learning, one is considered literate in most cases. The third factor is that in this country, the standard of literacy is set at a comparatively low level. (It) is based on subjective reports" Hamil Jong-gon Hwang, "Adult Education: Imperative for a New Society," *Korea Journal* 6.7:9–12, 19 (July 1966), pp. 9–10.

A similar drive to eliminate illiteracy took place in North Korea as well. Unlike the south, however, North Korea chose to eliminate entirely the use of Chinese characters, so that all reading material is comprehensible to a "literate" person. The north reported achieving universal literacy by 1956. Byung Soon Song, "Comparative Study of Ideological Influences in Educational Theory and Practice in North and South Korea," unpublished PhD dissertation, Wayne State University, 1974.

48. See Wilson.

49. Koh, p. 66.

50. Ibid.

51. Byung Hun Nam, p. 221.

52. See Byung Soon Song's "Comparative Study."

53. See Dodge's "History of U.S. Assistance."

54. Ibid., p. 61.

55. See William M. Williams, "Foreign Assistance to Korean Education," *Korea Journal* 2.1:16–18 (January 1962).

56. Dodge, p. 103.

57. Ibid., p. 276.

58. Arthur Feraru, "Korean Students in the United States." *School and Society* 86:60–62 (1974).

59. P. 284.

60. Tai-si Chung, "Korean Education."

61. Dodge, pp. 280–281.

62. Jagdish Bhagwati and William Dallalfar, "The Brain Drain and Income Taxation: A Proposal," Working Paper No. 92, Massachusetts Institute of Technology, Department of Economics, 1972.

63. Byung-hun Oh, "University Students and Politics in Korea," *Koreana Quarterly* 9.4:1–41 (winter 1967). College students later served only one and a half years in the military instead of three years. This exception lasted from 1955 to 1962.

64. For a good review of this history, see Norbert J. Tracy, "Education in this Remarkable Republic of Korea," in Society of Jesus, *Korean Sociological Survey,* Seoul, 1969.

65. Jin Eun Kim, p. 132.

66. Horace Underwood, "Korean Education: Master of the Future or Slave of the Past?" *Koreana Quarterly* 5.3:52–60 (autumn 1963), p. 54.

67. The following description could apply to the late 1950s, illustrating the ironies of history:

> There are not nearly enough appointments, official or otherwise, to go round, and you can see that the high schools and the university are aggravating the problem of unemployment; aggravating it in a particularly insidious way by loosing upon a simple and primitive people an increasing band of conceited young men, talented in their own manner, with a prestige of learning, naturally fluent and force-ful in speech, and hankering for an upheaval in the expectation of plunder in the form of lucrative offices in the new State.
>
> H. B. Drake, *Korea of the Japanese* (London, 1930), p. 138, cited in Chung Han Kim, "Changing Functions of Women's Higher Education in the Republic of Korea: A Study of Educational Equality Between Men and Women," unpublished PhD dissertation, George Peabody College for Teachers, 1975.

68. Hyun-ki Paik, "Present State of Education."

69. UNESCO, *Long-Term Projections for Education in the Republic of Korea* (Bangkok, 1965).

70. Seung-Shik Oh, "Economic Development and Human Resources: with Reference to University Education," *Koreana Quarterly* 8.1:37–48 (spring 1966).

71. Oscar Perez de Tagle, "The Stage Theory of Balanced Educational-Economic Development and its Application to Countries with Educated Unemployment," unpublished PhD dissertation, University of Wisconsin, 1973, quoting from *The International Migration of High-Level Manpower*, n. 72 below.

72. Heather Low Ruth, "Korea," in Committee on the International Migration of Talent, *The International Migration of High-Level Manpower* (New York, 1970), pp. 130–131.

73. "A Systematic Sub-optimization Model for Educational Planning."

74. These investments did not, apparently, always have rapid economic returns:

> The budget of the Korean School System was entirely inadequate to meet the objective of universal compulsory education for elementary school children as well as the demand at other levels of education. The American advisor to the Department of Education remarked bitterly in October 1948 that "the government had to make its choice between achieving the goal of universal elementary education and building a strong police force and military might." According to this advisor, the government "chose the latter course" and education suffered. Wilson, p. 129.

THREE   *Education and Growth of the Economy*

1. Cole and Lyman, p. 4.

2. Frederick H. Harbison, *Human Resources as the Wealth of Nations* (New York, 1973), p. 47.

3. UNESCO, *Republic of Korea: Educational Services in a Rapidly Growing Economy.*

4. See Edward F. Denison, "Measuring the Contribution of Education to Economic Growth," in E. A. G. Robinson and J. E. Vaizey, eds., *Economics of Education* (New York, 1966); G. U. Papi, "General Problems of the Economics of Education," in Robinson and Vaizey; Fritz Machlup, *Education and Economic Growth* (Lincoln, Nebraska, 1970).

5. See Garry S. Becker, *Human Capital and the Personal Distribution of Income: An Analytical Approach* (Ann Arbor, 1967); also Jacob Mincer, "The Distribution of Labor Incomes: A Survey with Special Reference to the Human Capital Approach," *Journal of Economic Literature* 8.1:1–26 (March 1970); and Surjit Bhalla, "The Education-Income Connection—An Investigative Report," Discussion Paper No. 40, Research Programs in

Economic Development, Woodrow Wilson School, Princeton University, 1973.

6. Curtis L. Gilroy, "Investment in Human Capital and Black-White Employment," *Monthly Labor Review* 98.7:13-21 (July 1975).

7. Randall Collins, "Functional and Conflict Theories of Educational Stratification," *American Sociological Review* 36.6:1002-1019 (December 1971).

8. See Thomas J. LaBelle and Robert E. Verhine, "Nonformal Education and Occupational Stratification: Implications for Latin America," *Harvard Educational Review* 45.2:160-190 (May 1975) for an elaboration of these hypotheses and their validation in other countries.

9. Kwang Suk Kim and Michael Roemer, *Growth and Structural Transformation, Studies in the Modernization of the Republic of Korea: 1945-1975* (Cambridge, Mass., 1978), pp. 22-23. The comparison was based on 1944 provincial statistics for land and population, and 1939-1940 data for production.

10. Ibid., pp. 26-28.

11. Ibid., pp. 32-33.

12. Yŏng-bong Kim, *Uri nara kyoyukpi, kyoyuk suyo hyŏngt'ae mit kyoyuk ŭi kyŏngje sŏngjang kiyŏ punsŏk* (Seoul, 1975).

13. Chang Young Jeong, "Rates of Return on Investment in Education," in Chuk Kyo Kim, ed., *Industrial and Social Development Issues,* Essays on the Korean Economy Vol. II (Seoul, Korea Development Institute, 1977).

14. Charles R. Frank, Kwang Suk Kim, and Larry E. Westphal, *Foreign Trade Regimes and Economic Development: South Korea* (New York, 1975).

15. Recently, the Korean economy has begun to experience a shortage of labor supply, especially in technical areas. The abundance of educated manpower has been denied, and manpower development has been stressed in recent plans. See Shin-Bok Kim, pp. 20-26, and Han'guk Kyoyuk Kaebal Yŏn'guwŏn, *Kyoyuk kyehoek e kwanhan kich'o t'onggye charyo* (Seoul, 1975).

16. See Youngkee Lee, "A Study on the Measurement of Education Investment to Economic Growth," in Ministry of Finance, *Reports Financed by the Academic Research Promotion Fund,* Vol. 3 (Seoul, 1969); Yŏng-bong Kim, *Uri nara kyoyukpi*; and Sin-bok Kim and Nae-yŏng Pak, "Kyoyuk kwa kukka palchŏn," *Kukka palchŏn e taehan kyoyuk ŭi kiyŏ (1945-1975),* (Seoul, Korea Educational Development Institute, 1976). Youngkee Lee, applying Schultz's approach, credited 15% of economic growth during 1962-1968 to education investment. Yŏng-bong Kim, applying Denison's methods, estimated that education increased

manufacturing production by 1.2% during the period 1960–1966, which accounted for 5.5% of the growth of manufacturing production. Han Heyn Kim, "On the Role of Human Capital in Optimal Growth (unpublished PhD dissertation, Stanford University, 1971), used a production function approach to estimate that 38% of the growth in GDP from 1955 to 1969 was attributable to wages paid, or the value of human capital.

17. Denison, "Measuring the Contribution" and in *Why Growth Rates Differ* (Washington, The Brookings Institution, 1967).

18. Marcelo Selowsky, "On the Measurement of Education's Contribution to Growth," *Quarterly Journal of Economics* 83.3:449–463 (August 1969).

19. Wontack Hong, "Statistical Data on Korea's Trade and Growth," Appendix to *Exports and Employment in Korea* (Seoul, Korea Development Institute, 1975).

20. See Denison, *Why Growth Rates Differ,* pp. 80–83, for the method and rationale. Age classes adopted here are different from those used by Denison. Indexes are constructed for age groups under 25, 25–34, 35–44, and over 45 considering the composition of labor force given below.

Percentages of Labor Force by Age Groups, 1974

	Under 25	25–34	35–44	Over 45
Male	21.4	27.7	25.1	25.8
Female	33.4	17.7	23.1	25.8

Source: Economic Planning Board, *Employment Statistics,* 1974.

21. Primary school dropouts constitute 7.3% of the workers with less than elementary school education, and the proportion of dropouts in secondary level is only 3.6% in 1970. It is customary in Korea that wages are determined on the basis of the level of schooling completed rather than years of education attained. The 70% assumption may not deviate much from reality since Denison's index of earnings for the United States and northwest Europe shows a similar pattern, 50% for 0 years and 80% for 5–7 years. (See Denison, *Why Growth Rates Differ,* pp. 83–85.)

22. Material presented in Chapter 4 will deal with the extent to which income differences result from differences generated by educational attainment as opposed to those attached to sex or class or region.

23. Denison, *Why Growth Rates Differ,* p. 190.

24. See Youngkee Lee, pp. 60–62 and Yŏng-bong Kim, *Uri nara kyoyukpi,* pp. 52–53.

25. Suggested by Dwight Perkins, in commenting on an earlier draft of this work.

26. For example, Collins in "Functional and Conflict Theories" and LaBelle and Verhine in "Nonformal Education."

27. For example, Samuel Bowles, "Schooling and Inequality from Generation to Generation," in Theodore Schultz, ed., *The Equity-Efficiency Quandary* (Chicago, 1972); Bowles and Herbert Gintis, "The Problem with Human Capital Theory—A Marxian Critique," *American Economic Review* 65.2:74–72 (May 1975); and Mark Blaug, "Human Capital Theory: A Slightly Jaundiced Survey," *Journal of Economic Literature* 14.3:827–855 (September 1976).

28. See, for example, Donald Adams, and Sung-hwa Lee.

29. Korea was known traditionally as "The Land of Scholars and Gentlemen"; see Sung-hwa Lee. Describing Korea in the 1950s after the war, Elaine Barnes wrote: "Traditionally, the prestige symbol has been education. Other symbols, too, are important, but the shortage of consumer goods makes these even harder to realize. Consequently, there is a great turning to education, bought at the price of sacrifice of food, housing, warmth—all the necessities" (p. 97).

30. Collins, p. 1015.

31. Simplistic as it may be, many educational plans are justified on exactly these grounds, that education will lead to growth.

32. Chong Ch'ol Kim, and Jin Eun Kim. See Chapter 1 for details of this plan.

33. A study of the relationship between technical education and economic growth in Taiwan has shown that expansion of technical education "generally has resulted from industrial development rather than leading such development." Ying Cheng Chuang, "Predicting the Optimum Requirements for Technical Education in Relation to Industrial Development in a Developing Country," unpublished PhD dissertation, University of California, Los Angeles, 1967.

34. Dodge, p. 103.

35. Bom Mo Chung, "Impact of American Culture."

36. Chapter 5 presents a more detailed review of research on the contribution of education to "modern" attitudes.

37. Sung Chick Hong, "Values of Korean Farmers, Businessmen and Professors," in *International Conference on the Problems of Modernization in Asia: Report* (Seoul, 1965), p. 799.

38. Sung-mo Huang, "The Role of Industrial Laborers in the Modernization of Korea," in *International Conference* (see n. 37 above), p. 775.

FOUR   *Education and Income Distribution*

1. For example by Irma Adelman, "South Korea," in Hollis Chenery et al., *Redistribution with Growth* (London, 1974).

2. See, for example, Raymond Boudon, *Education, Opportunity and Social Inequality* (New York, 1974).

3. Christopher Jencks et al., *Inequality* (New York, 1972).

4. See Harry T. Oshima, "Income Inequality and Economic Growth, The Postwar Experience in Asian Countries," *Malayan Economic Review* 15.2: 7–41 (October 1970); Num-Kyoo Chae, "Income Size Distribution in Korea," paper prepared for the Working Group Seminar on Income Distribution, Manila, January 1972; Montek S. Ahluwalia, "Income Inequality: Some Dimensions of the Problem," in Chenery et al., *Distribution with Growth*; and Bertrand Renaud, "Economic Growth and Income Inequality in Korea," paper presented for the Tenth Anniversary Conference of the Population and Development Studies Center, Seoul National University, January 1975.

5. See Mun-Kyoo Chae, and Renaud.

6. See Adelman.

7. Adelman; Renaud; and Hakchung Choo, "Some Sources of Relative Equity in Korean Income Distribution: A Historical Perspective," in Japan Economic Research Center/Council for Asian Manpower Studies, *Income Distribution, Employment and Economic Development in Southeast and East Asia* (Tokyo and Manila, 1975).

8. Hakchung Choo, "Some Sources of Relative Equity," Appendix; his "Review of Income Distribution Studies, Data Availability and Associated Problems for Korea, the Philippines and Taiwan," Monograph 7406, Seoul, Korea Development Institute, 1974; and William I. Abraham, "Observations on Korea's Income Distribution and the Adequacy of the Statistical Base" (mimeo, Harvard Institute for International Development, April 1976).

9. In *Size Distribution of Income: A Compilation of Data* (Washington, 1975).

10. Most estimates for this period are based on a small income and expenditure survey conducted in 1966 by Chungang University under a USOM contract. The authors of the survey report did not themselves compute a Gini ratio, and subsequent analysts, adjusting the survey results in different ways, have produced moderately different values: Oshima obtained a value of 0.265, while Chae put it as 0.335, and Jain cites a figure of 0.3416 computed by a World Bank consultant. There is even confusion about the reference period of the survey, which Oshima and apparently Adelman thought was 1964 but is now said to be January-March 1966. Hakchung Choo, "Some Sources of Relative Equity," Appendix.

11. Felix Paukert, "Income Distribution at Different Levels of Development: A Survey of Evidence," *International Labour Review* 108.203:97–125 (August-September 1973); and Ahluwalia, "Income Inequality."

12. Several historical factors, noted below, buttress the purely statistical evidence supporting this conclusion.

13. Adelman, p. 284.

14. Jain, pp. 65–66.

15. Adelman, p. 284; Renaud.

16. Renaud; Abraham.

17. Abraham, p. 18.

18. Hakchung Choo, "Review of Income Distribution Studies"; and Abraham.

19. There is reason to believe that rapidly growing countries are more likely to experience growing inequality than slowly growing countries, at least for a period of time. However, this proposition cannot be established with presently available data. Such time series data as the World Bank has been able to assemble suggest a wide variety of country experiences and no clear relationships (Ahluwalia, pp. 13–16).

20. Adelman; and Hakchung Choo, "Some Sources of Relative Equity."

21. Hakchung Choo, Ibid., pp. 54–58.

22. One chŏngbo = 2.45 acres.

23. Adelman, p. 280.

24. See Hakchung Choo, "Some Sources of Relative Equity," pp. 61–62. On the other hand, fortunes were also made during the war. Choo observes that businessmen from the southeastern part of the country, which escaped the destruction of the war, did especially well and remain prominent among leading industrialists and businessmen to this day (p. 63). Some of the wealth accumulated illegally during the war and immediate post-war years was confiscated after the Student Revolution of April 1960 (pp. 64–67), but it seems unlikely these confiscations amounted to more than a fraction of the money so earned.

25. See Harbison and Myers.

26. Irma Adelman and Cynthia Taft Morris, *Economic Growth and Social Equity in Developing Countries* (Stanford, 1973).

27. See Cole and Lyman; and Gilbert T. Brown, *Korean Pricing Policies and Economic Development in the 1960s* (Baltimore, 1973).

28. Paul Kuznets, "Labor Absorption in Korea since 1963," Working Paper No. 16, International Development Research Center, Indiana University, 1972; and David C. Cole and Larry E. Westphal, "The Contribution of Exports to Employment in Korea," in Wontack Hong and Anne O. Krueger, eds., *Trade and Development in Korea* (Seoul, 1975).

29. Adelman, p. 284.

30. Sedjo has documented the rise in real wages in both agriculture and industry from 1963–1964 on, a rise which he attributed to a transition from a labor surplus economy to conditions of labor scarcity. Roger A. Sedjo, "The Turning Point for the Korean Economy," in Sung-Hwan Jo and Seong-Young Park, eds., *Basic Documents and Selected Papers of Korea's Third Five-Year Economic Development Plan, 1972–1976* (Seoul, 1972).

31. Frederick H. Harbison, "Education and Income Distribution" (mimeo, 1973).

32. Highlighted here to stress its importance, the educational finance question will not be accorded a separate section in the discussion which follows because of overlaps with the other two subsections. The use of fees as a means of limiting access to post-primary schooling will be discussed in relation to the access question, while the effect of fees in limiting the net economic benefits of education will be mentioned in the discussion of education's effect on the incomes of the educated. Also, educational finance was discussed in Chapter 1.

33. A complication in interpreting the enrollment ratio for 18–21-year-olds is the fact that a significant number of males are still in college after age 21 as a result of delays in their education caused by compulsory military service. In a 1-percent sample of 1970 census data this group represented 16.6% of enrollment among those 18 or older. However, it seems probable that the effect of this phenomenon is relatively steady over time, so that the intertemporal comparison in Figure 8 should not be seriously distorted.

34. Ministry of Education, *Education in Korea 1974–75* (Seoul, 1975), p. 9.

35. See UNESCO, *Long-Term Projections for Education*, p. 11.

36. Charles Nam, "Group Disparities in Educational Participation," in Organization for Economic Cooperation and Development, *Conference in Policies for Education Growth IV. Group Disparities in Educational Participation and Achievement* (Paris, 1971).

37. In Korean practice these are called si (cities), ku (boroughs), or kun (counties). We use the term "county" to include all three categories.

38. Again using Charles Nam's data as a basis for comparison, we see that overall regional variation in enrollment ratios is relatively small in Korea. Dividing the country into ten regions (nine provinces and Seoul), we can calculate a 1960 mean enrollment ratio for the over-13 groups in each region, a standard deviation for the ten regional means and a coefficient of variation (standard deviation as a percentage of the mean) which comes out to be 11.2%. Nam has done similar calculations for secondary-level enrollments in OECD member countries, of which 14 (Austria, Belgium,

France, Germany, Greece, Ireland, Italy, Norway, Portugal, Spain, Sweden, Turkey, England and Wales, and Yugoslavia) turn out to have more relative variation among regional enrollment ratios than Korea and only 4 (Canada, Japan, the Netherlands, and the United States) have less.

39. However, students may also establish a residence in Seoul (e.g., with a relative) for the purpose of going to school there; the statistics would probably not reflect this practice.

40. Hyun-ki Paik, "Present State of Education."

41. "Changing Functions of Women's Higher Education," p. 166.

42. Ibid.

43. Academic "merit" may of course be unrelated to the requirements for life as a productive or happy citizen. We found no research on the entrance examinations used to select students for higher levels, although various foreign advisory groups have commented on the doubtful validity of the tests (e.g., UNESCO-UNKRA, *Rebuilding Education in the Republic of Korea,* Paris, 1954). Many employers select graduates from high school or the university on the basis of a company-manufactured test, rather than relying solely on grades or school examination results (Grant, p. 155).

44. Jacob Mincer, "On the Job Training: Costs, Returns and Some Implications," *Journal of Political Economy,* Supplement, October 1962.

45. In Han'guk chejoŏp ŭi imgŭm kyŏkch'a kujo (Seoul, Korea Development Institute, 1975).

46. Reported in University of Minnesota, *Annual Report: 1976,* Economic Development Center.

47. Kwang Suk Kim, "Rates of Return on Education in Korea" (mimeo, USAID/Korea, 1968).

48. John Chang, "Schooling and Earning Differentials: The Korean Experience," Appendix B to Morgan and Chadwick, eds., *Systems Analysis for Educational Change.*

49. Chang Young Jeong, "Rates of Return on Investment in Education."

50. George Psacharopoulos and Keith Hinchcliffe, *Returns to Education: An International Comparison* (Amsterdam and San Francisco, 1973).

51. Namely, 1) that the high rate of return on physical capital was possible only because of the large existing pool of skilled manpower (this is so, but it would be consistent with a low rate of return on human capital if the large supply of skilled manpower had driven down earnings differentials and would suggest increasing the supply of physical capital relative to human capital); and 2) that adding a 10% allowance for inflation makes rates of return on human capital comparable to returns on physical capital (one suspects that this is spurious, in that the estimated rate of return on physical capital—insofar as it *has* any sound basis—was probably already calculated in real terms).

52. All of the discussion above, as well as all the research we have reviewed, is concerned exclusively with social rates of return to education, but what matters to individuals is the private rate of return. By definition, the difference between these two concepts is educational costs borne by society. The private rate of return is therefore always higher than the social rate of return. In countries where most educational costs are publicly financed, this difference is great, and high private rates of return can coexist with low social rates. By contrast, in Korea, where households pay two-thirds of the direct costs of education and all the indirect costs, the private returns on educational investments cannot be much higher than the social returns to society.

53. Paul Kuznets has suggested that education may be an especially powerful selection device in the Korean case because of the unique ethnic, historical, linguistic, and cultural homogeneity of the people and because of the virtual destruction of the pre-war class structure by the end of the Korean War; unpublished ms. on education in Korea. Bae-Ho Hahn and Kyu-Taik Kim, "Korean Political Leaders (1952–1962): Their Social Origins and Skills," *Asian Survey* (July 1963), cited by Kuznets, found a university education to be a virtual prerequisite for obtaining a high-level political or bureaucratic position in the early 1960s.

FIVE   *Education as a Source of Values and Attitudes Conducive to Modernization*

1. Little is known about what students are actually learning in Korean schools. Apparently only one study has been done on the cognitive abilities that children acquire through education. This unpublished 1972 research by the Korean Institute for Research in the Behavioral Sciences was designed to compare the abilities of persons of different ages and length of schooling to carry out basic social tasks. For example, only 17% of high school graduates could write at a reasonable level.

One study sought to measure students' knowledge of the political process in Korea. Sae-gu Chung, "The Political Socialization of Selected Elementary and Middle School Students to the Republic of Korea: Political Knowledge, Political Trust, and Political Efficacy," unpublished PhD dissertation, Florida State University, 1973, gave 509 students in one primary and two middle schools in a suburb of Seoul a test measuring knowledge of national politics. He found little knowledge about the political process among 5th and 8th grade students, but high knowledge among 6th and 9th grade students. The 8th grade students knew only half as much as the

6th grade students. This finding makes sense if we can presume that the 6th and 9th grade curricula emphasize national politics, and the 5th and 8th grade curricula do not, and that students retain little of what they are taught.

2. C. E. Black, *The Dynamics of Modernization* (New York, 1966).

3. Marion J. Levy, *Modernization and the Structure of Societies*, 2 vols. (Princeton, 1966).

4. See also Patrick H. Irwin, "An Operational Definition of Societal Modernization," *Economic Development and Cultural Change* 23.4:595–614 (July 1975).

5. S.N. Eisenstadt, *Modernization: Protest and Change* (Englewood Cliffs, N.J., 1966).

6. Daniel Lerner, *The Passing of Traditional Society* (Glencoe, Ill., 1958).

7. W. Arthur Lewis, *The Theory of Economic Growth* (Homewood, Ill., 1965).

8. David Apter, *Choice and the Politics of Allocation* (New Haven, 1971).

9. Black, p. 77.

10. Ibid., pp. 77–78.

11. Theories of modernization based on historical analyses, which is all of them, end up defining in normative terms relationships that existed previously in other societies. Levy and Black, for example, convert their description of what has happened in the past to statements of what must happen in the future if a nation wishes to modernize. The theories pursue a strict determinism in which there is little or no room for choice by peoples or governments. Needless to say, this too is ideology, and has been used to justify a variety of actions, including violence and repression in the name of development.

12. Michael T. Hannan, "Societal Development and the Expansion of Educational Systems" (Washington, National Center for Educational Research, 1973).

13. Ibid., p. 7.

14. Alex Inkeles and David H. Smith, *Becoming Modern: Individual Change in Six Developing Countries* (Cambridge, Mass., 1974). Although not couched in terms of "modernization" many of the same individual variables are also discussed by David C. McCelland, in *The Achieving Society* (Princeton, 1961), "Does Education Accelerate Economic Growth?," *Economic Development and Cultural Change* 14.3:257–278 (April 1966), and *Motivating Economic Achievement* in terms of Need for Achievement. McCelland argues from cross-national data that increases in educational investment tend to be associated with increases in achievement

values, which in turn are associated with economic growth. But the direction of causality is not always that education leads to economic growth.

15. Alex Inkeles, "The Modernization of Man," in Myron Weiner, ed., *Modernization* (New York, 1966).

16. Inkeles and Smith, p. 143.

17. Ibid., pp. 272–273.

18. Ibid., pp. 312–313.

19. Ibid., p. 142. For similar arguments, see Ineke Cunningham, "The Relationship between Modernity of Students in a Puerto Rican High School and their Academic Performance, Peers and Parents," in Alex Inkeles and Donald B. Holsinger, eds., *Education and Individual Modernity in Developing Countries* (Leiden, 1974); Donald B. Holsinger, "The Elementary School as Modernizer; A Brazilian Study" and Richard Sack "The Impact of Education on Individual Modernity in Tunisia," both in the same volume.

20. Martin Carnoy, "A 'Landmark' from a 'Time of Optimism' for the Modern World," *School Review* 84:127–136 (1975).

21. Harvey Leibenstein, "Shortages and Surpluses in Education in Underdeveloped Countries," in Arnold Anderson and Mary Jean Bowman, eds., *Education and Economic Development* (Chicago, 1965).

22. Ross Harold Cole, p. 353.

23. Alejandro Portes, "Modernity and Development: A Critique," *Studies in Comparative International Development* VIII: 247–279 (1973), p. 269.

24. Suk-jo Kim and Quee-Young Kim, "Social Structure and Legal Culture in Korea," unpublished ms., 1977.

25. While not endorsing immoral or Machiavellian conduct, McClelland notes that individuals high in Need for Achievement may cut corners, act in a sly or cunning fashion. Inkeles, on the other hand, argues that city workers should be more, not less, religious than rural people.

26. Young-ho Lee, "The Political Culture of a Modernizing Society: Political Attitudes and Democracy in Korea," unpublished PhD dissertation, Yale University, 1970.

27. T'ae-gil Kim, *Han'guk taehaksaeng ŭi Kach'igwan, 1964* (Seoul, 1967.

28. Sŭng-jik Hong, *Han'guk kach'igwan yŏn'gu* (Seoul, 1969).

29. Wŏn-sŏl Yi, "Haksaeng undong Kwa Han'guk chŏngch'i," *Yŏngnam Taehakkyo nonmunjip* 4:127–166 (1970).

30. Sae-gu Chung, "Political Socialization of Selected Elementary and Middle School Students."

31. Ui-Yong Ham, "Democratization of Political Consciousness in Korea," *Korea Journal* 14.1:8–20 (January 1974).

32. Se-jin Kim, "Attitudinal Orientations of Korean Workers," *Korea Journal* 12.9:18–30 (September 1972), p. 20.

33. Kyu-pŏm Yi, Kyun-bo Kim, and Chae-hwan Ha, "Kakkŭp hakkyo haksaeng tŭl ŭi kukka ŭisik e kwanhan yŏn'gu," monograph, Pusan Teachers College, 1975.

34. The rejection of anti-communism and nationalism is a direct contradiction of educational policy as expressed in the National Charter of Education. The National Charter has three paragraphs. The first speaks of being born into a historical mission of national regeneration. The second paragraph lists the values that individuals must have to fulfill their obligation to serve and build the nation. The third paragraph reads as follows:

> The love of country and fellow countrymen together with the firm belief in democracy against communism is the way for our survival and the basis for realizing the ideals of the free world. Looking forward to the future when we shall have the honorable fatherland unified for the everlasting good of posterity, we, as an industrious people, with confidence and pride pledge ourselves to make new history with untiring effort and collective wisdom of the whole nation.
> (From Ministry of Education, *Educational Development in Korea,* 1975.)

The history and intent of the Charter is described by Hyung-jin Yoo, "The Charter of National Education," *Korea Journal* 9.8:4–7 (August 1969).

35. Hichul Henry Whang, "The Tasks of Public Education as Perceived by the Public in the Republic of Korea," unpublished PhD dissertation, University of Wisconsin, 1972.

36. See T'ae-gil Kim.

37. See Solomon Rettig and Benjamin Pasamanick, "Moral Codes of American and Korean College Students," *Journal of Social Psychology* 50:65–73 (1959), and their "Invariance in Factor Structure of Moral Value Judgments from American and Korean College Students," *Sociometry* 25:73–84 (1962); also Rettig and Jin-Sook Lee, "Differences in Moral Judgments of South Korean Students Before and After the Korean Revolution," *Journal of Social Psychology* 59:3–9 (1963).

38. Rettig and Lee.

39. H. J. Eysenck, *Sense and Nonsense in Psychology* (London, 1957).

40. O, Pyŏng-hŏn, Yŏng-bok Ko, and Yŏng-dŏk Yi, *Haksaeng munje yŏn'gu* (Seoul, 1970).

41. Ibid., p. 281.

42. And a disproportionate number of the jailed "subversives" are

Christians, supposedly more modern in their orientation than Buddhists or adherents of other religions.

43. Andrew J. Sofranko and Robert C. Bealer, "Modernization Balance, Imbalance and Domestic Instability," *Economic Development and Cultural Change* 22.1:52–72 (October 1973).

SIX   *Education and the Development of Korea*

1. See Boudon, *Education, Opportunity and Social Inequality.*

2. Nancy Baster and Wolf Scott, *Levels of Living and Economic Growth: A Comparative Study of Six Countries 1950–1965* (Geneva, 1969).

3. For example, Chang Young Jeong.

4. The best known of these studies are James Coleman, et al., *Equality of Educational Opportunity* (Washington, 1966); Torsten Husen, ed., *International Study of Achievement in Mathematics: A Comparison of 12 Countries* (Stockholm and New York, 1967); G. F. Peaker, *The Plowden Children Four Years Later* (Slough, U. K., 1971); Christopher Jencks, et al., *Inequality*, and Alan C. Purves and Daniel V. Levine, eds., *Educational Policy and International Assessment* (Berkeley, 1975).

5. Perhaps as a result of evaluative studies in the late 1960s, interest in skill training has increased. See Hyun-ki Paik, "Nonformal Education in Korea: Programs and Prospects," in Cole S. Brembeck and Timothy J. Thompson, eds., *New Strategies for Educational Development* (Lexington, Mass., 1973) and J. H. Lee, "Economic Value of Korean Farmers' Education: Their Productivity and Earnings," unpublished MA Thesis, Cornell University, 1969, for samples of studies showing a high return to training in industry and agriculture, respectively.

6. This section owes much to the work of John W. Meyer, "The Effects of Education as an Institution," *American Journal of Sociology* 83.1: 55–77 (July 1977).

7. W. Mischel, *Introduction to Personality* (New York, 1971).

8. Meyer, p. 55.

9. Ibid.

10. And late-developing countries place even greater reliance on formal education as a credential-bestowing device than countries which developed earlier; Ronald Dore, *The Diploma Disease* (Berkeley and Los Angeles, 1976).

11. Meyer, p. 67.

12. Previously, access to these newly preferred forms of higher education was controlled largely through competition for admittance to a few prestigious high schools. Now the most important selection point is university admission; those who get into Seoul National University particularly are regarded as being tagged for success.

13. Hahn Been Lee and In-joung Whang, "Development of Senior Administrators: The Korean Experience," *Koreana Quarterly* 13.3:1–18 (autumn 1973).

14. Meyer, p. 680.

15. Ross Harold Cole, pp. 301–302.

Bibliography

Abraham, William I. "Observations on Korea's Income Distribution and the Adequacy of the Statistical Base." Mimeographed. Harvard Institute for International Development, April 1976.

Adams, Donald K. "Education in Korea 1945-1955." Unpublished PhD dissertation, University of Connecticut, 1956.

Adelman, Irma. "South Korea," in Hollis Chenery et al., *Redistribution with Growth.* London, Oxford University Press, 1974.

—— and Cynthia Taft Morris. *Economic Growth and Social Equity in Developing Countries.* Stanford, Stanford University Press, 1973.

Ahluwalia, Montek S. "Income Inequality: Some Dimensions of the Problem," in Hollis Chenery et al., *Redistribution with Growth.* London, Oxford University Press, 1974.

Ahmed, Manzoor. "Republic of Korea: A Multipurpose Farmer Education Program," in M. Ahmed and P. H. Coombs, eds., *Education for Rural Development.* New York, Praeger, 1975.

Apter, David. *Choice and the Politics of Allocation.* New Haven, Yale University Press, 1971.

Bank of Korea. *National Income in Korea, 1975.* Seoul.

——. *Economic Statistics Yearbook, 1976.* Seoul.

Barnes, Elaine Milam. "The School of Taegu, Kyongsang Pukto [North Kyŏngsang] Province, Korea, in 1954-1955: An Investigation into the Interaction between Culture and Education." Unpublished PhD dissertation, University of Maryland, 1960.

Baster, Nancy and Wolf Scott. *Levels of Living and Economic Growth. A Comparative Study of Six Countries, 1950-1965.* Geneva, United Nations Research Institute for Social Development, 1969.

Becker, Garry S. *Human Capital and the Personal Distribution of Income: An Analytical Approach.* Ann Arbor, Institute of Public Administration Department of Economics, University of Michigan, 1967.

Beirn, Russell, David C. Kinsey, and Noel F. McGinn. "Antecedents and Consequences of Early School Leaving," *Bulletin of the International Bureau of Education* 46.182 (first quarter, 1972).

Bhagwati, Jagdish and William Dallalfar. "The Brain Drain and Income Taxation: A Proposal." Working Paper No. 92, Department of Economics, Massachusetts Institute of Technology, 1972.

Bhalla, Surjit. "The Education-Income Connection—An Investigative Report." Discussion Paper No. 40, Research Program in Economic Development, Woodrow Wilson School, Princeton University, 1973.

Black, C. E. *The Dynamics of Modernization*. New York, Harper and Row, 1966.

Blaug, Mark. "Human Capital Theory: A Slightly Jaundiced Survey," *Journal of Economic Literature* 14.3:827–855 (September 1976).

Boudon, Raymond. *Education, Opportunity and Social Inequality*. New York, Wiley, 1974.

Bowles, Samuel. "Schooling and Inequality from Generation to Generation," in Theodore W. Schultz, ed., *The Equity-Efficiency Quandary*. Chicago, University of Chicago Press, 1972.

—— and Herbert Gintis. "The Problem with Human Capital Theory—A Marxian Critique," *American Economic Review* 65.2:74–82 (May 1975).

Brown, Gilbert T. *Korean Pricing Policies and Economic Development in the 1960s*. Baltimore, Johns Hopkins University Press, 1973.

Carnoy, Martin. "A 'Landmark' from a 'Time of Optimism' for the Modern World," *School Review* 84:127–136 (1975).

Central Education Research Institute. "A Study of Education Administration in Korea." Research Bulletin No. 45, Seoul, 1967.

—— *A Comprehensive Study on the Contents of Higher Education*. Seoul, 1967.

Chae, Mun-Kyoo (Ch'ae, Mun-gyu). "Income Size Distribution in Korea." Paper prepared for the Working Group Seminar on Income Distribution, Manila, January 1972.

Chang, John. "Schooling and Earning Differentials: The Korean Experience," Appendix B to Robert M. Morgan and Clifton B. Chadwick, eds., *Systems Analysis for Educational Change: The Republic of Korea*. Tallahassee, Department of Educational Research, Florida State University, 1971.

Chang, Yunshik (Chang, Yun-sik). "Education in Korea 1945–1970: A Comparison of North and South Korea." Workshop on Korean Modernization: North and South, University of Puerto Rico, January 1976.

Choe, Byung Sook (Ch'oe, Pyŏng-suk). "The Impact of the Government Policy on the Development of Education in the First Republic of Korea, 1948–1960." Unpublished PhD dissertation, University of Pittsburgh, 1971.

Choi, Michyun. "Social Attitudes of Yonsei and Korea University Students." Unpublished MA thesis, Korea University, 1971.

Choi, Sun Pyo (Ch'oe, Sŏn-p'yo). "The Problem of Reconstructing Korean Education in Historical Perspective." Unpublished PhD dissertation, University of Illinois, 1960.

Chŏng, Ch'ang-yŏng. See Jeong, Chang Young.

Choo, Hakchung (Chu, Hak-chung). "Review of Income Distribution Studies, Data Availability and Associated Problems for Korea, the Philippines and Taiwan." Monograph 7406. Seoul, Korea Development Institute, 1974.

————. "Some Sources of Relative Equity in Korean Income Distribution: A Historical Perspective," in Japan Economic Research Center/Council for Asian Manpower Studies, *Income Distribution, Employment and Economic Development in Southeast and East Asia.* Tokyo and Manila, 1975. Subsequently reprinted, edited and without Appendix, in Chuk Kyo Kim (Chŏk-kyo Kim), ed., *Industrial and Social Development Issues.* Essays on the Korean Economs, Vol. II. Seoul, Korea Development Institute, 1977.

Chŏn, Yong-sin. "Han'guk taehaksaeng ŭi chŏngch'ijŏk t'aedo," (The political attitudes of Korean college students), Koryŏ Taehakkyo nonmunjip, che 15-gwŏn (Korea University thesis collection, Vol. 15). 1969)

Chŏng, Kang-su and Kwang-sŏk Kim (Kwang Suk Kim). *Han'guk chejoŏp ŭi imgŭm kyŏkch'a kujo* (Structure of wage inequalities in Korean manufacturing). Seoul, Korea Development Institute, 1975.

Chuang, Ying Cheng. "Predicting the Optimum Requirements for Technical Education in Relation to Industrial Development in a Developing Country." Unpublished PhD dissertation, University of California, Los Angeles, 1967.

Chung, Bom Mo (Chŏng, Pŏm-mo). "The Impact of American Culture on Korea through Education Exchanges," *Koreana Quarterly* 9.4:74–87 (winter 1967).

Chung, Sae-gu (Chŏng, Se-gu). "The Political Socialization of Selected Elementary and Middle School Students in the Republic of Korea: Political Knowledge, Political Trust and Political Efficacy." Unpublished PhD dissertation, Florida State University, 1973.

Chung, Tai-si (Chŏng, T'ae-si). "Korean Education: Yesterday and Tomorrow," *Koreana Quarterly* 12.3:66–76 (autumn 1970).

Chung, Yong Hwan (Chŏng, Yŏng-hwan). "A Study of Some Aspects of Educational Administration with Implications for the Korean Public School System." Unpublished PhD dissertation, University of Oklahoma, 1965.

Cole, David C. and Princeton N. Lyman. *Korean Development: The Interplay of Politics and Economics.* Cambridge, Harvard University Press, 1971.

—— and Larry E. Westphal. "The Contribution of Exports to Employment in Korea," in Wontack Hong (Wŏn-t'aek Hong) and Anne O. Krueger, eds., *Trade and Development in Korea*. Seoul, Korea Development Institute, 1975.

Cole, Ross Harold. "The Koreanization of Elementary Citizenship Education in South Korea, 1948–1974." Unpublished PhD dissertation, Arizona State University, 1975.

Coleman, James, et al. *Equality of Educational Opportunity*. Washington, U.S. Office of Education, 1966.

Collins, Randall. "Functional and Conflict Theories of Educational Stratification," *American Sociological Review* 36.6:1002–1019 (December 1971).

Cunningham, Ineke. "The Relationship between Modernity of Students in a Puerto Rican High School and their Academic Performance, Peers and Parents," in Alex Inkeles and Donald B. Holsinger, eds., *Education and Individual Modernity in Developing Countries*. Leiden, Brill, 1974.

Denison, Edward F. "Measuring the Contribution of Education to Economic Growth," in E. A. G. Robinson and J. E. Vaizey, eds., *Economics of Education*. New York, St. Martin Press, 1966.

——. *Why Growth Rates Differ*. Washington, The Brookings Institution, 1967.

Dodge, Herbert Wesley. "A History of U.S. Assistance to Korean Education: 1953–1966." Unpublished PhD dissertation, George Washington University, 1971.

Dore, Ronald. *The Diploma Disease*. Berkeley and Los Angeles, University of California Press, 1976.

Drake, H. B. *Korea of the Japanese*. London, John Lane, 1930.

Economic Planning Board. *Employment Statistics*. Seoul, 1974.

Eisenstadt. S. N. *Modernization: Protest and Change*. Englewood Cliffs, New Jersey, Prentice Hall, 1966.

Eversull, Frank L. "Some Observations on Higher Education in Korea," *School and Society* 65.1674:51–53 (January 1947).

Ewha (Ihwa) University. Student Guidance Center. *Research Review*. 1969.

Eysenck, H. J. *Sense and Nonsense in Psychology*. London, Penguin Books, 1957.

Farrell, Joseph P. "National Planning Systems in Latin America: Their Environment and their Impact," *Educational Planning* 1.1:20–33 (May 1974).

Feraru, Arthur. "Korean Students in the United States," *School and Society* 86:60–62 (1974).

Frank, Charles R., Kwang Suk Kim (Kwang-sŏk Kim), and Larry E. Westphal. *Foreign Trade Regimes and Economic Development: South*

Korea. New York, National Bureau of Economic Research, Columbia University Press, 1975.

Gilroy, Curtis L. "Investment in Human Capital and Black-White Employment," *Monthly Labor Review* 98.7:13–21 (July 1975).

Glazer, Nathan. "Social and Cultural Factors in Japanese Economic Growth," in Hugh Patrick and Henry Rosovsky, eds., *Asia's New Giant: How the Japanese Economy Works.* Washington, The Brookings Institution, 1976.

Gotkowski, Zygmont. "The Evolution of Developmental Gaps Between Rich and Poor Countries, 1955–65: A Methodological Pilot Study," *International Social Science Journal* 27.1:38–52 (1975).

Grant, Sidney R. "General Characteristics of the Formal Education System at the Primary and Secondary Levels in South Korea with Special Reference to the Feasibility for Innovation," Appendix A in Robert Morgan and Clifton B. Chadwick, eds., *Systems Analysis for Educational Change.* Tallahassee, Florida State University, Department of Educational Research, 1971.

Hahn, Bae-ho (Han, Pae-ho) and Kyu-Taik Kim (Kyu-t'aek Kim). "Korean Political Leaders (1952–1962): Their Social Origins and Skills," *Asian Survey*, July 1963.

Ham, Ui-Yong (Ham, Ŭi-yŏng). "Democratization of Political Consciousness in Korea," *Korea Journal* 14.1:8–20 (January 1974).

Han-guk Kyoyuk Kaebal Yŏn'guwŏn (Korean Educational Development Institute). *Kyoyuk kyehoek e kwanhan kich'o t'onggye charyo* (Basic statistics for education planning). Seoul, 1975.

Hannan, Michael T. "Societal Development and the Expansion of Educational Systems." Washington, National Center for Educational Research, 1973.

Harbison, Frederick H. *Human Resources as the Wealth of Nations.* New York, Oxford University Press, 1973.

——. "Education and Income Distribution." Mimeographed. 1973.

—— and Charles S. Myers. *Education, Manpower and Economic Growth.* New York, McGraw-Hill, 1964.

——, Joan Maruhnic, and Jane R. Resnick. *Quantitative Analyses of Modernization and Development.* Princeton University, Industrial Relations Section, 1970.

Holsinger, Donald B. "The Elementary School as Modernizer: a Brazilian Study," in Alex Inkeles and Donald B. Holsinger, eds., *Education and Individual Modernity in Developing Countries.* Leiden, Brill, 1974.

Hong, Sung Chick (Hong, Sŏng-jik). "Values of Korean Farmers, Businessmen and Professors," in *International Conference on the Problems of Modernization in Asia: Report.* Seoul, Asiatic Research Center, Korea University, 1965.

———. *The Intellectual and Modernization*. Seoul, Asiatic Research Center, 1967.

Hong, Sŭng-jik (Hong, Sung Chick). *Han'guk kach'igwan yŏn'gu* (A study of Korean value systems). Seoul, Asiatic Research Center, 1969.

Hong, Wontack (Hong, Won-t'aek). "Statistical Data on Korea's Trade and Growth," Appendix to *Exports and Employment in Korea*. Seoul, Korea Development Institute, 1975.

Huang, Sung-mo (Hwang, Sŏng-mo), "The Role of Industrial Laborers in the Modernization of Korea," in *International Conference on Problems of Modernization in Asia*. Seoul, Asiatic Research Center, 1965.

Husen, Torsten, ed. *International Study of Achievement in Mathematics: A Comparison of 12 Countries*. Stockholm, Almquist and Wiksell, and New York, Wiley, 1967.

Hwang, Hamil Jong-gon (Hwang, Chong-gŏn). "Adult Education: Imperative for a New Society," *Korea Journal* 6.7:9–12, 19 (July 1966).

Im, Sungkwun (Im, Sŭng-gwŏn) and Kwanyong Rhee (Kwan-yong Yi). "A Preliminary Study on the Occupational State of Graduates," *Seoul National University Research Review* 8.1:31–42 (June 1971).

Inkeles, Alex. "The Modernization of Man," in Myron Weiner, ed., *Modernization*. New York, Basic Books, 1966.

——— and David H. Smith. *Becoming Modern: Individual Change in Six Developing Countries*. Cambridge, Harvard University Press, 1974.

Irwin, Patrick H. "An Occupational Definition of Societal Modernization," *Economic Development and Cultural Change* 23.4:595–614 (July 1975).

Jain, Shail. *Size Distribution of Income: A Compilation of Data*. Washington, The World Bank, 1975.

Jencks, Christopher, et al. *Inequality*. New York, Basic Books, 1972.

Jeong, Chang Young (Chŏng, Ch'ang-yŏng). "Rates of Return on Investment in Education," in Chuk Kyo Kim (Chŏk-kyo Kim) ed., *Industrial and Social Development Issues*. Essays on the Korean Economy, Vol. II. Seoul, Korea Development Institute, 1977.

Chŏng Ch'ang-yŏng (Jeong, Chang Young) and Myŏng-hwi Kim, "Hyŏng-myŏng ŭi simnihak" (The psychology of revolution), *Han'guk ilbo* (Hankook Ilbo) 9:19, 1960.

Kang, Chu-Chin (Kang, Chu-jin). "Library System in Korea," *Koreana Quarterly* 11.4:62–66 (winter 1969–1970).

Kim, Chong Ch'ol (Kim, Chong-ch'ŏl). "Long-Range Educational Planning in Korea," *Korea Journal* 11.10:5–11, 15 (October 1971).

Kim, Chung Han (Kim, Chŏng-han). "Changing Functions of Women's Higher Education in the Republic of Korea: A Study of Educational Equality Between Men and Women." Unpublished PhD dissertation, George Peabody College for Teachers, 1975.

Kim, Han Heyn. "On the Role of Human Capital in Optimal Growth." Unpublished PhD dissertation, Stanford University, 1971.

Kim, Hong Yung. "A Comparative Analysis of Developmental Values Found in the Children's Stories from the Old and the New Language Arts Textbooks in the Republic of Korea." Unpublished PhD dissertation, Ball State University, 1974.

Kim, Jin Eun (Kim, Chin-ŭn). "An Analysis of the National Planning Process for Educational Development in the Republic of Korea, 1945–70." Unpublished PhD dissertation, University of Pittsburgh, 1973.

Kim, Kak. "Education Undergoes Drastic Revisions," *Korea Journal* 1.4: 19–20 (December 1961).

Kim, Kwang Suk (Kim, Kwang-sŏk). "Rates of Return on Education in Korea." Mimeographed, USAID/Korea, 1968.

—— and Michael Roemer. *Growth and Structural Transformation. Studies in the Modernization of the Republic of Korea: 1945–1975.* Cambridge, Council on East Asian Studies, Harvard University, 1978.

Kim, Myung Han (Kim, Myŏng-han). "The Educational Policy-Making Process in the Republic of Korea: A Systems Analysis." Unpublished PhD dissertation, North Texas State University, 1974.

Kim, Quee-Young (Kim, Kwi-yŏng). "Social Structure and Student Revolt: A Quantitative Analysis of the Korean Case." Unpublished PhD dissertation, Harvard University, 1975.

Kim, Se-jin. "Attitudinal Orientations of Korean Workers," *Korea Journal* 12.9:18–30 (September 1972).

Kim, Shin-Bok (Kim, Sin-bok). "A Systemic Sub-Optimization Model for Educational Planning: with Application to Korea." Unpublished PhD dissertation, University of Pittsburgh, 1973.

Kim, Sin-bok (Kim, Shin-Bok) and Nae-yŏng Pak, "Kyoyuk kwa kukka palchŏn" (Education and national development), in Han'guk Kyoyuk Kaebarwŏn (Korean Educational Development Institute), *Kukka palchŏn e taehan kyoyuk ŭk kiyŏ 1945–1975* (Contribution of education to national development, 1945–1975). Seoul, 1976.

Kim, Suk-jo (Kim, Sŏk-cho) and Quee-Young Kim (Kwi-yŏng Kim). "Social Structure and Legal Culture in Korea." Unpublished manuscript, 1977.

Kim, T'ae-gil. *Han'guk taehaksaeng ŭi kach'igwan, 1964.* Seoul, Ilchogak, 1967.

Kim, Uk Hwan (Kim, Uk-hwan). "An Examination of the Interplay of Culture and Education in Korea: A Comparative Study." Unpublished PhD dissertation, Claremont Graduate School, 1972.

Kim, Yŏng-bong (Kim, Yung Bong). *Uri nara kyoyukpi, kyoyuk suyo hyŏngt'ae mit kyoyuk ŭi kyŏngje sŏngjang kiyŏ punsŏk* (The demand for education and contribution of education to economic growth in Korea). Seoul, Korea Development Institute, 1975.

——. "Education and Economic Growth." Working Paper 7605, Korea Development Institute, October 1976.

Kim, Yungho (Kim, Yŏng-ho) et al. *Toward a New Instructional System.* Seoul, Korean Educational Development Institute, 1973.

Koh, Harold H. "The Early History of U.S. Economic Assistance to the Republic of Korea, 1945–1955." Harvard Institute for International Development, mimeographed. September 1975.

Korea Chamber of Commerce and Industry (KCCI). *See* Taehan Sanggong Hoeŭiso.

Korean Educational Development Institute (KEDI). *See* Han'guk Kyokyuk Kaebal Yŏn'guwŏn.

Korean Society for the Study of Education. *The Saemaul Education in the Republic of Korea.* Seoul, 1974.

Kuznets, Paul. "Labor Absorption in Korea since 1963." Working Paper No. 16, International Development Research Center, Indiana University, 1972.

——. Unpublished manuscript on education in Korea. N.d.

Kyungbuk (Kyongbuk) University. *Research Review 1968.*

LaBelle, Thomas J. and Robert E. Verhine. "Nonformal Education and Occupational Stratification: Implications for Latin America," *Harvard Educational Review* 45.2:160–190 (May 1975).

Lee, Hahn Been (Yi, Han-bin) and In-joung Whang (In-jŏng Hwang). "Development of Senior Administrators: The Korean Experience," *Koreana Quarterly* 13.3:1–18 (autumn 1973).

Lee, J. H. "Economic Value of Korean Farmers' Education: Their Productivity and Earnings." Unpublished MA thesis, Cornell University, 1969.

Lee, Sun-Keun (Yi, Sŏn-gŭn). "The Extent to Which the Japanese Colonial Policy toward Korea Contributed to Her Modernization," in *International Conference on the Problems of Modernization in Asia: Report.* Seoul, Asiatic Research Center, Korea University, 1965.

Lee, Sung-hwa (Yi, Sŏng-hwa). "The Social and Political Factors Affecting Korean Education, 1885–1950." Unpublished PhD dissertation, University of Pittsburgh, 1958.

Lee, Won-Sul (Yi, Wŏn-sŏl). "The Impact of United States Occupation Policy on the Socio-political Structure of South Korea, 1945–1948." Unpublished PhD dissertation, Western Reserve University, 1961.

Yi, Wŏn-sŏl (Lee, Won-Sul). "Haksaeng undong kwa Han'guk chŏngch'i" (The student movement and Korean politics), *Yŏngnam Taehakkyo nonmunjip, che 4-gwŏn* (Yŏngnam University thesis collection, vol. 4), pp. 127–166, 1970.

Lee, Young-ho (Yi, Yŏng-ho). "The Political Culture of a Modernizing Society: Political Attitudes and Democracy in Korea." Unpublished PhD dissertation, Yale University, 1970.

Lee, Youngkee (Yi, Yŏng-gi). "A Study on the Measurement of Education Investment to Economic Growth," in Ministry of Finance, *Reports Financed by the Academic Research Promotion Fund,* Vol. 3. Seoul, 1969.

Leibenstein, Harvey. "Shortages and Surpluses in Education in Underdeveloped Countries," in Arnold Anderson and Mary Jean Bowman, eds., *Education and Economic Development.* Chicago, Aldine, 1965.

Lerner, Daniel. *The Passing of Traditional Society.* Glencoe, Illinois, Free Press, 1958.

Levy, Marion J. *Modernization and the Structure of Societies.* Princeton, Princeton University Press, 1966.

Lewis, W. Arthur. *The Theory of Economic Growth.* Homewood, Illinois, Richard D. Irwin, 1965.

McClelland, David C. *The Achieving Society.* Princeton, Van Nostrand, 1961.

——. "Does Education Accelerate Economic Growth?" *Economic Development and Cultural Change* 14.3:257–278 (April 1966).

—— and D. G. Winter. *Motivating Economic Achievement,* New York, Free Press, 1971.

Machlup, Fritz. *Education and Economic Growth.* Lincoln, University of Nebraska Press, 1970.

Meyer, John W. "The Effects of Education as an Institution," *American Journal of Sociology* 83.1:55–77 (July 1977).

Mincer, Jacob. "On the Job Training: Costs, Returns and Some Implications," *Journal of Political Economy,* Supplement, October 1962.

——. "The Distribution of Labor Incomes: A Survey with Special Reference to the Human Capital Approach," *Journal of Economic Literature* 8.1:1–26 (March 1970).

Mun'gyobu (Ministry of Education). *Ŭima Kyoyuk Wansŏng 6-gae nyŏn kyehoek, 1954–1959* (6-Year Accomplishment Plan of Compulsory Education, 1954–1959), Seoul, 1954.

Ministry of Education (Mun'gyobu). *Education Monthly* 41:106–107 (September 1958).

——. *Statistical Yearbook of Education, 1965, 1970, 1973, 1974, 1975.* Seoul.

——. *Education in Korea 1973.* Seoul, 1974.

——. *Education in Korea, 1974–75.* Seoul, 1975.

——. *Educational Development in Korea.* Seoul, 1975.

Mun'gyobu (Ministry of Education). *Hyŏngmyŏng chŏngbu mun'gyo sich'aek* (Educational policies of the Park Military Government). Seoul, Chŏngbu Kanhaengmul (Government publications), 1961.

Mischel, W. *Introduction to Personality.* New York, Holt, Rinehart and Winston, 1971.

Morgan, Robert and Clifton B. Chadwick, eds. *Systems Analysis for Educational Change: The Republic of Korea.* Tallahassee, Florida State University, Department of Educational Research, April 1971.

Nam, Byung Hun (Nam, Pyŏng-hun). "Educational Reorganization in South Korea under the United States Army Military Government, 1945–1948." Unpublished PhD dissertation, University of Pittsburgh, 1962.

Nam, Charles. "Group Disparities in Educational Participation," in Organization for Economic Cooperation and Development, *Conference on Policies for Educational Growth, IV. Group Disparities in Educational Participation and Achievement.* Paris, 1971.

Office of Labor Affairs. *Report of Occupational Wage Survey, 1972.* Seoul.

——. *Wage and Employment Survey, 1972.* Seoul.

Oh, Byung-hun (O, Pyŏng-hŏn). "University Students and Politics in Korea," *Koreana Quarterly* 9.4:1–41 (winter 1967).

O, Pyŏng-hŏn (Oh, Byung-hun), Yŏng-bok Ko, and Yŏng-dŏk Yi. *Haksaeng munje yŏn'gu* (A study of student problems). Seoul, UNESCO, 1970.

Oh, Seung-Shik. "Economic Development and Human Resources: with Reference to University Education," *Koreana Quarterly* 8.9:37–48 (spring 1966).

Osgood, Cornelius. *The Koreans and their Culture.* New York, Ronald Press, 1951.

Oshima, Harry T. "Income Inequality and Economic Growth, The Postwar Experience of Asian Countries," *Malayan Economic Review* 15.2:7–41 (October 1970).

Paik, Hyun-ki (Paek, Hyŏn-gi). "The Present Status of Education," *Korea Journal* 3.4:4–15 (April 1963).

Paek, Hyŏn-gi (Paik, Hyun-ki), "Han'guk kyoyuk kyehoek ŭi pyŏnch'ŏn" (Changes in Korean educational planning), *Chungang Kyoyuk Yŏn'guso sobo.* (Bulletin of the Central Education Research Institute), 9.4:37 (December 1968).

——. *A Content Analysis of Elementary School Textbooks and a Related Study for Improvement of Textbook Administration.* Seoul, Central Education Research Institute, 1969.

——. "Nonformal Education in Korea: Programs and Prospects," in Cole S. Brembeck and Timothy J. Thompson, eds., *New Strategies for Educational Development.* Lexington, Massachusetts, Lexington Books, 1973.

Pak, Hyung Koo (Pak, Hyŏng-gu). "Social Changes in the Educational and Religious Institutions of Korean Society under Japanese and American Occupations." Unpublished PhD dissertation, Utah State University, 1964.

Papi, G. U. "General Problems of the Economics of Education," in E. A. G. Robinson and J. E. Vaizey, eds., *Economics of Education*. New York, St. Martin Press, 1966.

Passin, Herbert. *Society and Education in Japan*. New York, Bureau of Publications, Teachers College, Columbia University, 1965.

Paukert, Felix. "Income Distribution at Different Levels of Development: A Survey of Evidence," *International Labour Review* 108.203: 97–125 (August-September 1973).

Peaker, G. F. *The Plowden Children Four Years Later*. Slough, National Foundation for Educational Research in England and Wales, 1971.

Perez de Tagle, Oscar. "The Stage Theory of Balanced Educational-Economic Development and its Application to Countries with Educated Unemployement." Unpublished PhD dissertation, University of Wisconsin, 1973.

Portes, Alejandro. "Modernity and Development: A Critique," *Studies in Comparative International Development* VIII:247–279 (1973).

Psacharopoulos, George and Keith Hinchliffe. *Returns to Education: An International Comparison*. Amsterdam, Elsevier Scientific, and San Francisco, Jossey-Bass, 1973.

Purves, Alan C. and Daviel V. Levine, eds. *Educational Policy and International Assessment*. Berkeley, McCutchan, 1975.

Renaud. Bertrand. "Economic Growth and Income Inequality in Korea." Paper prepared for the Tenth Anniversary Conference of the Population and Development Studies Center, Seoul National University, January 1975.

Rettig, Solomon and Benjamin Pasamanick. "Moral Codes of American and Korean College Students," *Journal of Social Psychology* 50:65–73 (1959).

——, "Invariance in Factor Structure of Moral Value Judgments from American and Korean College Students," *Sociometry* 25:73–84 (1962).

Rettig, Solomon and Jin-Sook Lee (Chin-suk Yi). "Differences in Moral Judgments of South Korean Students Before and After the Korean Revolution," *Journal of Social Psychology* 59:3–9 (1963).

Rhee, Kwanyong. "A Study on Mooney Problem Check List," *Research Review*, Seoul National University 7:2 (June 1970).

Rim, Han Young (Im, Han-yong). "Japanese Totalitarian Education in Korea, 1910–1945," *Koreana Quarterly* 1 2:85–92 (1960).

Ruth, Heather Low. "Korea," in Committee on the International Migration of Talent, *The International Migration of High-Level Manpower.* New York, Praeger, 1970.

Sack, Richard. "The Impact of Education on Individual Modernity in Tunisia," in Alex Inkeles and Donald B. Holsinger, eds., *Education and Individual Modernity in Developing Countries.* Leiden, Brill, 1974.

Schiefelbein, Ernesto. "Repeating: An Overlooked Problem of Latin American Education," *Comparative Education Review* 19:468–487 (1977).

Sedjo, Roger A. "The Turning Point for the Korean Economy," in Sung-Hwan Jo (Sŏng-hwan Cho) and Seong-Young Park, (Sŭng-yong Pak) eds., *Basic Documents and Selected Papers of Korea's Third Five-Year Economic Development Plan (1972–1976).* Seoul, 1972.

Selowsky, Marcelo. "On the Measurement of Education's Contribution to Growth," *Quarterly Journal of Economics* 83.3:449–463 (August 1969).

Sofranko, Andrew J. and Robert C. Bealer, "Modernization Balance, Imbalance and Domestic Instability," *Economic Development and Cultural Change* 22.1:52–72 (October 1973).

Song, Byung Soon (Song, Pyŏng-sun). "Comparative Study of Ideological Influences on Educational Theory and Practice in North and South Korea." Unpublished PhD dissertation, Wayne State University, 1974.

Sukmyong (Sungmyŏng) University, Student Guidance Center. *Problems of the Korean College Students and Some Approaches in Guidance and Counseling.* 1971.

———. *Research Review,* 1973.

Taehan Sanggong Hoeŭiso (Korea Chamber of Commerce and Industry-KCCI). *Kyŏngje kaebal kwa kyoyuk t'uja* (Economic development and educational investment) Seoul, January 10, 1973.

Tracy, Norbert J. "Education in this Remarkable Republic of Korea," in Society of Jesus, *Korean Sociological Survey* Seoul, 1969.

Underwood, Horace. "Korean Education: Master of the Future or Slave of the Past?" *Koreana Quarterly* 5.3:52–60 (autumn 1963).

United Nations Statistical Yearbook, 1974.

United Nations Educational, Scientific and Culture Organization-United Nations Korean Rehabilitation Administration Educational Planning Mission to Korea. *Rebuilding Education in the Republic of Korea.* Paris, 1954.

United Nations Educational, Scientific and Cultural Organization. *Long-Term Projections for Education in the Republic of Korea.* Bangkok, UNESCO Regional Office for Education in Asia, 1965.

———. *Progress of Education in the Asian Region: Statistical Supplement* Bangkok, UNESCO Regional Office for Education in Asia, 1972.

——. *Republic of Korea: Educational Services in a Rapidly Growing Economy.* 2 vols. Paris, 1974.

——. *Statistical Yearbook, 1974.*

University of Minnesota. *Annual Report: 1976.* Economic Development Center, University of Minnesota, 1976.

Werth, Richard. "Educational Developments under the South Korean Interim Government (SKIG)," *School and Society* 69.1793:305-309 (April 1949).

Whang, Hichul Henry. "The Tasks of Public Education as Perceived by the Public in the Republic of Korea." Unpublished PhD dissertation, University of Wisconsin, 1972.

Williams, William M. "Foreign Assistance to Korean Education," *Korea Journal* 2.1:16-18 (January 1962).

Wilson, Elizabeth Cecil. "The Problem of Value in Technical Assistance in Education: The Case of Korea, 1945-1955." Unpublished PhD dissertation. University of Maryland, 1959.

Yi, Kyu-bŏm, Kyun-bo Kim, and Chae-hwan Ha. "Kakkŭp hakkyo haksaeng tŭl ŭi kukka ŭisik e kwanhan yŏn'gu" (A survey of the national consciousness of students at schools of various levels). Monograph, Pusan Teachers College, 1975.

Yi, Un-Hwa (Yi, Un-hwa). "Pre-school Education in Korea," *Korea Journal* 12.12:28-31 (December 1972).

Yi, Wŏn-sŏl. *See* Lee, Won-Sul.

Yoo, Hyung-jin (Yu, Hyŏng-jin). "The Charter of National Education," *Korea Journal* 9.8:4-7 (August 1969).

——. "New Entrance Examination for High Schools in Korea, 1973." Paper presented at the World Congress of Comparative Education Societies, Geneva, June 28, 1974.

Zymelman, Manuel. "Patterns of Educational Expenditures." The World Bank, Staff Working Paper No. 246. Washington, November 1976.

Index

Abraham, William I., 142

Academic high schools, 6, 48-49; classrooms in, 51; enrollments in, 131; graduates of, 168, 181. *See also* High schools

Adams, Donald K., 86

Adelman, Irma, 141, 144-145

Adult education: in civic schools, 8-9; in College of Air and Correspondence, 9-10; by voluntary organizations, 10

Age, wages by, 102, 119, 120; and educational attainment, 109

Agriculture: education for, 10; production at Liberation, 105; incomes in, 142; and land reforms, 144; related jobs, 206; College of, graduates, 207

Bealer, Robert C., 216

Black, C. E., 186-187, 216, 239

Capital: aid from U.S., xxv, 70, 89-90, 92; as factor in economic growth, 123; effect of foreign aid upon, 79, 97, 100; control by Japanese, 144

Carnoy, Martin, 193

Central Board of Education, 14

Chadwick, Clifton B., 71

Chang, John, 177, 178

Chang Myon Government: educational administration under, 11

Chŏng, Kang-su, 176

Chung, Bom Mo, 137

Chung, Sae-gu, 202

Civic schools: enrollments in, 8-9

Coeducation, 227; in primary schools, 8, 9; under U.S. Military Government, 12, 86, 87

Cole, David C., 61-62

Cole, Ross Harold, 37, 41, 43, 194, 239

Colleges (4-year), 7; admission to, 7-8; enrollments in, 8, 29, 47, 131-133, 135, 152; financing of, 26, 27; objectives of, 32; student-teacher ratios of, 51; founding of, 86; graduates of, 111; cost per household, 156

Compulsory Education Accomplishment Plan (1954-1959), 37

Constitution of the First Republic, 12

Counties, school districts in, 13

Curriculum, 12; and national budget, 45; compared to other countries, 75, 77, 136-137, 228; and examinations, 75-76; changes in, 136-138; and modernization, 192, 212, 231; major influences on, 221; effect of upon social values, 231

Denison, Edward F., 116, 117, 119, 124, 125

Dodge, Herbert Wesley, 89, 92, 93

Economic growth: and human resources, xxv, 60-66, 99-100, 104-116, 204, 230; and education, 1, 60-61, 99-138, 139, 146-184, 194, 216, 220, 224-230, 240; comparison of with other countries, 4, 60-68, 99, 128-129, 143; human-capital perspective of, 101-126; and the labor force, 101, 123, 143; and technology, 103-104, 240; periods of, 104; indicators of, 105; alternative perspectives of, 126-129; and income distribution, 139-184

Education: high levels of, xxv; strengths of for South Korea, xxv-xvi; and

Harvard East Asian Monographs

46. W. P. J. Hall, *A Bibliographical Guide to Japanese Research on the Chinese Economy, 1958–1970*

47. Jack J. Gerson, *Horatio Nelson Lay and Sino-British Relations, 1854–1864*

48. Paul Richard Bohr, *Famine and the Missionary: Timothy Richard as Relief Administrator and Advocate of National Reform*

49. Endymion Wilkinson, *The History of Imperial China: A Research Guide*

50. Britten Dean, *China and Great Britain: The Diplomacy of Commerical Relations, 1860–1864*

51. Ellsworth C. Carlson, *The Foochow Missionaries, 1847–1880*

52. Yeh-chien Wang, *An Estimate of the Land-Tax Collection in China, 1753 and 1908*

53. Richard M. Pfeffer, *Understanding Business Contracts in China, 1949–1963*

54. Han-sheng Chuan and Richard Kraus, *Mid-Ch'ing Rice Markets and Trade, An Essay in Price History*

55. Ranbir Vohra, *Lao She and the Chinese Revolution*

56. Liang-lin Hsiao, *China's Foreign Trade Statistics, 1864–1949*

57. Lee-hsia Hsu Ting, *Government Control of the Press in Modern China, 1900–1949*

58. Edward W. Wagner, *The Literati Purges: Political Conflict in Early Yi Korea*

59. Joungwon A. Kim, *Divided Korea: The Politics of Development, 1945–1972*

60. Noriko Kamachi, John K. Fairbank, and Chūzō Ichiko, *Japanese Studies of Modern China Since 1953: A Bibliographical Guide to Historical and Social-Science Research on the Nineteenth and Twentieth Centuries, Supplementary Volume for 1953–1969*

61. Donald A. Gibbs and Yun-chen Li, *A Bibliography of Studies and Translations of Modern Chinese Literature, 1918–1942*

62. Robert H. Silin, *Leadership and Values: The Organization of Large-Scale Taiwanese Enterprises*

63. David Pong, *A Critical Guide to the Kwangtung Provincial Archives Deposited at the Public Record Office of London*

64. Fred W. Drake, *China Charts the World: Hsu Chi-yü and His Geography of 1848*

65. William A. Brown and Urgunge Onon, translators and annotators, *History of the Mongolian People's Republic*

66. Edward L. Farmer, *Early Ming Government: The Evolution of Dual Capitals*

67. Ralph C. Croizier, *Koxinga and Chinese Nationalism: History, Myth, and the Hero*

68. William J. Tyler, tr., *The Psychological World of Natsumi Sōseki*, by Doi Takeo

STUDIES IN THE MODERNIZATION OF THE REPUBLIC OF KOREA: 1945–1975

91. Leroy P. Jones and Il SaKong, *Government, Business, and Entre-preneurship in Economic Development: The Korean Case*

92. Edward S. Mason, Dwight H. Perkins, Kwang Suk Kim, David C. Cole, Mahn Je Kim, et al., *The Economic and Social Modernization of the Republic of Korea*

RITTER LIBRARY
BALDWIN-WALLACE COLLEGE